THE PRACTICE OF
WORKPLACE PARTICIPATION

THE PRACTICE OF WORKPLACE PARTICIPATION

Management–Employee Relations at Three Participatory Firms

S. Lance Denning

Q

QUORUM BOOKS
Westport, Connecticut • London

Library of Congress Cataloging-in-Publication Data

Denning, S. Lance, 1961–
   The practice of workplace participation : management–employee relations at three participatory firms / S. Lance Denning.
     p.   cm.
   Includes bibliographical references and index.
   ISBN 1–56720–195–4 (alk. paper)
   1. Industrial management—Employee participation. 2. Industrial sociology. 3. Industrial management—Employees participation—United States—Case studies. I. Title.
HD5650.D454   1998
658.3'15—dc21   97–32990

British Library Cataloguing in Publication Data is available.

Copyright © 1998 by S. Lance Denning

All rights reserved. No portion of this book may be reproduced, by any process or technique, without the express written consent of the publisher.

Library of Congress Catalog Card Number: 97–32990
ISBN: 0–56720–195–4

First published in 1998

Quorum Books, 88 Post Road West, Westport, CT 06881
An imprint of Greenwood Publishing Group, Inc.

Printed in the United States of America

The paper used in this book complies with the Permanent Paper Standard issued by the National Information Standards Organization (Z39.48–1984).

10 9 8 7 6 5 4 3 2 1

Copyright Acknowledgments

The author and publisher gratefully acknowledge permission for use of the following material:

Passages from *Exit, Voice, and Loyalty* by Albert O. Hirschman. Copyright © 1970 by the President and Fellows of Harvard College. Reprinted by permission of Harvard University Press.

Passages from *Democracy in America* by Alexis de Tocqueville. Edited by Richard E. Heffner. New York: Penguin Books, 1956.

Passages from *The Social Contract* by Jean-Jacques Rousseau. Translated by Maurice Cranston. Reprinted by permission of the Peters Fraser & Dunlop Group Ltd. Copyright: The Estate of Maurice Cranston.

*For my family and friends, who saw me
through these often frustrating times,
who listened and understood, and better yet,
who acted to provide warmth and love*

CONTENTS

ACKNOWLEDGMENTS		xi
Introduction The Complexity of Democratic Change		1
1	WORKPLACE PARTICIPATION	
	The Issues, the Literature, and the Democratic Concern	15
	Participation, Productivity, and Political Efficacy	17
	The "Leap" from Private to Public Behavior	20
	The Participatory Literature	22
	Broader Issues and the Need for Caution	24
	Conceptions of the Market System	31
	Voice and Choice	36
	The Research Agenda	38
	Notes	41
2	DEFINITIONS AND RESEARCH METHODOLOGY	43
	Notes	54
3	THE FRUSTRATION AT STANDARD KNAPP	55
	The Employee Buyout and the Participatory Design	57
	From Participatory Design to Worker Attitudes	62
	A Language of Division, Points of Frustration	66
	The Number Four Quandary	68

	Testing Participatory Theory's Activity Hypothesis	70
	Conclusion	72
	Notes	74
4	EMPLOYEE PARTICIPATION IN THE QUAD/GRAPHICS CULTURE	77
	Rousseau's General Will and the "Quad" Culture	77
	Quad/Graphics' Participatory Design	81
	Two Views of Quad/Graphics	84
	Transformation and Political Activity: Quad/Graphics Evidence	87
	Rousseau's Prescription	90
	Conclusion	92
	Notes	93
5	THE ZARITSKY BROTHERS Furthering Employee Ownership and Participation at Orange Handling	95
	Orange Handling's Atmosphere	96
	Orange Handling's History and Participatory Design	98
	Employee and Management Frustration at Orange Handling	100
	Attitudes the Participatory Design Creates	104
	Is Testing For Transformation and Political Activity Possible?	109
	The Ability for Change, the Ability to Change	112
	Notes	114
6	THE CONTRADICTIONS OF PARTICIPATORY DEMOCRATIC THEORY	117
	Theoretical Expectations and Practical Concerns	120
	The Causal Path Analyzed	124
	Exit, Voice, and Loyalty	126
	Internal Structural Effects on Participation and Efficacy	133
	The Misleading Effect of Economic Success	137
	Conclusion	141
	Notes	142
7	THE "ROUGH MIX" OF A PARTICIPATORY WORKPLACE	145
	Notes	159

Appendixes

A	SURVEY AND INTERVIEW NUMBERS	161
B	SAMPLE SURVEY QUESTIONNAIRE	165
	SELECTED BIBLIOGRAPHY	169
	INDEX	173

ACKNOWLEDGMENTS

I must first acknowledge the firms that allowed me to study their participatory attempts. My work was welcomed with openness and respect. Also, the employees who answered the surveys and granted interviews are the most important part of this research. Without their interest and concern about their workplaces, my inquiry would have stalled.

I would like to thank the Benevolent Association and the Graduate Student Organization at the University at Albany/SUNY for offsetting many of my research costs.

I also want to thank Alan Sturmer of Greenwood Publishing Group, who guided me through the initial stages of publication with graciousness and respect. John Beck, book producer, was helpful and very responsive to any query. Mark Edwards certainly deserves recognition for the time and effort he spent improving the flow and questioning the details of this work. These people, and I am certain there are more at Greenwood who have helped with this project, have made the publication process a true labor of love.

I extend my utmost gratitude toward the committee members who have contributed their time and energy in making this project more enlightening and more enjoyable. Todd Swanstrom and Mort Schoolman gave constructive comments that forced me to question assumptions and reassess some ideas that had become too "well worn." Anne Hildreth challenges the methodology to this day, and because of her concerns the work prospers. Peter Breiner labored endlessly on each draft—and there were several—and he was and remains a source of intellectual stimulation. Even better to ward off my insecurities, he is both kind and forgiving.

Also, I want to thank many others who have supported me over the course of this project. This work benefited from Lori Hewig's computer knowledge, research assistance, and astute guidance. Randy Winn and Scott Lowry provided long-distance diversion. Linda Kiley and Neil Kraus helped me through my days in Albany. Vicki Ash Hunter gave me hope for the future as this project drew to its end. My brother Craig compromised his routines so that I could pursue my educational and personal goals. My parents have supported my efforts quietly for years, often hearing only my exasperation. I will remember always their love and cautious interest. Finally, Angela King provided optimism and warmth during this endeavor. With a calming, sensitive influence, she encouraged patience and relieved troublesome worries.

Introduction   **THE COMPLEXITY OF
                                 DEMOCRATIC CHANGE**

Twenty five years ago, American society was anything but quiescent. Sprouting from the counterculture protests in the 1960s, the early 1970s were characterized by vehement and fatal protests over Vietnam War policies, by an increasingly factionalized but growing women's movement which focused debate on the control of women's bodies, and by a burgeoning resentment toward political power and its abuse after Watergate. Senator George McGovern and Governor George Wallace, two candidates far from the Democratic Party's center, had captured a majority of Democratic rank and file votes as the 1972 primaries rolled into summer.[1] McGovern became the party's nominee but was crushed by the incumbent president who paradoxically campaigned as an "outsider" fighting an entrenched liberal establishment. However, Nixon's support crumbled under charges of criminal wrongdoing, cover-ups, and ethical violations. If American society looked for government guidance and moderation in this time of social change, it found few answers from a Democratic Party too divided to offer leadership and even less from a Republican Party that disgraced the presidency by abusing its responsibilities. Thus, while social movements were challenging how society had thought about a range of issues and constituencies, established institutions were, through their errors, dubiously legitimating many of the movements' critiques.

During these turbulent years participatory democratic theorists argued for empowering individuals to regain control over their lives and the political realm. Pluralism had a truncated concept of social and political activity. The task for participatory theorists became not only to describe who and what was left out of the liberal concept of political activity, but also to prescribe a course of action to include the dramatic social changes taking place. Carole Pateman's work, *Participation and Democratic Theory* (1970) followed the increasing criticism of pluralist politics—among others, Bachrach in 1962 and 1967). Her message, which was neither revolutionary nor new, claims that industrial work based on undemocratic authority relations produced passive and politically apathetic citizens. She stated that if the workplace was structured on democratic principles, a more participatory politics would soon replace the current politics of democratic elitism. Societal problems would be resolved by dispersing power to where it originated, in the people. The problems of the 1960s and 1970s showed, as participatory theorists argued, that the people were the necessary repository of power and action. Civil rights, peace demonstrations, women's and gay issues, and the nuclear freeze and environmental movements provided evidence that the people felt underrepresented and were willing to reclaim their power. As it existed, the social contract between a large segment of society and government, perhaps with corporate America as the government's accomplice, was being rethought and refought.

Since then, the participatory workplace alternative has drawn considerable attention. Just as the early 1970s grappled with change, including social issues like abortion and civil rights to internal Congressional change toward openness and equal representation, a wealth of studies explored the means to and the ends of a more participatory workplace. But the academic literature studied two different agendas. On the one hand, research poured out of the management and economic journals detailing the advantageous results of various work structures, in effect how much participation was "beneficial" and how each work design affected productivity requirements. The emphasis was on the institutional changes and how the changes would help or hinder the business firms. On the other hand, the participatory democratic literature, supported by psychological and sociological studies, concentrated on employee attitudes as the crucial variables that transformed helplessness and alienation to commitment and activity. Perhaps because any research attention was better than none, these divergent agendas and their objectives were hardly questioned at first. In addition, this rift between research on employee paticipation and/or ownership structures and research into individual attitudes affecting employee involvement speaks to the difficulty of measuring how a firm changes from extrapolating from attitudinal investigations. The relative ease in revealing how a firm changes after a change in ownership or management control contrasts with the less certain paths of causality from individual attitudes before and after employee control occurs.

Attitudinal data support the participatory democratic claims of empowerment. The theory focuses on the individual's perceived sense of efficacy over immediate decisions and how the individual becomes energized to participate in broader public concerns. By giving employees more control over their work, employees begin to participate in resolving problems. They begin to offer reforms, create new strategies, and perhaps support each other. Examples of success in worker decision-making control breed sustained commitment and energy; and as workplace issues are resolved, these actuated workers turn their commitment to more communal issues which demand action. In essence, participatory theory argues that part of the answer to the 1960s and 1970s democratic abuses is to provide more democratic opportunities for people.

Since the late 1970s, employee ownership has become less the preserve of radical conceptions of democratic politics and more the haven for "cutting edge" corporate policy. Stock ownership and methods of participation are now viewed as attractive corporate strategies and, at times, attractive labor strategies, as the 1980s and 1990s business climate struggles with increasing competition, changes in technology, and the need always to be market responsive. In fact, what better policy to reduce costly middle management than to motivate "the shop floor" to think out and decide for themselves what hampers and helps their efficiency? Corporate America's experimentation with worker involvement has fostered numerous innovative ownership and participative schemes. Corporate policies to build worker loyalty and participation fall under many different labels, from quality circles, total quality management, and reengineering to team-based empowerment and activity-based management; but plans such as these often become an end in themselves and neglect the workers' concerns and interests. Also, corporate goals often remain decidedly different than participatory democrats' goals. What Pateman prescribed as a strategy to reinvigorate citizenship and a democratic political process has become a corporate strategy to fight off global economic competition. Consequently, the concepts "participatory democracy" and "a Democratic workplace" today carry widely divergent meanings depending on whether democratic advocates or corporate management are using the terms.

I intend to analyze participatory theory's propositions in light of several variables that I think the theory undervalues. With a better understanding of how participation affects workers and firms, the theory can better forecast both success and failure, thereby reducing the effects of unwarranted or overzealous expectations. We must first recognize that democratic citizenship is still the final public objective from this democratic process of change. But an active citizenry should not be the sole measure of employee participation's success. Democratic citizenship can be viewed as the culmination of a series of successful processes or developments to which participatory schemes aim. Initial or intermediate accomplishments include individual self-development, the creation of efficacious workers, and the reestablishing of an active, local politics. If the ultimate goal remains to engage people toward some form of public awareness and action by empowering them to control their work space, then participation may be best viewed as a series of concentric circles emanating outward from the individual to other employees, then to the workplace itself, then perhaps to issue-orientated associations or fraternal groups, onto local public issues, and then to regional, state, and national concerns. Some may question why the individual remains at the center of these conceptual circles if the objective is to foster a truly civic culture. My response can only be that change begins incrementally, and today's culture focuses without question on individual rights and freedoms. My argument stresses that workplace democracy should not be assessed favorably only when it either achieves active citizenship or when it boosts economic productivity. It must also be assessed in light of "smaller," perhaps less ambitious but more immediate individual changes such as the creation of empowerment and efficacy—especially given the social and economic obstacles which inhibit or pervert its development.

What are some of these obstacles? For one, participatory changes must take account of the climates in which people work, in which people perceive themselves as in control or "out of the loop," as empowered or powerless, and in which people are or are not motivated. In tune with the cries of participatory theory to empower individuals and reduce the scope of distant corporate and bureaucratic control, the success of participatory changes must be assessed on a small, perhaps individualized scale. Second, participatory theory needs to account for the power of the market system to inhibit even willing participants from feeling empowered or efficacious. Given that the market remains a persistent external force to which every firm must respond, and given that most every worker has been acculturated to the "wisdom" of market relations, it is questionable whether participatory firms can control and perhaps isolate market behavior from participatory desires. Third, participatory theory needs to account for the power of the larger individualistic culture to also limit participation's benefit to the worker. As with the market, the culture fosters certain attitudes and ideas that workers bring to the workplace which can conflict with participatory designs and aspirations. Or, if some workers hail a participatory workplace as a refuge from the individualistic, materialistic culture, their unmet expectations can frustrate the entire participatory experiment. In a sense, these employees become the most derisive of what they perceive as "ersatz change," while they were at one time the most supportive of the participatory attempt. Given these potential obstacles, the question that first needs an answer is what presently hinders individual citizen action. The following examples illustrate conditions which make citizenship difficult. They also reveal a continuity of debate about unbridled economic power and the effects of capital's privileged position that harkens back to the debates of the tumultuous 1960s.

The 800 employees of Whitehall Labratories in Elkhart, Indiana, sued the parent company, American Home Products Corporation, after the company decided to shut down in 1991 and move operations to Puerto Rico. The company denied accusations that it benefited from unfair tax breaks though it agreed to a $24-million out-of-court settlement. In May 1993, the village of North Tarrytown, New York, passed a law that created costly environmental cleanup restrictions on General Motors Corporation (GM) after the company decided to close its local factory by 1996. By November 1993, GM filed suit against the village claiming the local ordinance violated federal and state constitutions. While GM viewed the law as a form of "economic protectionism," the village's mayor stated, "They [GM] seem to believe they can just clap their hands and walk away."[2] These examples show not just the effects of capital's mobility but a questioning of capital's preeminent privileges, a questioning of its communal effects, and a questioning of its social responsibility. While participatory theory advocates that all bureaucratic and hierarchical social structures need an infusion of participatory change, the workplace is one of the most obvious bases from which to dramatically change the inequalities that present relations foster. Former Labor Secretary Ray Marshall challenges that "We ought to have a more equitable sharing of the costs and benefits of change."[3]

However, when corporate policies extend to the work force, substantial prospects for capital helping individuals and communities exist. The Lowes' Companies, a building supply chain, has made many of its employees millionaires, no matter their skill, upon retirement through their long-term participation in the firm's stock ownership plan. Even without the benefits of start-up capital, the Community Service Center in the South Bronx created Cooperative Home Care Associates in 1985 to provide better paying and more secure jobs in the home health care field. Starting with a few employees, today it employs over 200, pays at the highest wage-level in the industry, and provides health insurance and vacation time. Its profit margins outperform the national average and turnover remains at less than half the national average.[4] Finally, a 1993 study by the Northeast Ohio Employee Ownership Center reports that, of the approximately 195 employee-owned firms that responded to their questionnaires, 41 percent of the respondents increased employment. The authors conclude, "If the rest of Ohio's companies had matched Ohio's ESOP firms during the last three years, the state would have full employment."[5] These examples prove that capital itself is not always the adversary. Rather, what people and communities fight against is when capital directs socioeconomic relations without consideration for any other values than profit maximization.

Profit maximization, though, remains capital's principal if not sole motive. But to pit empowered workers against a firm's profit maximization motive oversimplifies the tension. Participatory workers, who gain control of the firm's decision making, may in effect seek to maximize their gain. This possibility notes that potential difficulties may intensify even after participatory changes are made. The question is not just how to implement participatory change but also how to sustain commitment to the principles of the changes after power has shifted to the workers.

Profit, to be sure, remains essential, but it must be one of several considerations that form an successful modern business operation. Too often capital's commitment to employee involvement remains tied principally to a firm's "bottom line." Ironically, though, despite the examples which question capital's profit and power, capital clearly maintains the ability to dictate its agenda. The movement toward employee participation is quite often muted by the lack of employee control. The examples of people's and communities' discontent created by the unrestricted power of a large local employer quite often contrasts with the very same communities' associations, sometimes regional associations, that actively seek to convince firms to relocate to their areas—usually with strong enticements like favorable tax rates and modest land prices. Despite some seeds of capital's reevaluation, then, capital still sets the business, and thus the political and social, agenda. However, within the strong tendency of capital to enhance its power, made stronger in some ways by its contraction in recent years, a vital undercurrent persists.

Moving from the economic to the psychological level, the debate over human motivation has recently been fueled by antibehaviorist psychologists like Alfie Kohn and Charles Garfield. They claim incentives such as money often do not create happiness and can inhibit people's motivation to perform as best as they can. As Kohn explains, "When you do something for a reward you tend to become less interested in what you're doing. . . . It comes to seem like a chore, something you have to get through in order to pick up the dollar or the A or the extra dessert. What this means is that millions of well-meaning teachers and parents and managers are killing off creativity and curiosity in their attempt to bribe people to do a good job."[6] The authors' argument is not that corporate America should refrain from offering incentives, but the examples of using rewards to produce behavior begins to reassess socioeconomic institutions and much of human relations. The authors propose that such a reward system perverts human development and creates individuals who find meaning or satisfaction—and less and less meaning over time—only in the reward and not in the act of the endeavor. In fact, the examples question the motivational bases for the vast majority of both public and private activity. As an example, Charles Reich's *The Greening of America* was one of the first to capture what was labelled as a "new breed" of worker. The new breed rejected the necessity of the work ethic proferred by their parent's generation, rejected the rat race mentality, and rejected the corporate personality and lifestyle. Instead, this new breed chose paths where they would express themselves in their work and perhaps help their fellow man.

Worzalla Publishing Company, an employee-owned printer and bindery business since 1986, is an example where wages were not a principal priority. At the outset of the change to employee ownership, workers agreed not to raise wages for five years and went further in debt with the necessary acquisition of new capital so that no bonuses were paid until 1991.[7] In addition, participation programs based on work teams have initiated hundreds of ideas, and a monthly newspaper involves close to 20 percent of the firm's workers. In December 1993, the board of directors, pilots, and machinists of United Airlines approved a plan to trade majority ownership for five-year wage and benefit cuts totaling $4.5 billion and work-rule concessions.[8]

If money is not the sole motivator, if community is established only by fighting the dominant local employer as job security becomes an economic anachronism, then these changes indicate a possible reevaluation of capital's position and of the concentration of economic power. Though debate rages over whether this reevaluation remains an individualistic response to specific problems at the workplace or whether it is an emerging social trend, examples that question social and economic relations also rearticulate a competing ideology that runs as an undercurrent throughout American history. Whether we look to the Jacksonian era, the farmer's and Populist movements, or the tumultuous 1960s, people typically bond when they recognize similar perceptions of difficult circumstances.

These democratic movements have difficulty in maintaining commitment and even effectively enunciating their concerns because of the power of the American ideology supportive of individualism and free enterprise. The power of capitalism in some ways reaches its zenith in its ability to deflect criticism, or even analysis, from its actions to those who raise the issues. The few who cry out that the system is unjust, or that the industrial process serves to "manufacture worker consent," often find themselves labelled by either society as a whole or by those who maintain power as a noisy cabal who are fortunate to have the opportunity to make their grievances.[9] Moreover, demand for change in the socioeconomic structure is usually misconstrued as a challenge to the fundamental rights, particularly political rights, of the individual. My intention here is not to denounce individual rights but to call attention to how social and economic relations infringe upon not only individual development, but also the collective good as well.

Michael Walzer captures how late-twentieth-century liberalism molds people more for consumer activity and less for any notion of common activity:

> We are perhaps the most individualist society that ever existed in human history. Compared certainly to earlier, and Old World societies, we are radically liberated, all of us. Free to plot our own course. To plan our own lives. To choose a career. To choose a partner or a succession of partners. To choose a religion or no religion. To choose a politics or an anti-politics. To choose a life-style—any style. Free to do our own thing, and this freedom, energizing and exciting as it is, is also profoundly disintegrative, making it very difficult for individuals to find any stable communal support, very difficult for any community to count on the responsible participation of its individual members. It opens solitary men and women to the impact of a lowest common denominator, commercial culture. It works against commitment to the larger democratic union and also against the solidarity of all cultural groups that constitute our multi-culturalism.[10]

Walzer's contemporary insights reiterate Tocqueville's views of America 160 years ago. Tocqueville wrote, "The first thing that strikes the observation is an innumerable multitude of men, all equal and alike, . . . each of them, living apart, is as a stranger to the fate of all the rest, he is close to them [fellow-citizens], but he sees them not; . . . he exists but in himself and for himself alone, . . . he may be said at any rate to have lost his country."[11] While some may argue that Walzer speaks to the effects of liberalism and market relations while Tocqueville described the despotism of popular opinion, Tocqueville did recognize that the American propensity toward industrial callings and market activities could easily give rise to a "permanent inequality of conditions" that would spell trouble for American democracy.[12]

Walzer's and Tocqueville's accounts of individualism have been understood by Jurgen Habermas as the source of crisis tendencies.[13] In brief, Habermas argues that social needs and expectations emerge to which the state cannot respond because of a deficit of legitimation. A variety of paradoxes results revealing that the state functions to protect its own power while it aids only a fraction of the population. Given the aforementioned examples, it seems communities are not consciously bonding together to experiment with alternative forms of socioeconomic relations as much as they are reacting to the negative consequences of capital's power. Capitalist firms have backed these communities into a dire economic corner, and the communities' lawsuits are their immediate and desperate response. The difference between a planned form of experimentation and a desperate reaction to economic dislocation reveals the motivational commitment people have to democratic alternatives. If they pursue employee ownership principally as a strategy to ward off economic catastrophe, the work force will likely vary considerably in their level of attachment to the plan and its success.

At the individual level, well before any unified social action occurs, Habermas forecasts tendencies which produce a "motivational" crisis. This develops when the civil and familial–vocational privatism central to the state's reproduction are challenged. In the previous examples, a prominent paradox that faces the individual is that the tradition of both possessive individualism and the market's equitable outcomes contrasts with an increasingly intrusive set of government policies which allocate numerous social benefits to particular interests. Again, when these paradoxes emerge and political practice no longer conforms to American ideology, people are left to question, and in some examples actively challenge, what appears as unjust conditions—for instance, the injustice that people claim for both the creation and abolition of affirmative action quotas. Habermas argues that what can result is a society contemptuous of its culture and lacking any ideological attachment or underpinning, a society ready to rethink its social, economic, and political contract and act to recover its definition of democratic control. Or perhaps more characteristic of American society today, a society that does not rethink its cultural contracts becomes increasingly cynical of all its social institutions and public officials and turns into bitterly segregated groups, each demanding that others acknowledge and respect their particular group's differences.

These representative examples of community action and individual questioning of economic power and, in turn, the government's lack of an effective response, backed by the numerous participatory workplaces already in place, reveal Habermas's crises. The calls for participatory democracy at work, in the community, and in politics in general are the necessary signs that society has reached a crucial divide. However, to assume that workplace participation and other fundamental changes in the loci of power will develop misses the ability of both capital and the government to either—choose your preference—assuage or deflect society's crises. In general, the growth of interest group politics and identity-based politics reflects the inaction of the state to adequately respond to the worsening position of many groups in society. In turn, interest group politics, which some believe overloads the representational apparatus, more accurately represents the increasingly competitive environment for increasingly scarce resources for society in general. If the government has not responded adequately, groups have organized and pressed their interests less in the Tocquevillian sense of spontaneous accommodation and more in the vein of Social Darwinism, which demands ferocious and consuming competition in order to merely survive. Finally, given that many people tune out politics precisely because of its ferocious competition, capital exerts its power when people focus their disdain and anger on the political process to the exclusion of the state's necessary support of capitalist prerogatives. As a consequence, the legitimation crises that create social discontent and even calls for change often go unanswered.

In their study of the growing breed of cynical Americans, Kanter and Mirvis report that,

> Within the species known as the cynic we can identify two distinct brands of cynicism. First, there are cynics who seem to be broken-hearted about life. These are estranged cynics . . . [who] cope by distancing themselves from other people. They include the truly lonely crowd, those who suffer in quiet desperation, and the many lonely hearts. . . . Furthermore, in the affairs of commerce and politics they are the outsiders and the voiceless. A second prominent verson of the cynical types is neither estranged from the world nor connected to it. Instead, they seem to be tough-minded about life. . . . They bring to mind Sydney J. Harris's dictum: "You may be sure that when a man begins to call himself a realist [as these cynics often do] he is prepared to do something he is secretly ashamed of doing."[14]

The question becomes which option do cynical Americans pursue: that of the estranged cynic, who mirrors the isolated individualist path that Tocqueville notes undermines associational life and thus democracy's vigor; or that of a realist cynic, who assumes that others are only "out for themselves" and so he too must selfishly pursue his interests? In the latter case, if an issue motivates the person to act politically, he perceives his actions in the narrowest sense, to satisfy his interests. Neither option addresses the underlying conditions which cause cynicism and the individual's actions, although both options exacerbate social dysfunction and increase at least political friction.

The times may or may not appear as tumultuous as the 1960s and early 1970s, but in Habermas's language, the varied community and organized worker protests show that tendencies for crisis exist. These tendencies produce several important questions if people are ready to change their commitment to their social contract. For example, if employees seek to restructure their workplace to encourage participation but at the expense of capitalist norms, do these actions indicate that individuals are willing to forego a degree of economic individualism in the name of economic equality and efficiency? Do employees recognize that these changes fundamentally alter relations in economics and politics, or do they understand a more participatory workplace as a legitimate right of equal opportunity as ingrained by the current culture? Specifically, for those who change their workplace, and for those who participate in these changed environments, are the participatory changes due to a conscious effort to supplant the dominant forms of employee control with a more active and educated employee? Or are these changes based on narrow self-interest: to save a job, to get rid of a difficult employer, or to grab control from a faceless corporation?

As previously noted, participatory democratic theorists typically make the assumption that a more engaged, informed individual at the workplace will be more likely to be socially active as well. Participation at the workplace encourages the individual to develop a broader perspective in answering company decisions. In turn, this perspective eventually extends to society and helps to build a stronger communal sentiment. However, questions about the motivations for employee participation persist, and employees typically do not view their changing work environments as challenges to the capitalist system but justify the changes with the same values upon which the capitalist system prospers. In this light, the claims that participatory theorists make about participation's effects are at least questionable.

My task is not to dismiss workplace participation as idealistic. It remains a powerful alternative to the problems associated with capital's concentrated power with numerous examples of success. But just as participative schemes need to develop a series of graduated criteria to measure their successes, beginning with the improvement in the individual's motivation at work and in private affairs and ending in a truly active democratic citizenry, so must expectations for workplace democracy be assessed within the culture it attempts to reform. Although Habermas sees crisis tendencies in all late capitalist societies, he states flatly that crises do not occur simply because the causes are apparent. In effect, the crises are necessary but not sufficient causes for societal change. In turn, workplace democracy may represent necessary but not sufficient change in how society determines its economic and political relations. I argue that workplace democracy finds justification as a method to begin to resolve present feelings of powerlessness and anomie. This justification remains well within the American ideology beholden to individualism and free market enterprise. The distinction, then, is that participatory theory proposes work conditions that employees themselves may not support because the workers may not agree with the wholesale societal changes the theorists seek. The alternative I propose reduces the scope of change to a series of graduated contexts. This scope still allows change to occur but with less ambitious or fundamental social implications, which may be the only method which allows for cautious individuals to democratically come to decide for themselves for fundamental change. What does my alternative improve? It provides for a series of analyses of participation's effects in various degrees and in various social settings—for instance, the workplace, the city hall, and the state legislature. What does this alternative overcome? The unrealistic expectations that can develop and then create frustration when they go unrealized by calls for dramatic, fundamental change.

To decipher what motivates employees, this work recognizes two underappreciated contentions within the participatory and the economic research literature: (1) that employees, even established worker–owners, bring different sets of personal attitudes and different motivations to participatory attempts, and these differences affect both the economic and cooperative success of the company and the individual's sense of well-being; (2) that the creation of educated individuals with a newfound awareness of and concern for political activity not only depends on the different motivations each individual brings to the endeavor but also depends on the economic and cultural obstacles that exist in a society not familiar with worker ownership and participation. Workplace participation should not be written off as a mistake if it does not produce the engaged citizens participatory theory claims it will. For it to encourage citizenship, people must forego much of the ideological baggage that inhibits workers acting as owners. But even more paradoxically, it is the individualist ideology and concern for equality that generates a crisis for reform against the culture which itself is predicated on individualism and equality. A crisis may, in fact, occur, but how each individual interprets that crisis, whether to call for fundamental changes or to reform current practices, affects how the changes develop. It is these interpretations which I argue determine how change develops, and these interpretations exist within profound cultural constraints which participatory theory undervalues. While Habermas provides reasons why the demands for workplace participation can mushroom, society's traditional commitment to individualistic and free-market ideologies present contradictory attitudes that mute the cries for change. Thus, workers may proclaim their avid support for participatory involvement but do little to initiate such changes or halfheartedly accept such changes at their workplace.

But interestingly, workplace participation also maintains support in the United States because it expresses the tradition—some argue it is more an undercurrent to American history—of individual freedom to rule one's environment equally with others. Thus, employee involvement as a force of social change revives the ongoing tenuous balance between the freedom to pursue one's economic interests unencumbered in the marketplace against the recognition of some measure of economic and political equality. Today the problems with an oppressive social equality result in part from the excesses of freedom which have concentrated economic and political resources. This result shifts Tocqueville's concerns about the tyrannical designs of popular opinion to the destructive amount of liberty for a select few. Tocqueville felt associational life would constrain the few to tyrannize, but today's associational life has been constrained by the sheer number of social institutions, by a responsive government, and by an unresponsive market economy. While Tocqueville saw equality as a more pernicious and relevant problem in his time than inequality, he at least recognized the latter's potential for tyranny: "I am of opinion . . . that the manufacturing aristocracy which is growing up under our eyes is one of the harshest which ever existed in the world; but, at the same time, it is one of the most confined and least dangerous. Nonetheless, the friends of democracy should keep their eyes anxiously fixed in this direction; for if ever a permanent inequality of conditions and aristocracy again penetrate into the world, it may be predicted that this is the gate by which they will enter."[15] My perspective is that this potential for tyranny is less confined and more dangerous than it was 160 years ago. What results when inequality becomes a permanent feature of society, when the manufacturing elite develops and uses its power against its employees and their actions as citizens? Tocqueville provides an answer when he states that "the manufacturing aristocracy of our age first impoverishes and debases the men who serve it, and then abandons them to be supported by the charity of the public. . . . Between the workman and the master there are frequent relations, but no real association."[16] Since associations are for Tocqueville how citizens interact and help produce public policy, the consequences of industrial relations inhibits associations between people and between classes. If associational life is absent, then partial or special interests determine public issues. His analysis describes today's legislative process at all levels of government.

In essence, a vicious cycle emerges. First, manufacturing relations dehumanize the working class. Tocqueville agrees that this dehumanization suppresses associational life. Next, people rely on public welfare because they lack the inclination to combine with others. But manufacturing interests mold the system of public welfare because business interests dominate the political sphere when peoples' associations decline. Finally, individuals isolated without associational life find fault primarily with themselves and their abilities as Tocqueville's oppressive public opinion judges them as somehow "unfit." As Kanter and Mirvis argue, many Americans follow this isolating path and have become, simply, too cynical to be part of society. In short, for many individuals, manufacturing relations inflict a personal injury and then public opinion rubs salt into it. Tocqueville worried about the effects of public opinions, as he saw only a minor, containable manufacturing aristocracy. Today, though, the wound from corporate policies and market activities may be more pronounced. However, public opinion, by acknowledging workplace participation as a viable economic option, can provide a salve rather than salt.

In its ideal form, employee participation redistributes economic and political power and thereby remedies some of the effects described by Tocqueville. My concern is whether these changes can compete against the established institutions as well as the established ideologies supportive of capital and individual freedom. Moreover, raising the issue of individual motivations recognizes that employee participation can compete economically against traditionally operated capitalist companies. But these work reforms must also compete against the established ideologies inherent in the capitalist culture and supported by the political process.

Consequently, if employee ownership and involvement produces fulfilled and satisfied workers but not necessarily active citizens, what does this mean for our democracy? It is possible that satisfied workers will direct their energies to change their larger social environment, or will employee ownership leave them locally satisfied without any regard for the public interest. If this rift between one's immediate vision and the public arena persists, then public policy remains subject to special and protected interests. Without an extension to public issues, workplace participation remains an effective agent for creating self-worth but at the cost of neglecting persistent social concerns. If this is what occurs, do the changes workplace participation promise demand a reevaluation of what values we as a society recognize? Although my tone appears less optimistic than participatory democrats' proposals, my answers seek to distinguish between what is immediately possible and what is optimistically argued. We have the same objective of advocating and reinvigorating citizenship; the task is to understand how individuals cope with a culture that contains mixed messages on the importance of citizenship.

NOTES

1. Denis G. Sullivan, Jeffrey L. Pressman, Benjamin I. Page, and John J. Lyons, *The Politics of Representation: The Democratic Convention 1972* (New York: St. Martin's Press, 1974), 20–22.

2. Benjamin Weiser, "When the Plant Closes," *Washington Post National Weekly Edition*, 10–16 January 1994, 6–7.

3. Quoted in ibid., 6.

4. "Employee Ownership and Community Economic Development," *National Center for Employee Ownership Report* 14 (January–February 1994): 5.

5. "Encouraging Results from Major Ohio Study," *National Center for Employee Ownership Report* 13 (July–August 1993): 4.

6. Quoted in Jay Mathews, "For Love or Money," *Washington Post National Weekly Edition*, 13–19 December 1993, 22.

7. "Case Study: Worzalla Publishing Company," *National Center for Employee Ownership Report* 13 (November–December 1993): 7.

8. "United Buyout Moves Closer," *National Center for Employee Ownership Report* 14 (March–April 1994): 1.

9. Michael Burawoy, *Manufacturing Consent: Changes in the Labor Process under Monopoly Capitalism* (Chicago: University of Chicago Press, 1979), 77–94, 193–203.

10. Michael Walzer, "Citizenship and Civil Society," Part 1, New Jersey Committee for the Humanities Series on the Culture of Community, New Brunswick, New Jersey, 13 October 1992, 11–12.

11. Alexis de Tocqueville, *Democracy in America*, ed. Richard D. Heffner (New York: New American Library, 1956), 303.

12. Ibid., 219. One of the most interesting research questions for participatory and democratic theorists is whether the system of Yugoslavian worker control survives the ethnic cleansing and nationalist barriers erected by the newly created governments in Croatia and Bosnia–Herzegovina. On one hand, worker control was more the economic method for interaction and not the economic structure itself. If this is accurate, it seems that even the development of market reforms will still rely on the traditional methods of worker participation. But the introduction of a market economy changes both economic and political institutions, and the possibility of sweeping change seems to rest with those who have power—sometimes political power, other times military might. At any rate, worker participation most likely has greater legitimacy than any political system at this stage.

13. Jurgen Habermas, *Legitimation Crisis*, trans. T. McCarthy (London: Heinemann, 1976), 62–92.

14. Donald L. Kanter, and Philip H. Mirvis, *The Cynical Americans: Living and Working in an Age of Discontent and Disillusion* (San Francisco: Jossey-Bass, 1989), 186–187.

15. Tocqueville, *Democracy in America*, 219.

16. Ibid.

Chapter 1 # WORKPLACE PARTICIPATION
The Issues, the Literature, and the Democratic Concern

For the past three decades, workplace democracy has been advocated as one possible remedy for the social, economic, and political problems which critics claim plague American culture. For employees, participation combats social alienation, job stress, and even encourages self-actualization. However, democracy in the factory or office has meant everything from participation at the shop-floor to acquiring and voting for stock options. More involvement at work, where most people attach some degree of personal meaning, has been viewed as the first step toward overcoming its isolating and perhaps dehumanizing aspects. Also, whether in small work groups or in enterprises based wholly on employee ownership, bringing people together to make decisions about a company's health changes the way people approach and interpret problems and solutions. Some researchers, especially participatory theorists, believe workplace democracy breeds a communitarian outlook that counters the individualism that the market and the political system support. They suggest that empowerment at work translates into a sense of political efficacy. Simply put, involvement in the decision-making process at work translates into an active and engaged citizenry.

Different supporters define workplace democracy differently.[1] At one extreme, participatory theorists like Peter Bachrach, Carole Pateman, and C. B. MacPherson emphasize the rights of each individual to participate in society and develop as a productive member. These authors contend that in a democratic society based on equal rights, a reciprocity between society and the individual exists. Broadly conceived, people create the institutions through which they express themselves, and, in turn, they remain responsible for attending to the issues which guide institutional behavior. Participatory theorists believe that present institutions and processes do not foster participation. They argue that in an increasingly bureaucratized world with a politics based on competitive parties, the political rights of citizenship remain meaningless or at least fundamentally incomplete. Also, at the individual psychological level, they suggest that because people feel government is both remote and impenetrable, citizens either never develop or lose any sense of political efficacy. But the workplace remains an arena where people can express their individual rights as well as their rights of citizenship, developing their political capabilities as they participate in a comparatively smaller "political" environment.

At another extreme, companies in the last fifteen years have developed numerous employee participatory schemes. What these plans have in common is not a singular form of participation but rather the corporate motivation to increase worker productivity. The concern is not foremost individual development or the realization of basic, common rights. Quality of life programs, quality circles, job enrichment plans, and work teams are examples of participation which generally involve a voice in only the methods of an employee's immediate work. Participation in this sense does not extend to company decision-making control and fosters little change in individual efficacy. Even in regard to employee ownership, significant differences exist between mere ownership and employee participation in a company's decision making. Despite these substantial differences between wholly participatory endeavors and corporate "enrichment," corporate attempts do integrate the individual with other workers in some form of participatory unit. Employee participation demands that the individual think and act on more than simple self-interest. Given the growth of worker ownership and corporate participatory plans, both management and employees appear receptive to these work changes.

But the success of employee participation schemes remains mixed. Certainly, workplace democracy advocates have hundreds of financially prosperous and personally fulfilling examples. The National Center for Employee Ownership (NCEO) states over eleven million employee–owners exist and over ten thousand Employee Stock Ownership Plans (ESOPs) operate in the United States. Worker-owned and operated businesses successfully compete in numerous industries from services, like Avis, Inc., to retail, like Fred Schmid Appliances, to manufacturing, like Stone Construction Equipment, Inc. But to lump together the variety of participatory designs and ownership structures to buttress the claim that employee participation is an unqualified successs misleads as much as it simplifies. Christopher Eaton Gunn's research on the Northwestern plywood firms is a relevant example. Gunn found that despite the cooperative symbols of shared control and material incentives, worker–owners retained some methods of the conventional capitalist process, such as the use of hired labor and the vesting of membership rights to stock ownership. Also, members remained motivated by profit, sometimes at the expense of cooperative principles. Gunn recognizes, as did Greenberg's earlier research, that the plywood firms compete against conventionally owned firms and that the externally hostile, competitive market structure permeated thinking inside the cooperative.[2] What the plywood firm's research shows is that different forms of worker ownership and employee participation produce different measures of success. The notion of success itself remains an important definitional issue, as the plywood firms are typically regarded as "successful" examples of employee ownership. Greenberg's and Gunn's research are startling reevaluations of what constitutes the relationships between participation, control, success, and worker democracy.

To recognize that success is contingent upon the firm's objectives does not undervalue the worker's importance. Some argue that in privately owned firms, participation remains controlled by capital and capitalists. Employees have no voice over how management designs participation. But if the definition of success extends beyond corporate goals, the recognition of a variety of participatory endeavors as successful may mean that management recognizes a variety of employee identities and interests. The workplace is but one of many arenas where individuals express themselves. Employees find satisfaction and make commitments in their family, their church, and their local American Legion. Commitment to decision-making control may wax and wane given the priorities individuals ascribe to other interests in their lives. Often, a common reason to forego participation in even small-scale political or work-related issues is the need to spend more time with one's family. This may overdramatize the time and effort required to participate in one's firm, yet it shows that employee participation competes with other objectives that comprise a person's life. Thus, the causality that participatory theorists cite between participation and political activity is uncertain given the demands on workers which these changed workplaces create.

PARTICIPATION, PRODUCTIVITY, AND POLITICAL EFFICACY

Participation means both a form of ownership and company control by its worker–owners. Although this definition generally refers to industrial democracy, or the complete reordering of social, economic, and political relations, my focus is to first understand how less complete or thoroughgoing participatory attempts affect democratic participation and how established social structures and beliefs affect participation. I believe these initial participatory experiments are crucial in understanding not only whether people willingly adjust but also what are the most significant impediments to implementing reform. By recognizing what resistance exists and how it develops, and whether participatory changes are assimiliated into society in a modified form as workplace involvement evolves, we can uncover the strengths of the participatory challenge to the present system and how the system attempts to control the challenge.

Despite confusion over research definitions and in ordinary social usage, employee participation schemes share some fundamental concerns. Advocates claim that involvement breeds commitment. The growth of worker ownership reveals that employees seek control over an increasingly complex world. Given the often primary role of the workplace in an individual's life, decision-making input and voting rights reclaim the power that an individual feels is lost in the larger political environment.[3] In turn, it is reasonable to assume that corporate participatory strategies admit to a problem of employee purposelessness.[4] Reestablishing a commitment between the worker and the company's operation or product reduces absenteeism, turnover, carelessness, and even waste and small theft. While a firm benefits by combating these ills, the principal corporate interest in participation focuses on increasing productivity. Bennett Harrison's report in a *Technology Review* article epitomizes the exclusive corporate interest in worker output. As he concentrates on the short-term results, he writes that employee involvement "not only fails to help efficiency but actually appears to hurt it."[5] The article makes no mention of whether the employees or the firm find satisfaction with their participatory attempts.

Participatory advocates believe such statements focus too narrowly on economic concerns. To base participation's success only on efficiency measures keeps an analysis within the constraints of the system which creates employee difficulties. To be sure, a firm exists to produce a product or provide a service within a competitive market. If this remains the sole motivation, a company's profit remains the guidepost. Employee grievances and subsequent employee involvement are then only methods of internal tinkering with the established corporate structures. However, if corporate agendas are expanded to include empowered employees, or if employees run the companies where they work, then efficiency may be just one of several measures of success. If the employee becomes as important or essential as the company, factors such as efficacy and control become substantial company concerns. To dichotomize the debate between corporate concerns with efficiency and the concerns of employee-operated firms with other measures of "success" or "profitability" overlooks both the subtlety of corporate control and the numerous issues confronting labor-run businesses.

For example, one strand of research emphasizes an apparent tradeoff between participation and productivity. According to this view, a firm that exists in a capitalist market must attempt to maximize efficiency to stay competitive. Hierarchical control streamlines information flow and allows for a strict accounting of responsibilities and output. Productivity suffers as participation increases the number of actors and the time necessary to inform them and make a consensual decision. In their highly acclaimed work, Alchian and Demsetz argue that this tradeoff directly affects production costs and encourages "shirking" or "free-riding." They state, "It is possible to increase productivity through team-oriented production, a production technique for which it is costly to directly measure the marginal outputs of the cooperating units. This makes it more difficult to restrict shirking through simple market exchange between cooperating inputs. It is economical to estimate marginal productivity by observing or specifying input behavior. The simultaneous occurrence of both these preconditions leads to the contractual organization of inputs, known as the classical capitalist firm."[6]

What Alchian and Demsetz may misunderstand is that participation provides additional information that management may not be able to observe or dictate. In addition, a wealth of recent research overwhelmingly disproves the apparent tradeoff. Christopher Eaton Gunn states that there "is a growing body of empirical literature that is generally supportive of claims for the economic efficiency of the labor-managed firm. Much of this literature focuses on productivity, frequently finding it to be positively correlated with increasing levels of participation" (Cable and Fitzroy 1980; Jones and Backus 1977; Granrose, Applebaum, and Singh 1986; Rosen and Quarrey 1987; Estrin, Jones, and Svejnar 1987). Though Gunn recognizes the difficulty in developing accurate comparisons of "traditional" versus "cooperative" firms, he finds "on balance, theoretical debates have done little to shake the basic case for the efficiency of the labor-managed firm, and empirical findings have tended to support that case."[7] As Bruce K. MacLaury, President of Brookings, reports, "A major finding . . . [of their study] is that whatever compensation scheme is used, meaningful worker participation, beyond labor representation in boards of directors, enhances productivity."[8] Finally, in a 1993 Sage publication, John Cotton concludes that "employee ownership can (but not always) have a positive impact on organizational productivity and employee attitudes . . . the weight of the evidence suggests that employee ownership (plus employee participation) is more likely than not to have a positive effect."[9]

Moreover, the attention given to the efficiency debate obscures the more complex relationship between social activity and the capitalist creed. While the efficiency debate centers on economic relations, the power of society to promote specific economic relations over others broadens the scope of the debate. Jackall and Levin aptly describe the social forces at work:

It is a commonplace of social analysis that every society promotes, both explicity and tacitly, certain forms of productive organization by reinforcing the conditions for growth and survival of some types of enterprise while ignoring or even opposing other possibilities. Specifically, in the United States, the very forms of legal structure, access to capital, entrepreneurship, management, the remuneration of workers, and education all favor and reinforce the establishment and expansion of hierarchical corporate forms of enterprise and simultaneously create barriers to cooperative ones. Worker cooperatives are anomalies to these mainstream trends.[10]

In this light, the claims that participatory firms are less efficient than traditionally owned capitalist firms appear quite hollow. Even given the constraints that our predispositions for hierarchical business organizations place on cooperative firms, that latter in many studies outperform the traditionally designed firms on their most important criterion, productivity. Another irony is that the workplace remains one of the few, if not the only, realm where Americans willingly accept a modification of their fierce individualism. Or, perhaps one could argue that Americans express their individualism as a reaction to their stultifying work lives. The pertinent issue here focuses on how participatory firms, as anomalies to the present system, can in fact exist, and then effectively compete, within a setting designed to discourage their existence.

THE "LEAP" FROM PRIVATE TO PUBLIC BEHAVIOR

It appears that workplace democracy, or at least participation, shows encouraging results. But before enthusiastically supporting these reforms, it is essential to separate the economic findings from the theoretical assumptions and aspirations of participatory advocates. Understanding the complexity of the debate over the merits of workplace participation involves unraveling practical advantages from theoretical advocacy. Participatory advocates make two debatable claims. The first is that individual involvement at the shop-floor, in managerial decision making, and in determining remuneration spurs efficacy. Simply put, increased involvement in an endeavor enhances one's sense of purpose in or control over the endeavor. The enhanced sense of purpose increases employees' satisfaction not just with their jobs but first of all with themselves. Participation increases people's perceived sense of influence, and the subsequent power gives people's lives meaning. Although this contention has its critics, Spector's meta-analysis of eighty-eight studies examining employee perceptions of control concludes that employee participation was associated with improvements in general satisfaction, as well as satisfaction with the work, organizational involvement, promotion and growth possibilities, pay, and supervision.[11] The relationship assumes that participation produces feelings of control and satisfaction. Obviously, debate continues as participation itself depends on other variables.

The second claim is that workplace efficacy "spills over" to political participation. On one hand, it seems reasonable that the increased sense of power at work easily translates into individuals working to resolve problems beyond work—in their neighborhoods, cities, and even nationally. On the other hand, the assumption of efficacy in one's economic environment extending to the larger, more abstract, and, as Jackall and Levin recognize, the more antagonistic political realm misreads the basic difference between private and public goods, between private and public activity.

It is this "leap of faith" from workplace efficacy to political participation that demands scrutiny. To do so, the first contention, that participation builds efficacy, also needs analysis because different actors with different motivations define workplace democracy differently. Participants reveal a variety of interpretations of what participation means to them. Some partisans for decision-making control extend it only to narrow economic interests; others advocate workplace democracy to alter the competitive marketplace as a whole. Jackall and Levin note that, "Countercultural enterprises have generally drawn their members through friendship networks.... Unfortunately, an organization using such an inexplicit selection process often ends up with persons whose only common value is negativism toward the traditional workplace, rather than a positive commitment to create and sustain a positive alternative. When demands are made upon such persons, they often become divisive, using their well-honed destructive energies to undermine the organization."[12] For the authors, alternative work organizations, such as employee participation schemes, remain as much a haven for generally disgruntled people as an outlet for those workers committed to recreating their work relationships. If so, it seems that a firm needs to establish its requirements and responsibilities with its employees. With an indication of how a participatory and/or employee-run firm operates, employees begin to see their changing roles and the potential influence of their efforts. This does not mean the firm can be run from the "top-down," as this will incite all the employees no matter their level of negativity.

Perhaps employees must rethink their expectations. This latter change, if it occurs midstream, encourages an embittered few who stay to become the firm's constant source of criticism. While Albert O. Hirschman notes that a firm benefits from employee "loyalty" by their willingness not to leave the firm or choose another product but to voice their concerns, Jackall and Levin begin to recognize a group of workers who do not necessarily help a firm by exercising their voice option.[13] Though Jackall and Levin do not clarify the conditions that encourage these "negative" people to become divisive, it seems that any company decision that smacks of "exploitation" or "exclusivity," however they define these broad terms, presents problems of this type. More generally, Rothschild and Whitt recognize the difficulty of establishing a workplace that involves a number of individual differences, whether negative or not. They claim that "the task of any collective workplace . . . is to eliminate all bases of individual power and authority, save those that individuals carry in their own persons."[14] Existing within a market economy that compensates individuals for specific skills and educational backgrounds, the ability of a participatory workplace to overcome an individual's tacit support of the external system, which translates into a worker who feels exploited or undercompensated in the internal democratic workplace, remains crucial. For without this transformation to participatory and/or democratic principles, the employee-run firm never approaches any significant internal change and, thus, breeds various levels of negativity.

My argument is not just that there is a host of reasons for joining cooperatives or participating in decision making. My argument is that when workplace participation occurs, participation's transformative effect to produce civic-minded individuals depends on the identities and motivations individuals associate with participation and what they bring to the process from outside the workplace. The issue here is not only whether people act for the common good once they participate in the workplace. My concern is with the additional assumption that people are in fact transformed by participation. Before any public activity occurs, the individual must undergo a decisive change in motivation and in attitude to combat the social forces which stress individualistic behavior. But the interrelationship between these changes, moving from the indvidual's pyschological perceptions to activity in the public arena, presents a difficulty in deciphering how these changes occur, or if they occur at all.

If an initial uncertainty exists over the relationship of purely economic motivations to broader public interests, then the task becomes how to distinguish actions based on one or the other and whether in fact such delineation is appropriate. The rationale for not marking substantive differences relates to the earlier argument that individuals have a host of interests which remain in a constant and intermixed flux. Engaged and motivated workers often justifiably alter their preferences for public service or participation given the individual importance of the issues involved. Not all workers will remain primarily economically interested, and not all workers will become and remain politically interested. If an issue's salience affects public activity, then it is necessary to examine, not when workers act publicly, but why they act publicly when they do. If workers who participate in decision making at work feel empowered to act on those public issues of personal salience, then workplace democracy may be the variable to overcome collective action problems. However, an individual's concern for decision-making control at work is but one important variable that competes with several other motivations that typically change over time.

THE PARTICIPATORY LITERATURE

Carole Pateman's *Participation and Democratic Theory* epitomizes the participationist's strong association between workplace involvement and civic behavior. Her insights, though, do not differentiate public action according to specific issues or according to individual motivations. Rather, in keeping with the Rousseauean tradition, she suggests that participation allows the individual to develop both individually and politically. Pateman infers that, without participation, individuals are lacking in their potential as not only citizens, but as fulfilled, whole people. She intricately links participation with self-development in the workplace:

The theory of participatory democracy is built round the central assertion that individuals and their institutions cannot be considered in isolation from one another. . . . The major function of participation . . . is therefore an educative one, educative in the very widest sense, including both the psychological aspect and the gaining of practice in democratic skills and procedures. . . . The most important area [for a participatory society] is industry; most individuals spend a great deal of their lifetime at work and the business of the workplace provides education in the management of collective affairs. . . . The second aspect of the theory of participatory democracy is that spheres such as industry should be seen as political systems in their own right. . . . A further reason . . . relates to the substantive measure of economic equality required to give the individual the independence and security necessary for [equal] participation. . . . Finally, the justification for a democratic system in the participatory theory of democracy rests primarily on the human results that accrue from the participatory process.[15]

Pateman interprets Rousseau to mean that participation affects the individual's psychological makeup. Participation transforms individuals through their experiences by "managing collective affairs." She claims, "The central function of participation in Rousseau's theory is an educative one . . . designed to develop responsible, individual social and political action through the effect of the participatory process."[16] For participatory theorists in general, workplace involvement is one of many necessary prerequisites which ultimately forecast a dramatic change between private and public concerns.

Peter Bachrach echoes Pateman in arguing that the workplace needs consideration as a forum for political activity. He believes that democracy and its researchers typically define the term using the biases of the elitist, procedural "Schumpeterean" language. For Schumpeter, democracy is "a method bound neither to interests nor to ideals," but Bachrach recognizes that often the method contains inherent power inequalities.[17] Earlier, Bachrach and Baratz also argued that the pluralist model cannot describe adequately the democratic process because people or groups can exercise power by either establishing or reinforcing barriers to the airing of public policy.[18] From them, nondecisions or nonissues reveal the exercise of power as much as the more obvious, everyday political decisions and agenda setting.

Bachrach's workplace remedy challenges the assumption that indifference would only be extended if the workplace became a political arena. He writes:

For many individuals political issues and elections appear either as trivial or remote and beyond the reach of their influence. Of a different magnitude are issues which directly affect them in their place of work, issues which are comparatively trivial, yet are overlaid with tensions and emotions that often infuriate and try men's souls. . . . I am not suggesting that the average worker . . . if given the opportunity to share in the making of factory decisions, would be magically transformed, in the fashion of Rousseau's common man, from an unimaginative, parochial, selfish human being to a broad-minded, intelligent, public-spirited citizen. I am saying that political education is most effective on a level which challenges the individual to engage cooperatively in the solution of concrete problems affecting himself and his immediate community. In the past this task was ideally performed in the New England town meeting; in twentieth-century America it can effectively be performed in the factory community.[19]

In a vein similar to J. S. Mill, Bachrach believes that reducing the scale but widening the scope of what is political will increase citizen attention. Democracy cannot remain as a simple accounting of elite preferences. Rather, it must be extended by its diffusion to the individual's work environment. Although Bachrach appears less optimistic about participation's effects than Pateman, his acknowledgment of man's selfish tendencies give greater credence to his argument. True, man can be selfish, but if he regularly participates with others in deciding their future, Bachrach argues that man will see no advantage in selfishness.

What form Bachrach's participatory "diffusion" takes points to one of the crucial elements of participatory theory. Bachrach and Botwinick claim "The underlying premise of participatory democracy . . . is that [it] encompasses self-exploration and self-development by the citizenry. . . . [For instance, for] people from lower classes . . . to become conscious of their interests, they must actually become involved in the political process."[20] The educative component of participation places both individual action and democratic results in an ongoing state of change and interpretation. This makes democracy and what constitutes democratic success difficult to define, but it places its power in those who comprise it. Democracy, then, becomes both a process of decision making and a collective state of mind.

Similarly, C. B. MacPherson states that the democratic workplace could provide a more meaningful avenue for development and fulfillment than the formalized processes of citizenship. He also believes that democratic values learned at the workplace could translate to the larger political arena. The implication is that participation inculcates efficacy, not only at work, but also in the political process itself. He does not argue for a dramatic alteration in the political system, only that participation can make the present system stronger, more relevant and effective. He states:

Those who are involved in it [workplace participation] are getting experience of participation in decision-making in that side of their lives—their lives at work—where their concern is greater, or at least more immediately and directly felt, than in any other.... Those who have proved their competence in one kind of participation, and gained confidence there that they can be effective, will be less put off by the forces which have kept them politically apathetic, more able to reason at a greater political distance from results, and more able to see the importance of decisions at several removes from their most immediate concerns.[21]

MacPherson believes that workplace participation links worker–citizens to the representational system. In understanding the problems of scale that Bachrach may deemphasize, MacPherson promotes participation as a method to develop workers capable of holding elected officials responsible. In this model, development at a local level encourages "true" representation at the national level. Also, as is true of the other theorists, the central tenets of participation's educative effects, the individual's capacity for development, and the changing character of the political system remain constant.

BROADER ISSUES AND THE NEED FOR CAUTION

But to advocate participation requires more than granting people the rights to control decision making. It also necessitates obligations and duties of the populace to be informed and engaged. Pateman, among others, assumes that participation breeds not only knowledge but interest.[22] In essence, all issues in society become political matters, forums for political judgment. By recognizing all interaction as political, participatory theory seeks to uncover the biases and inequalities inherent in present society. This extention of democracy, or more precisely of citizen interest, in a complex and confusing world is an example of the claims that need scrutiny.

To question citizen interest and development does not imply a Schumpeterean view of democracy. Participatory theorists look to participation as encouraging public mindedness, and they view workplace democracy as one arena where the private individual transforms into a public being. But the relationship between workplace participation and public behavior is clouded by the interests and expectations individuals bring to their work. To control one's immediate work environment is usually more important, and therefore more likely, than to concern oneself with local, regional, or national affairs. In addition, for public issues that encompass a diverse set of interests, individuals, despite strong feelings for an issue, often decide to spend their time on other topics where their effect is more probable and more tangible.

The motivation individuals have to pursue immediate interests rather than public concerns underscores the problem inherent in producing collective goods. It makes the calculation of when people participate and when people choose to be "free riders" difficult at best. But there are immediate gains for participating at work for the costs incurred. However, to infer that participation educates and develops Rousseauean citizens sidesteps the demands the "father" of participatory theory believed were compulsory—and today improbable—to create the general will. While Rousseau labels democracy as a government suitable only to a nation of gods, he states that his ideal republic requires a relative economic equality and independence.[23] Though these practical conditions make Rousseau's republic improbable, they do not make the republic impossible.

More important, though, he argues that the general will represents what is common to all citizens, yet it is not the mere aggregation of interests. Citizens determine the will, but they have no say on any particular policy or case. The distinction between the general legislative power—the sovereignty of the people—and its administration recognizes the difference between deciding on guiding principles and then administering them justly. Democracies are suspect for Rousseau because they combine both the legislative and executive functions. Instead, in the republic

The general will, to be truly what it is, must be general in its purpose as well as in its nature; that it should spring from all for it to apply to all; and that it loses its natural rectitude when it is directed towards any particular and circumscribed object—for in judging what is foreign to us, we have no sound principle of equity to guide us. For, indeed, whenever we are dealing with a particular fact or right, . . . it is a conflict in which private interests are ranged on one side and the public interest on the other; and I can see neither the law which is to be followed nor the judge who is to arbitrate . . . it cannot as a general will give a ruling concerning any one man or any one fact.[24]

Rousseau's insights are significant, but not because they show the inapplicability of individual interests in nurturing democracy. Rather, Rousseau himself recognizes that individuals have a host of interests which permit citizenship—but only for what everyone commonly shares, not on specific issues. His theory makes the crucial distinction between issues which remain partial concerns for individuals and issues which call for the collectivity's deliberation. For Rousseau, not all issues are appropriate for public consideration because some individuals or groups will have more concern for certain decisions than others. In contemporary politics, this distinction recognizes that some groups have developed an organizational or a resource bias to advantageously press their special interests often at the expense of the common good. The issues worthy of public assemblies are ones "intended not so much to uphold the general will there as to ensure that it [the general will] is always questioned and always responds."[25] This formulation of what constitutes the public good allows Rousseau to claim that the general will is inalienable and indestructible. As long as the social contract exists, a contract which produces the rule of law arising from equal participation, the general will is supreme, and any contention to the will is the result of either a question wrongly asked or an individual's partial reading of the will.

At first blush, it seems participatory workplaces cannot meet the requirements of Rousseau's general will. As is often the case in today's legislative politics, workers will employ selfish calculations to define their positions, as the general will becomes what best suits oneself. However, while Rousseau's theory seems too impractical and too homogeneous for modern times, the theory begins to reconcile the problems of information, education, and deliberation caused by a polity's scale. If citizenship is defined as the activity of seeking and clarifying the public good, leaving its enactment to an administrative body, Rousseauean citizenship can still occur today. Granted, this definition of citizenship alters the conception of face-to-face interaction common to New England town meetings and Swiss cantons. But citizenship occurs when people decide common principles and evaluate social actions in light of mutually accepted guidelines, in essence commiting to the guidelines as the basis for their interaction. My extrapolation from Rousseau's ideas is that as the polity grows, citizenship remains possible if it focuses on broad rules, on issues that unite people and not on issues that divide them. To be sure, this interpretation remains difficult to fathom today, as all our issues tend to divide and not unite us. Rousseau's republican response may well be that we do not ask ourselves the right questions. That is, collectively we fail to define and discuss what we seek to share and what we intend to accomplish together as a society. Rather, public policy today is a continual fight in a zero-sum game over scarce resources.

At base, Rousseau seeks to avoid the tyranny of man over man. The social contract is the agreement by men not to be ruled by men, as in monarchies and aristocracies, but rather to be ruled by laws. Men determine what these laws shall be and decide on them through their constant participation. Participation, then, becomes the act of reinforcing the rule of law, of upholding the social contract. As Pateman notes, this participation in deciding how one shall live and be ruled is not an infringement upon one's freedom. It is only an infringement upon what Rousseau calls independence, and independence only exists in the state of nature. Independence is subject to the whims of nature and of other men (i.e., might makes right), whereas freedom is the rational determination to unite for common and individual purposes.

Participation, and its sense of control of one's fate, becomes the avenue for guaranteeing "true" freedom. Pateman claims, "Rousseau argues that unless each individual is forced through the participatory process into socially responsible action then there can be no law which ensures everyone's freedom, i.e. there can be no general will."[26] For Rousseau, freedom is not the liberal definition of negative freedom—freedom from interference or from government rule. It is not the mere recognition and acceptance of individual diversity because no general will can result from only distinct interests. Again, today's interest group politics can never hope to foster a common will. Freedom becomes the degree of control that the individual has as he participates in directing how he shall live, being his own "master." It is the sense of "freedom feeling" in that he, and no one else, actively decides his freedom and the ability to self-legislate the general will which creates the individual's moral autonomy. With Rousseau's definition of freedom, diversity is not suppressed by a conformist general will. Because all participate in articulating the general will, all submit to it, for it is in each individual's interest—where the individual's notion of interest comes to mean that each seeks to avoid a life under the partial or arbitrary will of others. In fact, submitting to the social contract and producing the general will creates the environment for man's ultimate freedom, control over one's world without the arbitrary exercise of another man's will. In the workplace this means that employees make collective decisions that benefit everyone in the firm equally; in turn, everyone's needs are satisfied as a result. In today's workplace, though, the workers often think of themselves and their satisfaction first rather than any other worker or more generally the firm's health.

Freedom, though, dictates caution about the motivations to participate and participation's effects for both the individual and the polity. Rousseau believed that only a small, roughly equal state could produce the delicate republic. His solution sought to ensure freedom by each adhering to general laws and not to other men. Rousseau's thoughts display sensitivity to the tension between partial interests and the necessary structure and expression of people's sovereignty. Today, the cultural preference for individual's interests—in competition with other individuals, multinational corporations, and state policies—decreases the likelihood of achieving Rousseau's positive freedom. In short, participatory theory undervalues the effects of an economy and a society which frustrate positive freedom in favor of negative freedom.

America's individualistic culture today grants the individual Rousseauean independence but not freedom. Often, society calls for less interaction with or through government and, thus, less participation and voice over what government and multinationals do. In the name of freedom, then, people abstain from the processes that Rousseau thought are the only possible avenue toward freedom. These actions result in the view that the creation of a general will infringes upon diversity and freedom because some measure of freedom is sacrificed.

Also, under such conditions, participation often does not educate and transform individuals, as Rousseau and Pateman claim. Rather, participation isolates people into rigid groups and intensifies their differences. Whether participatory theory upholds Rousseau's notion of freedom or not, the theory needs to address precisely how and when participation educates, transforms, and frees the individual. It seems that today's social and political actions identify what Rousseau called independence as true freedom and, thus, we unknowingly submit, in the name of democracy, to the power of the few over the many. Even if we begin to recognize what Habermas calls our "crisis tendencies," we know of no substantive alternatives because we are acculturated to a perverted form of what we think is democracy. Our practice of democracy does not allow us to realize our democratic aspirations, if in fact we do support democratic ideals. Our ideals are worth questioning because it seems that we uphold a concept of democracy that falls apart when we attempt to implement it. Thus, our democratic definitions are inadequate when compared with Rousseau's notion of thorough commitment and true freedom.

Tocqueville's analysis of American democracy also draws attention to problems associated with individual diversity and public claims. Participatory advocates find support for their views in Tocqueville's assertion that

Feelings and opinions are recruited, the heart is enlarged, and the human mind is developed, only by the reciprocal influence of men upon each other. I have shown that these influences are almost null in democratic countries; they must therefore be artificially created, and this can only be accomplished by associations. . . . Among the laws which rule human societies, there is one which seems to be more precise and clear than all others. If men are to remain civilized, or to become so, the art of associating together must grow and improve in the same ratio in which the equality of condition is increased.[27]

The implication is that people find true freedom when they band together and that people develop their political faculties and become public regarding through this interaction. The two principal claims that participatory theory makes, one of an individual transformative effect and the other of subsequent public activity, emerge from Tocqueville's insights about how civil associations produce public-spirited citizens. However, he also understands that individualism, which can degenerate into selfish egoism—which is another name for Rousseau's independence—undermines democracy. He states, "The same social condition which renders associations so necessary to democratic nations, renders their formation more difficult amongst those nations than amongst all other. . . . It is true that, in these ages, the notion of human fellowship is faint, and that men seldom think of sacrificing themselves for mankind. . . . In democratic times, . . . when the duties of each individual to the race are much more clear, devoted service to any one man becomes more rare; the bond of human affection is extended, but it is relaxed."[28] If individualism is a double-edged sword—in that it is an integral part for democracy's development, and yet it can devolve and foster social disintegration—the questions are how does individualism operate today and what are its social effects? For Tocqueville, American democracy of the 1830s had begun to develop "relaxed" loyalties, but "by dint of working for the good of one's fellow-citizens, the habit and the taste for serving them is at length acquired."[29] Without that habit and taste today, as indicated by statistics that show the paucity of associational life, how does individualism affect 1990s American democracy? Rousseau and Tocqueville would respond that today's partial interests undermine almost every attempt at creating a truly free, truly democratic citizenry.

Because Tocqueville remained optimistic about associations translating private interests into public concerns, his thoughts centered on the troubling aspects of social equality. In fact, Tocqueville's concerns with the majority imposing its will upon individual interests is in response to Rousseau's idea that individuals may have to be "forced to be free,"[30] in a sense forced to see that their views are not in accord with the general will. However, Rousseau's majority is determined not by the aggregation of individual interests, which is Tocqueville's destructive individualism, but by each person's general recognition of the public interest. Rousseau emphasizes how partial interests destroy the common good and, thus, he wants to restrain private interest in creation of the public good. Tocqueville emphasizes how majority tyranny destroys individual diversity and, thus, seeks to restrain the "perverted" general will or the authority of numbers over the deliberative general interest. Tocqueville's authority of numbers epitomizes Rousseau's concerns about the misguided effects of the mere aggregation of interests. Tocqueville seeks to protect political liberty through associational life against the intrusions of an administrative state. In fact, Tocqueville sees associational life as providing what Rousseau claims the general will could provide. Their concerns are hardly antithetical but coexist as components of what Tocqueville sees as ambiguous and conflictual desires. He states, "Our contemporaries . . . want to be led, and they wish to remain free . . . by this system, the people shake off their state of dependence just long enough to select their master, then relapse into it again."[31] As Rousseau describes how selfish interests stifle the hopes of finding freedom, Tocqueville reveals how public opinion can destroy the necessary social interaction that fosters true freedom.

Tocqueville sees people surrendering their sovereignty to the state to pursue what Rousseau calls partial interests. Tocqueville seeks to protect political liberty in the face of a growing bureaucratic, administrative state. Yet Rousseau believes individuals must surrender the independence that forms partial interests, as they must commit to the common good. Only in this manner can freedom exist and sovereignty be legitimate. Finally, of critical importance for today, Tocqueville sees the starting point of tyranny in the actions of the majority, not in the actions of a minority. He focuses on the power of popular opinion to smother difference, as the democratic concern for equality takes license over maintaining the attachments and commitments that a rich and direct associational life builds. In a sense, Tocqueville fears that the rush to equality translates into the rule by mere numbers which, in turn, replaces the truly public principles and strong associational life necessary for democracy's health. In short, Tocqueville worries that men no longer abide by laws. Rather, they either conform to what others think if they are in the minority or, if in the majority, they unduly exert their power of rule by ostracizing those who think differently.

It is important to recognize that Tocqueville offers a more amenable prescription for ensuring democratic society. Rousseau demands a commitment to the public good that subsumes partial interests. In our age of individualism, such a rigorous commitment seems difficult to achieve and to sustain. On the other hand, Tocqueville provides a less consuming commitment to the common welfare and, thus, a less "maximal" program for democratic society. In response to Rousseau, Tocqueville bases the notion of democratic fulfillment on the constant interaction of partial interests and associations. In a sense, he turns Rousseau on his head, in that a society of strong individualists can in fact develop and support democracy through their constant political activity, which ensures their political freedom. For Tocqueville, then, individualism does not have the disastrous consequences that Rousseau claims undermines democracy. The distinction, though, is that Tocqueville defines individualism in two ways; and while he agrees with Rousseau that individualism "wrongly understood" and expressed as selfish egoism does undermine democracy, individualism "rightly understood" as the continual expression of political liberty has beneficial results.

Tocqueville adds definitional complexity that allows individualism to flourish in the name of democratic health. Tocqueville's distinction, then, allows me to argue for both participatory democratic values and today's individualistic actions. I argue for individualism's place in participatory theory—out of necessity, given its ingrained support in society—but the question that persists today is whether American individualism is for Tocqueville an individualism this is "rightly" or "wrongly" understood. Participatory theorists, using Rousseau as their base, believe that today's individualism represents selfish egoism and invoke participatory democracy to ward off the preference to pursue narrow interests. By employing Tocqueville's idea of individualism, I provide a less rigorous and consuming commitment to participatory democratic principles in comparison to Rousseau's dictates, but I do so in hopes that participation creates an individualism "rightly" understood.

As for aristocracy and inequality arising from manufacturing, Tocqueville claims "The object [of the aristocracy created by business] is not to govern that population [which it directs], but to use it. An aristocracy thus constituted can have no great hold upon those whom it employs; . . . it knows not how to will, and it cannot act."[32] But to "use a population" implies a form of control over their lives. Even more troubling is that while governing is an overt method of control that people recognize and thus can readily evaluate, the "use of workers" that Tocqueville notes is a more insidious, less tangible form of control which appears haphazard and diffuse. In a representational or democratic contract, the people understand that government acts on their behalf. In a capitalist economic system, it is less clear to the workers that employers must concern themselves with their "subjects." And so it appears that employers do not have to have concern for their workers but do need to control them to produce.

Tocqueville argued in the 1830s that we must not forget the importance of striking a balance between equality and liberty, between equality of condition and political liberty. Given the tremendous economic inequalities that have emerged since the 1830s, the balance that Tocqueville prescribes for social and government interaction needs, if not a revision, then an update to account for the unequal economic relations between capitalist and worker. It is participatory theory's argument, though, that a workplace of involved employees, in essence a workplace of greater balance between the capitalist's and the worker's interests, serves both interests better. So, while Tocqueville calls attention to the beguiling but harmful effects of democratic equality, he, in turn, underestimates the power that economic relations exert on social interaction and government rule. In a sense, the astuteness he conveys about majority tyranny—that we must be vigilant in protecting political liberty from the arbitrary rule by numbers—habituates society to the inequalities under which the economic system operates. While it may be accurate today to describe the business class as without a consolidated, specified class interest, what remains worth consideration is whether capital itself, and the social and political power it commands, negatively affects both Tocqueville's notion that associations fulfill public functions and Rousseau's formulation of how a common will must arise.

CONCEPTIONS OF THE MARKET SYSTEM

Robert Lane recognizes not only the diversity of individuals' opinions but the different expectations that individuals have of both the economic and political realms. He argues that because Americans hold conflicting views of the fairness of these arenas, people create different measures of justice. In deciphering the potential and the problems of economics and in determining rulers from ruled, less clarity exists. Lane writes:

On balance . . . it seems that the public tends to believe that the market system is a more fair agent than the political system. People tend to include the problem cases in the political domain and exclude them from the market. . . . They prefer the market's criteria of earned deserts to the polity's criteria of equality and need, and believe that market procedures are more fair than political procedures. They are satisfied that they receive what they deserve in the market, but much less satisfied with what they receive in the polity. . . . They are much more satisfied with the general income distribution among occupations than with the distribution of influence among social groups in the polity.[33]

Society, it seems, spends less time evaluating economic relations and more time denouncing political decisions. Perhaps politics creates such division because it is the most obvious arena of choice where winners and losers are immediately known. Perhaps, too, because the political arena remains under public control, in theory at least, while economy activity remains privately operated and, thus, not subject to public review. Market relations certainly create winners and losers too, but its results are accepted as more equal because they are perceived as individual and impersonal in nature. Supply and demand determine profit, not the influence of one particular legislator or powerful interest group. Ironically, economics receives fair reviews because people do not consider or question its collective effects, whereas politics typically receives derisive reviews because people recognize an individual effect from most public policies.

Given these views, it seems likely that people avoid participating in the polity because of its less than clear outcomes for the effort expended. Even if we consider the opposite conclusion, for instance, that discontent with the distribution of power would provide a motivation for workplace participation if it could be seen as remedying unequal social influence instead of only income distribution, it still would have to overcome the individual's assessment that, given the indeterminable social outcome, the private costs are too high in rectifying the situation. In addition, because of the conflicting standards of justice people hold for the market and the political arena, people will pursue economic ends for far different reasons than political ends. The pursuit of economic interest involves fairly immediate and measurable gains, with the "nondescript" market acting as arbiter. People must perceive significant inequalities before they enter the political arena. In addition, people take action when faced with either a bureaucratic decision, which they often view as impersonal, or a judge who they view as fallible. These conceptions of the political generate slogans such as "fighting city hall" and "bucking the establishment." From this, I believe two issues emerge: One is that the different evaluations of the market and the political demand reappraisal; the other is that the participatory theorists' assumption that participation in market relations breeds political concern and activity cannot be sustained.

However, Lane asserts that people can develop more communitarian views which unite both considerations of economic and political fairness. He cites research results which challenge the apparent nonrelationship between economic concerns and political, or other, regarding behavior:

1. Research showing that concepts of justice are only loosely related to perceptions of self-interest.
2. Research showing that people seem to vote more according to national news of unemployment and inflation than according to their own perceived benefits and burdens.
3. Research documenting ... that it is their ideologies, quite independent of of their relative incomes, that determine people's attitudes toward income distribution and their perceptions of social advantage and disadvantage.[34]

Lane believes evidence exists that supports the transformative effects and public interest participatory theorists espouse. The task remains to recast the social structures which serve as barriers. Since, for Lane, people's perceptions legitimate social structures, the alternative he offers focuses on a communitarian viewpoint where, for instance, "Viewing from the bottom up, people see processes rather than outcomes, emphasizing individual deserts rather than the overall shape of a resulting distribution. The community point of view restores a more egalitarian attention to distribution."[35]

In addition to Lane's proposal for reconceptualizing our notion of justice, participatory democrats claim that, despite collective action problems, civic-minded behavior occurs in healthy doses. The issue cannot be evaluated as a clear dichotomy between concern for public issues and preferences for individual diversity. This represents an all too simplistic conceptualization of individual identity at the microlevel and of national ideology at the macrolevel. In fact, as Robert Dahl assesses Tocqueville's concern for political liberty's protection from majority tyranny, he argues, "The problem of liberty and equality that we face is not precisely the same. The conditions for reconciling liberty and equality that he advanced are, I think, still necessary. But since equality is as problematic as liberty, the conditions he specified are no longer sufficient. The question we confront is whether we can create conditions as supportive of liberty as those Tocqueville thought Americans . . . could provide, and as conducive to equality as he believed American society to be at a historical moment that is irreversibly behind us."[36] Though Dahl conceives of liberty as individual freedom whereas Tocqueville wrote of ensuring political liberty, Dahl believes equality is the value that needs attention today. He argues that private property cannot be justified as an inalienable right because it interferes with the more elemental right of self-governance. Acquiring or holding property, then, is justified only by its ability to increase the right to self-governance.

But Dahl's argument significantly alters the demands of participatory democrats. Typically, the assumption underlying calls for workplace democratization is that participation breeds egalitarian and cooperative behavior. To employ Benjamin Barber's terms, a strong democracy inculcates "common talk, common-seeing," and an unacknowledged—by Barber—agreement to agree.[37] Dahl, on the other hand, allows the individualist disposition toward ownership, yet he uses it to enhance his case for equality and, ultimately, for democracy. He claims, "If a right to property is understood in its fundamental moral sense as a right to acquire the personal resources necessary to political liberty and a decent existence, then self-governing enterprises would surely not, on balance, diminish the capacity of citizens to exercise that right; in all likelihood, they would greatly strengthen it. . . . It could entail a shift of ownership from stockholders to employees."[38]

Dahl recognizes that democratic reform does not occur in a cultural vacuum. The dominant ideology of individualism that Lane notes cannot be systematically replaced by a supposedly more "advanced" set of egalitarian practices. Change occurs slowly, and democratization must either grow from cultural attitudes or incorporate such attitudes into its processes. Dahl attempts not to transcend the dominant individualist ideology but to incorporate the participatory changes within it, perhaps in a manner similar to Gramsci's "periphery into the center" conception of a politics of inclusion. His plan, however, remains ambitious because of the apparent difference between his emphasis on political equality and present society's concern for maintaining liberty, especially when confronted with his calls for reassessing property rights.

Robert C. Grady also captures the tension within the participatory literature and within the social structure. He claims participatory theorists "assume that democratic values can be enhanced by economic growth and technological progress and that they can be divorced from the possessive individualist values that pervade U.S. political culture."[39] In fact, advocates often label participatory workplaces as successful but fail to recognize that individualistic behavior—such as in hiring additional members or employees and in selling shares for a short-term profit—still runs much of the firm's behavior. Greenberg, in his conclusions about the plywood firms, notes that "The expectation held by many theorists of industrial democracy that self-managed work environments might serve to nurture feelings of cooperation, equality, generosity . . . in one's fellows is only partly met within the plywood cooperatives. The expectation that such feelings would spill over the walls of the workplace so as to incorporate society, economy, and government is decidedly not met. . . . Indeed, the findings point to the opposite results."[40]

Participatory theorists would respond that individualist values would be redirected toward collective interests after democratic changes. But there is, and will continue to be, an interplay between the cooperative principles which underscore democractic reform and the individualist principles which guide present economic activity. In fact, given that the individualist values are part of the established culture, it remains uncertain whether democratic reform could outlast difficult economic times. Finally, Grady contends that although participatory democrats claim that educational reinforcement will lead to the development of cooperative behavior, "Their faith that participatory values can be transferred to the larger political system is . . . insufficient as long as the possessive individualist values that help define both political citizenship and corporate membership are discounted."[41] Perhaps "discounted" is too strong given the fact that, despite their different emphases, Rousseau, Tocqueville, and participatory democratic theorists are well aware of the power of possessive individualism. Grady's concern, however, is that because individualism of the sort that Rousseau and Tocqueville feared dictates much of political and economic action, modest participation at work will do little to effect broad social change. If anything, the effect may be to turn workers away from public life and exacerbate the strident individualism that already exists.

The tension is clear. If workplace democracy is to become a solution to the "possessive individualist" ideology under present market conditions, it must incorporate that ideology within its cooperative alternative. What differentiates participatory advocates is the degree to which they claim workplace democracy must accept and operate within the prevailing culture. Some proponents ultimately seek to replace the present social structure by replacing the preeminence of capitalism and the importance of individual interests. Less ambitious sympathizers seek modest changes in worker control and still adhere to the advantages of a "free market" economy. Because of these different agendas and because of the subsequent variety of applications of workplace involvement, it remains necessary to develop definitional rigor for participation and to recognize the implicit assumptions and effects that evolve from an engaged work force. Grady states, "To discount these values [individualist ones] . . . is to risk relegating the participatory aims of workplace democracy to the realm of idyllic proposals that lack a program of action—an arena in which too much political theory finds itself when it confronts the constraints of the political system and of contemporary political practice and policy."[42] My outlook agrees with this claim: Participatory alternatives are best understood not according to their idealistic assumptions but rather according to the practical constraints in which they must develop.

My task is therefore twofold. Not only do the relationships between workplace involvement, individual efficacy, and subsequent public activity need clarification, but also the more general issue of the assumptions and methods which guide participatory endeavors needs attention. Participatory democrats suggest that there exists a positive relationship between work involvement and public activity. But this study questions to what degree or under what circumstances worker participation causes even immediate political activity. In fact, the former issue cannot be resolved until we discuss the latter concern. The political activity proposition distinguishes participatory attempts, which seek to remake present social structures, from attempts (like Dahl's) which use established and legitimatized social beliefs to support participatory changes. To wholly remake social institutions to advance participation and democracy may be the object of both methods of reform, but the difference in the methods may mean that one makes inroads into society to encourage change while the other is written off—usually by those who hold power but also by reformers—as too dramatic and idealistic. The changes participatory theorists advocate are often disregarded as idealistic, and I intend to follow Dahl's and Grady's methods in developing these participatory changes to ward off such claims. I understand that this approach fails to live up to the complete economic and social transformation that some participationists advocate; but given the individualistic culture, my idea for participation is to understand how, when, and where it can be employed effectively. In a sense, then, my understanding of change is today piecemeal, and I believe change can only occur under these methods.

To address these concerns ultimately forces us to ponder whether democracy in general and participatory democracy in particular can operate if society also accepts the tenets of the market economy. While Lane details the different notions of justice which arise from these separate realms, MacPherson presents us with yet another tension:

The dilemma of modern liberal-democratic theory is now apparent: it must continue to use the assumptions of possessive individualism, at a time when the structure of market society no longer provides the necessary conditions for deducing a valid theory of political obligation from those assumptions.... The individual in market society is human as proprietor of his own person. However much he may wish it to be otherwise, his humanity does depend on his freedom from any but self-interested contractual [sic] relations with others. His society does consist of a series of market relations.... But the maturing of market society has cancelled that cohesion [a degree of class cohesion which made possible a viable political authority] which is a prerequisite for the deduction of obligation to a liberal state from possessive individualist assumptions. No way out of the dilemma is to be found by rejecting those assumptions while not rejecting market society.... The dilemma remains. Either we reject possessive individualist assumptions, in which case our theory is unrealistic, or we retain them, in which case we cannot get a valid theory of obligation. It follows that we cannot now expect a valid theory of obligation to a liberal-democratic state in a possessive market society.[43]

The dilemma arises because the structure of market society has changed. The tension between possessive individualism and a liberal-democratic state is irreconcilable, and that the rationale for any sense of attachment (i.e., obligation) to the state is mediated by an increasingly self-centered market economy. For MacPherson, economics and sociopolitical authority are interwoven, and his implied program is to alter fundamentally current market relations.

Participatory democrats claim workplace participation resolves MacPherson's dilemma by rebuilding political obligation and commitment on nonpossessive individualist assumptions, and most advocates believe that individualist values will submit to cooperative, egalitarian ones. However, this leaves me with a "practical" quandary, given my acceptance of the barriers of the individualistic culture: Can workplace participation develop political responsibility or obligation and still retain individualist values? Or, to acquiesce to MacPherson's forecast, are the values that the market creates irreconcilable with the values necessary for public activity and attachment?

Perhaps workplace democracy's multiple definitions result from participatory advocates', businesses', and political leaders' avoidance of MacPherson's dilemma. If his insights are accurate, workplace democracy becomes a trite, catch-all phrase without substantive meaning to evade the more fundamental contradiction between democratic values and market relations. If the market system necessitates a culture antithetical to democratic and participatory values, then workplace involvement operates in opposition to American culture. But the democratic values of the culture also affect the market; and, given that a historical current supportive of participation exists, involvement in one's work is often considered both just and truly democratic by society. Obviously, the power of this participatory current is constrained by the larger acceptance of the market ideology. Acceptance, though, does not necessarily mean societal approval through democratic deliberation, and this difference allows for the contradictory agendas and objectives of both market relations and participatory reforms. Participatory changes need not emasculate individualist values, but individualist values cannot predominate in a participatory society as they do in today's market society.

VOICE AND CHOICE

The questions this study raises are whether workplace participation does build employee efficacy and whether personal efficacy extends to action in the political realm. Participatory theorists claim that both changes occur. What drives my reappraisal of these claims is the lack of attention to individual personalities and the cultural barriers which influence paticipatory results. As John Cotton, in his survey of the literature, explains, "The issue of individual differences is still a greatly underresearched topic within job involvement."[44]

For example, it is unclear how information itself alters the link between attitudes and action. It may be too optimistic to assume that a worker–owner who becomes more knowledgeable of the important variables required in determining company decisions develops either an ability to apply this knowledge to the broader public domain or recognizes the connection between the abstract political realm and one's specialized workplace. Or, as Lane reveals, if a connection does occur, perhaps the individual maintains different measures for each distinct area. As for personal development, there may be a discrepancy between participatory theory's assumption that participation yields cumulative lessons in becoming a citizen and the individual's motivation to choose to behave publicly. Given the educational effects of the market system, in contrast to Rousseau's educational effects of participation, and given some of the dominant values of American culture which stress self-interest and self-reliance, the link between participation and citizenship fails to materialize.

Because this research emphasizes individual motivation and attitude, the central concern is the concept of choice. Just as Lane's work deciphers the varying attitudes toward politics and economics, Albert Hirschman's analysis of worker "exit," "voice," and "loyalty" behavior clarifies the relationship between the two realms.[45] For instance, he argues that a firm benefits in their market relations by seeking out employee "voice" (i.e., participation) instead of relying solely on their exit, which means leaving the firm or not choosing to buy the firm's product. The conclusion is that, while society, business, and political leaders tend to isolate economic, exit behavior from political, voice behavior, economic activity becomes more efficient and productive if it employs elements of political interaction. Such a conclusion should come as little surprise, as corporate America today embraces the notion of worker involvement and interaction to boost productivity.

Hirschman details the effects of choice. There is, however, a crucial difference between what Hirschman argues and how this study extends his argument to more subtle and limited conclusions. Hirschman's argument centers on the firm's ability to implement employee choice, a kind of structural reorientation that involves the employees to ultimately profit the firm. Loyalty, then, is the firm's ability to build trust and commitment—two wholly noneconomic terms—which encourages employees not to engage in typical market fashion. The ingenuity of his argument comes from the insight that implementation of typically nonmarket behavior—voice and loyalty—actually benefits the firm's market position.

But trouble arises because Hirschman treats voice behavior as an equal substitution for exit behavior. In effect, he assumes employee participation as voice carries roughly the same "power of choice" as exit behavior. Angered workers express their dissatisfaction through the firm's communication pipeline, and management notices and responds. But participation has a wider variety of practices and expressions than the one management establishes. Employees may exercise voice not out of choice, but out of perceived necessity. For instance, workers may believe that participating (i.e., company classes, outside functions, networking, attending additional policy meetings) remains one of the sure ways to advance. In such a case, if one wants to "climb the company ladder," there is little choice as to what to do. Or, because the firm structures itself for the employees to participate, the employee has little choice over how to exercise voice. In a sense, the worker perceives participation more as a part of the job requirement and less as the ability to engage or develop one's work with others.

G. A. Cohen captures this difficulty in his related description of how the labor market structures the working environment to apparently offer employees' opportunities to escape their class. But, in effect, what results is the lack of "the choice of voice." As I apply Cohen's analysis to the idea of particiation, the recognition that voice necessitates specified boundaries or thresholds, whereas exit is less constricted, arises from the observation that each worker's ability to exercise voice is contingent upon another worker not exercising this choice. Cohen then claims, "Each is free [to choose to voice] only on condition that the others do not exercise their similarly conditional freedom. Not more than one [or some small segment of the work force] can exercise the liberty they all have. If, moreover, any one were to exercise it, then . . . all the others would lose it."[46]

Robert Putnam's recent work on the democratic differences between Northern and Southern Italy exhibits another case where "the choice of voice" is less than what we expect. Putnam argues that Northern Italy remains decidedly more democratic and, thus, more prosperous than its Southern region because of its history of fraternal and civic organizations.[47] His argument, then, is that to encourage democracy, similar developments need to be in effect. But the difficulty is that, while it is relatively simple to structure either government or economics to involve participation, it is uncertain how to replicate a history of democratic interaction. Putnam answers that participation is essential to democracy without realizing that democracy is not essential to participation. The former Soviet Union's democratization epitomizes the lack of choice in creating an effective system of political and economic interaction when a newly created voice option emerges. Putnam assumes that initiating civic life will create democratic possibilities. Most likely it will, but how to establish the unique geographical and demographic preconditions for civic life remains nearly unanswerable for each part of the world.

THE RESEARCH AGENDA

Participatory democrats do acknowledge the adverse effects of the market system and the individualist culture. This often necessitates a list of conditions which, if created, facilitate their optimistic proposals. For example, Paul Bernstein determines that workplace democratization involves six necessary components, the sixth being the creation and maintenance of a participatory, democratic consciousness. While noting several important tensions within each individual (i.e., self-reliance versus receptivity to others' needs) and within a firm (i.e., economic goals versus humanitarian or democratic priorities), he maintains, "The fact that participatory consciousness is so susceptible to these external forces . . . some . . . argue that democratization of enterprises will be a hopeless aim until the surrounding society is changed in a participatory direction first. But there is much evidence to show that external factors need not predominate over the internal consciousness of a democratized firm. They are but conditioning influences which can facilitate or burden the otherwise relatively autonomous company mentality."[48] But the assumption Bernstein makes which remains questionable is whether the company can develop a "mentality" which exists independently of and quite powerfully in contradistinction to the external forces.

This issue has two interrelated considerations. One centers on the type of selection process, the other analyzes the participatory work scheme and how it nurtures participation. In a sense, the former factor deals with the kind of raw material available, the latter issue concerns what structure best suits the raw material. My concern is that often the composition of the raw material, its individualist nature, does not lend itself easily to the processes and the output the structure seeks. If correct, does a specific structure advantageously alter the raw material to satisfy the desired ends? This question does not assume that the raw material, or human nature, is immutable; that it is only self-interested. But it does ask whether the measure of individual control and perhaps power gained at a participatory workplace spreads to other facets of life and society in general, given the educational and cultural forces that stress individualism and a boundless Rousseauean independence.

A first step to uncover the interaction between the attitudes and actions of workers and the participatory structures—the kinds of workplace involvement—begins with their actions both before and after their participatory experiences. However, to infer generalizations from these complex relationships is fraught with uncertainty. For example, a body of research claims that what promotes individual worker efficacy is ownership in the company (i.e., to vote one's stock). According to this reasoning, ownership focuses attention on the profit margin. Worker–owners become not only employees but managers, looking to reduce waste and costs and encourage efficiency. The result has been the 1980s surge, with the support of massive tax incentives, in employee stock ownership programs.

Conversely, another body of research views efficacy as the product of not just ownership, but participation. Immediate decision-making control over one's work, and in concert with others, produces the mindset Bernstein claims is necessary for participatory success. To be clear, efficacy itself can be defined either by subjective feelings of empowerment or by the occurence of objective results. For instance, it seems participatory theory makes two claims for workplace participation, the first claim of building personal efficacy implies a subjective appraisal, while the second claim of subsequent public activity implies an objective test. If accurate, it becomes essential to distinguish between the two definitions of efficacy because they affect measures of the concept of "success." Often, if no apparent or objective changes occur (i.e., no public activity occurs given the change to employee participation), the changes are judged as ineffective. But if employee involvement produces satisfied workers who remain indifferent to politics, the conclusions are at least mixed. Given the complexity of social problems which affect individuals both outside and inside the work environment, an expansive definition of efficacy to recognize any positive changes in employee perceptions toward work or themselves seems appropriate.

My research concern is that the variety of participatory structures and their variety of ends, along with the variety of individual motivations to work voluntarily within these structures, precludes a high level of generalization. This necessitates a case-by-case analysis of employee involvement with a history of the circumstances under which the participatory "experiments" begin. With an awareness of the difficult circumstances that make up the employee buyouts of financially-troubled businesses or the predispositions of cooperative workers toward political activity, I can best assess the causality between workplace participation and political action.

To evaluate attitudes and actions of individuals in participatory workplaces, I conduct surveys and interviews. Of utmost methodological concern is that, while the research attempts to reveal longitudinal change of increasing levels of political activity as affected by the variable workplace participation, I employ methods more relevant for a snapshot approach. Historical analysis must help overcome this difficulty, as well as surveys which encourage evolutionary or long-term assessments of company direction and individual development.

My agenda is as follows: evaluations of participatory companies using survey and interview data to clarify the connection between workplace involvement, individual efficacy, and civic activity. My cautionary, alternative argument to participatory theory is that the diversity of individual preferences, the educational effects of the market system, and the socializing forces of individualism and freedom from external or legislated control modify the link between workplace participation and civic behavior. Moreover, I do not advance a theory as much as recognize the power of the status quo. The participatory democrat's generalization that there exists a relationship between involvement at work and public action forecasts a change in individual efficacy and in democratic rule. I believe these potential changes must battle the powerful forces that guide present society.

If the participatory alternative does not have readily apparent individual and economic benefits, social change is improbable. The one advantage that participatory democrats can claim, however, is that the culture has in part accepted the participatory experiment, and, recently, society has embraced the experiment as more than an unusual or atypical practice of economic activity. The following research seeks to resolve related issues which may generate a greater degree of public support, issues which alter the present relationships between worker and owner, between economic equality and political liberty, and between workplace paticipation and democratic citizenship. In order to address these larger issues, my next step is to clarify what participation means, what efficacy is, and when success occurs.

NOTES

1. Edward S. Greenberg, "The Consequences of Worker Participation: A Clarification of the Theoretical Literature," *Social Science Quarterly* 56, no. 2 (September 1975): 191–209. Greenberg details the principal advocates of workplace participation and how their agendas and values differ from each other.

2. Christopher Eaton Gunn, *Workers' Self-Management in the United States* (Ithaca: Cornell University Press, 1984), Chapter 4.

3. Peter Bachrach, *The Theory of Democratic Elitism* (Boston: Little, Brown, 1967), 4–9, 98–106.

4. Barry A. Macy, Mark F. Peterson, and Larry W. Norton, "A Test of Participation Theory in a Work Re-Design Field Setting: Degree of Participation and Comparison Site Contrasts," *Human Relations* 42, no. 12 (1989): 1095–1165.

5. Bennett Harrison, "The Failure of Worker Participation," *Technology Review* (January 1991): 74.

6. Armen A. Alchian and Harold Demsetz, "Production, Information Costs, and Economic Organization," *American Economic Review* 62 (1972): 783.

7. Gunn, *Workers' Self-Management*, 42–43. Also, see some of the cited works in the quotation: John R. Cable and Felix R. Fitzroy, "Cooperation and Productivity: Some Evidence from the West German Experience," *Economic Analysis and Workers' Management* 14, no. 2 (1980): 163–180; Derek C. Jones and David K. Backus, "British Producer Cooperatives in the Footwear Industry: An Empirical Evaluation of the Theory of Finance," *Economic Journal* 87 (1977): 488–510.

8. Alan S. Blinder, ed., *Paying for Productivity: A Look at the Evidence* (Washington, D.C.: The Brookings Institution, 1990), vii.

9. John L. Cotton, *Employee Involvement: Methods for Improving Performance and Work Attitudes* (Newbury Park, Calif.: Sage Publications, 1993), 229.

10. Robert Jackall and Henry M. Levin, eds., *Worker Cooperatives in America* (Berkeley and Los Angeles: University of California Press, 1984), 10.

11. Cited in Cotton, *Employee Involvement*, 17.

12. Jackall and Levin, *Worker Cooperatives*, 229.

13. Albert O. Hirschman, *Exit, Voice, and Loyalty: Responses to Decline in Firms, Organizations, and States* (Cambridge: Harvard University Press, 1970), 76–105.

14. Joyce Rothschild and J. Allen Whitt, *The Cooperative Workplace: Potentials and Dilemmas of Organizational Democracy and Participation* (New York: Cambridge University Press, 1986), 71.

15. Carole Pateman, *Participation and Democratic Theory* (London: Cambridge University Press, 1970), 42–43.

16. Ibid., 24–25.

17. Bachrach, *Democratic Elitism*, 23.

18. Peter Bachrach and M. S. Baratz, "The Two Faces of Power," *American Political Science Review* 56, no. 4 (1962): 942–952.

19. Bachrach, *Democratic Elitism*, 103.

20. Peter Bachrach and Aryeh Botwinick, *Power and Empowerment: A Radical Theory of Participatory Democracy* (Philadelphia: Temple University Press, 1992), 10–11.

21. C. B. MacPherson, *The Life and Times of Liberal Democracy* (Oxford: Oxford University Press, 1977), 104.

22. Pateman, *Democratic Theory*, 52–59.

23. Jean-Jacques Rousseau, *The Social Contract*, trans. Maurice Cranston (New York: Penguin Books, 1968), 113.
24. Ibid., 75–76.
25. Ibid., 151.
26. Pateman, *Democratic Theory*, 26.
27. Alexis de Tocqueville, *Democracy in America*, ed. Richard D. Heffner (New York: New American Library, 1956), 200–202.
28. Ibid., 193, 199.
29. Ibid., 197.
30. Rousseau, *Social Contract*, 64.
31. Tocqueville, *Democracy in America*, 304.
32. Ibid., 219.
33. Robert E. Lane, "Market Justice, Political Justice," *American Political Science Review* 80, no. 2 (1986): 387.
34. Ibid., 398.
35. Ibid., 399.
36. Robert A. Dahl, *A Preface to Economic Democracy* (Berkeley and Los Angeles: University of California Press, 1985), 51.
37. Benjamin Barber, *Strong Democracy: Participatory Politics for a New Age* (Berkeley and Los Angeles: University of California Press, 1984), 167–178, 209–212.
38. Dahl, *A Preface to Economic Democracy*, 112–113.
39. Robert C. Grady, "Workplace Democracy and Possessive Individualism," *Journal of Politics* 52, no. 1 (1990): 162.
40. Quoted in Dahl, *A Preface to Economic Democracy*, 96–97.
41. Grady, "Workplace Democracy," 162.
42. Ibid.
43. C. B. MacPherson, *The Political Theory of Possessive Individualism* (Oxford: Clarendon Press, 1962), 275.
44. Cotton, *Employee Involvement*, 18.
45. Hirschman, *Exit, Voice, and Loyalty*, Chapters 1–3, esp. 15–20; 36–43.
46. G. A. Cohen, *History, Labour, and Freedom: Themes from Marx* (Oxford: Clarendon Press, 1988), 263.
47. Robert D. Putnam, *Making Democracy Work: Civic Traditions in Modern Italy* (Princeton, N.J.: Princeton University Press, 1993), 121–185.
48. Paul Bernstein, *Workplace Democratization: Its Internal Dynamics* (Kent, Ohio: Kent State University Press, 1976), 107.

Chapter 2 **DEFINITIONS AND RESEARCH METHODOLOGY**

Researchers who are skeptical of worker participation's effects often cite Edward S. Greenberg's research on the Northwest plywood cooperatives as support. His research concludes that, despite cooperative behavior within the plywood enterprises, market demands force workers to remain attached to "possessive individualist" values. This conclusion reinforces the theme of the present study. But I take a somewhat stronger position: It remains unlikely that participatory structures transform workers, not only because of market forces, but also, and more important, because of the different conceptions of the role of work or the different identities each individual brings from the outside "individualist" culture to the participatory experience. Participation's educative effects must be called into question given the power of both the competitive market and the individualist culture.

However, given the frequency that Greenberg's results are cited, it is crucial to understand how some critics would find his study to be misleading. Peter Bachrach argues that Greenberg's definition of democracy focuses too narrowly on processes and neglects the relationship between democratic means and democratic ends. Bachrach claims that such a conceptualization limits a fully democratic analysis of behavior. He explains:

By conceptualizing participatory democracy largely in "process" terms . . . [there are] no means of evaluating the democratic import of ongoing participatory structures. Outside of a context of continuing assessment in relation to the democratic ends of self-development of all individuals together with a growing commitment to the well-being of the participatory community, participation can lead to an intensification of competitive, anti-democratic outcomes. . . . [Greenberg] does not consider the effect of the attitudes of the workers on the nature of the political process in which they as decision makers participate. Thus, his position permits a political process to be characterized as democratic even while producing consistently anti-democratic results.[1]

Bachrach's criticism makes two important points. The first is that Greenberg's work does not consider worker attitudes and, thus, fails to measure the transformative effects that Bachrach believes participation induces. Apparently, in Greenberg's approach, participation has no effect. The second point is that by excluding the effects of participation on democratic procedure itself, Greenberg's definition of democracy is incomplete.

Bachrach uncovers some fundamental flaws in Greenberg's definitions and throws his conclusions into doubt. Workers' attitudes need assessment in any definition of participatory democracy. However, they need assessment not for the reasons Bachrach believes. He claims that "the principal end [is] the self-development of all individuals in the participatory and not the possessively individualist sense."[2] But given that self-development today is not possible for most workers—indeed, it is not a reality within the vast majority of participatory workplaces—Bachrach's argument that workplace democratization mobilizes class consciousness appears as utopian as the participatory theorists and theories he discredits as too utopian. The key to class mobilization is the educative effects of participation; but participation, as Bachrach states, can foster antidemocratic results. Bachrach assumes, as do most other participatory thinkers, that education produces positive, productive, and progressive outcomes. Greenberg generalizes from this case that participation's educative effects are illusory.

But Greenberg's message carries little weight because his definition of democracy is faulty. As Bachrach claims, Greenberg's definition lacks a robust, healthy, engaged contribution from the firms' workers. However, while Bachrach argues that ends associated with democratic participation are excluded in Greenberg's definition, Bachrach does not see that this inadequate concept of democracy is based, ultimately, on the nondemocratic structure of the plywood cooperatives. In effect, it is useless to speak of ends when the original structure, the foundation of the firms, begins as antidemocratic. Thus, a more potent criticism of Greenberg's research is that his definition of democracy is too broad—not, as Bachrach assumes, too narrow.

By understanding the plywood firms as democratic, Greenberg adds to the definitional confusion of democratic and participatory workplaces. As David Ellerman states,

The plywood co-ops use one legal instrument, the membership share, to carry the membership rights and the rights to the member's accumulated share of the net book value of the corporation. . . . New workers often do not have the resources or credit to buy a membership share so they are hired as non-member employees. Hence in this traditional worker cooperative legal form, the membership rights are effectively capital-based, not labor-based. . . . The Mondragon-type worker cooperatives . . . create another legal instrument, the internal capital account, to carry the value of each member's accumulated capital. With that capital stripped of the membership shares and recorded in the internal accounts, those shares can be treated as "value-less" and non-salable membership certificates. These certificates signify that the holder qualifies for the personal right of membership in the cooperative.[3]

Greenberg's definition of democracy mixes worker participation with worker control. Indeed, the plywood firms do exhibit democratic characteristics. Voting is on a one-member, one-vote basis, and profits are distributed according to labor hours of the members. Where it retains an antidemocratic element is in the ability of capital to control membership rights. One's labor is not as important in determining membership rights as one's initial capital outlay. For instance, membership shares in some of the successful plywood firms are in the $100,000 range, with roughly one-fifth of the price as a down payment. Given such large sums of money, it is not hard to imagine why cooperative members remain "attached to market forces." From this capital-controlled beginning, it appears that additional nonparticipatory and nondemocratic scenarios will develop. Participatory measures will become secondary concerns to worker–owners' profit measures. Also, a dwindling membership, which inhibits member growth and decision-making participation, will result if a firm becomes increasingly profitable and the worker–owners choose to maximize their profit. These conclusions are what concern Bachrach, but he does not recognize where they emerge from. They emerge from the plywood firms' structural conditions, conditions that inhibit workplace democracy.

An obvious conclusion from Bachrach's review is that concepts such as participation and democracy require definitional consistency, and they must include both attitudes and democratic outcomes. More broadly, in workplace democracy research, the elusive character of the concepts that ground the debate has produced a literature mired in contention. If researchers cannot agree on definitions and measurements, theories and findings do not support what they claim to support. Consequently, much of the research on employee participation notes the "peculiar" or "special" attributes of the companies under scrutiny and concludes, in almost knee-jerk fashion, that additional research is necessary. For example, after analyzing the studies that examine the contextual factors that affect employee participation, John Cotton concludes:

Those studies examining the most powerful forms of employee involvement are also the studies that tend to include factors in addition to participation and to have the weakest methodologies.... Wagner and Gooding (1987a, 1987b) found that studies using more questionable methodology led to stronger findings for employee participation. Are the stronger findings due to a more direct (perceptual) methodology, or are they simply artifacts? We have no way of determining this. If employee involvement operates through affective reactions to the participation, it seems reasonable that the perception of participation would be a more sensitive measure than more "objective" measures of participation. In addition, greater control and more objective measures are easier in short-term laboratory studies, but would be less likely to find significant results.... This controversy seems to be an insolvable problem.[4]

Cotton points not just to the troubles of research consistency but to the operationalization of participation itself. He argues that its effects are perhaps best captured by methods which are less scientifically rigorous than most researchers allow. In turn, the research paradox is that when strong participation effects occur, critics attribute the effects to a flawed methodology—and yet "strong" methodologies often cannot capture participation's influence. Thus an impasse exists. Research has not found a consistent method to study the effects of participation. By the same token, studies that claim to uncover participation's effects are often undervalued. In a sense, this methodological uncertainty reiterates the differences that Lane and Hirschman note in societal perception of economics and politics. The market and science are neutral, objective arbiters, while participation and politics—Hirschman's voice option—are subjective and not generalizable.

In addition to slippery concepts and questionable methodologies, the difficulty inherent in the literature results from bridging divergent academic specialties. J. Maxwell Elden recognizes that "political scientists and political sociologists interested in participation tend to define it in relation to the electoral system. They use occupational titles rather than looking inside organizations. . . . Conversely, psychologists, sociologists, and organizational researchers have produced an enormous body of research and theory about the inner dynamics of work organizations without paying the least attention to possible political ramifications outside the organization."[5] Research agendas tend to define terms in relation to the questions raised and the issues considered. With worker participation, participatory theory and political scientists view the issue ultimately in terms of creating active citizens, perhaps even developing civic virtue. Other researchers, though, concentrate on the individual effects of participation and its organizational effects. Participationists may argue that the "political citizenship" approach can be the final stage in the individual developmental approach, but little if no research asks whether workplace involvement generates political activity. Advocates argue that it does. It seems commonsensical that motivated workers will be motivated in other areas of their lives. But few studies address the connection.

If different academic specialties study different aspects of a larger process, terms will not be generalizable across research agendas. In turn, few results will extend beyond the narrow terms of a specific discourse. The bulk of research on workplace participation has been directed toward productivity questions through decision-making power. The present study seeks to redress the split between the two kinds of studies by addressing worker efficacy or empowerment, both at the work site and in the public arena beyond the workplace. It evaluates an assumption that participatory democratic theorists either accept as true or simply overlook: that participation with others educates each individual to think less of selfish interests and more of common concerns, and that participation transforms each individual by building self-respect, as each person's "circle of ideas" increases.

Given the lack of research on these participatory connections, and given the differences between the numerous participatory plans in place today with the objectives that participatory theory advances, I present two types of definitions for the concepts involved. The first set of definitions provide a "maximum" participatory workplace, one where participation finds root and becomes the most common form of interaction. A democratic workplace entails five factors: equality, ownership, control, participation, and efficacy.

1. *Equality*: Each and every worker has an equal vote in electing a board of directors, if one is deemed necessary, and in voting on shareholder matters. The philosophy is one person, one vote; not one share, one vote.
2. *Ownership*: Workers must own at least a majority of the company's stock, typically through an ESOP, and preferably own 100 percent of the firm. Though workers usually elect a trustee to oversee stock ownership plans, worker–owners must retain the ability to determine the trustee's actions.
3. *Control*: This differentiates conventional ESOPs, which typically are legal structures that remain capital based, from democratically structured ESOPs or worker cooperatives. Conventional ESOPs base ownership on the number of shares held in the ESOP, determined by either work tenure or wage amount. Thus, those with more shares receive proportionally more in profits and have more "control" in determining the firm's policies. In democratic ESOPs, where all workers have an equal voice, profit is distributed by issuing new shares to the ESOP in the amount equal to the profit. In addition, if profit is distributed in this manner, the profit is deductible from taxable corporate income as deferred labor compensation. Through the legal structures that guarantee the ability to vote and own the firm, worker control also entails the necessary information and communication channels to present clearly the issues on which workers deliberate and decide. Control means that the responsibility for the enterprise falls to its employees–owners and that the employees understand their role in governing the firm.
4. *Participation*: This is the crucial element of any democratic workplace; unless it exists or the enterprise perishes as a wholly democratic firm. It comprises the structural requirements of granting all employees, most likely after a short probationary period, the right to voice their ideas through clearly defined processes which allow for the flow of information from the "bottom-up" and from the "top-down." It must be measured by the firm's institutional processes of disseminating information—newsletters, meetings, and promoting of discussion, as well as the harder-to-assess creation of a climate or culture of interaction.
5. *Efficacy*: The perception of the ability to voice one's views and to feel that one's efforts can contribute to or affect an issue's deliberation and resolution. It can exist at two distinct levels. One is the individual's sense of empowerment over his or her immediate work and work relations. The other is a feeling of influence, but not necessarily control, over broader public issues beyond the workplace. Efficacy will be assessed in a graduated scale, given the ability of the firms to meet the other definitional requirements. In participatory theory, if an enterprise can be labeled as a democratic, participatory workplace, then efficacy must be measured in terms of both an individual's efficacy over his or her immediate environment and the individual's efficacy in larger public concerns.

These definitions attempt to distinguish the most successful participatory workplace examples from other less participatory examples. Success, under this definition, means that a firm has a relatively long history of worker ownership and control—which usually means it is profitable—and that a firm has established the mechanisms to maintain a participatory environment. These definitions limit the number of cases that come under study, but they do so in order to concentrate on the healthiest examples of workplace democracy, the same cases on which participatory theory rests its claims. Oftentimes, employee ownership of a firm results because the firm's owners intend to either sell it off or shut it down. Under these circumstances, the firm is economically troubled, and the employees or the community incur a significant debt in taking over a failing business. The rigorous definitions seek to exclude these struggling examples.

However, if I adhere to these standards, all three firms in this research would be excluded from the study, including Quad/Graphics, which is routinely referred to by researchers in the field as one of the most participatory firms in the country. The degree of control—typically management decisions and the firm's forecasting—is where the firms commonly fail to meet the definitional standards. All three have well-established participatory avenues and offer at least moments of participatory ingenuity and accomplishment. The question is, though, can these firms still adequately test participatory theory's propositions although they fail to meet the maximal definition of participation and control? In other words, are there minimum participatory standards that these firms satisfy to test the developmental and public-spiritedness assumptions of the theory? In some respects, participatory theory does provide a minimal assertion: A recognizable degree of sustained, consistent participation at work has a transformative effect on the individual worker. Each firm, then, must provide the structural conditions and the informal environment to generate consistent participation. The structural conditions are easy to measure, but the interpretations of what constitutes a "participatory environment" leads back to the methodological ambiguity that characterizes the research field. At the least, workers must note that management wants to hear from them, and that they have access to the people and processes that influence their work. This is a sign of efficacy in its most elemental form. The minimal expectation appears as a change in worker attitude, and most likely worker expectations and behavior, given the recognizable change in workplace involvement.

But can participation transform and foster efficacious workers if they sense influence only over immediate job-related issues and not over the most significant company decisions? Participationists would argue that some individual change should occur despite the lack of widespread employee influence over the firm's "most important" decisions. Or, as with the present cases, the move to greater employee influence is an incremental process decided by management's approval of employee participation. In effect, then, management assesses whether worker involvement should continue. As I have noted, though, this analysis often does not conform to participatory theory's objectives.

From the beginning, then, the cases show how practice often limits what participatory theory proposes. This does not mean that participation would necessarily produce more beneficial results if the conditions were more conducive for participation. Nor should we assume that the less-than-maximal participatory firms cannot produce noticeable changes in attitudes and behavior. The cases simply bring into greater relief the power of the market system, the power of the "typical" attitudes of managment and employee functions, and the power of the conservative or status quo thinking of those who have power. With this as a starting point, changes toward participatory workplaces must clear considerable obstacles even to reach minimal definitional requirements.

Another problem must be considered. It remains unclear what function employee stock ownership plans provide. The Department of Labor views an ESOP as an employee benefit plan; however, the IRS views an ESOP as a corporate finance tool to gain significant tax breaks. As Peter Pitegoff cites, recent management uses of ESOPs show their varied applications, none of which have to do with participatory democracy:

1. Defending against corporate takeovers.
2. Financing plant expansion.
3. Acquiring or disposing of a business.
4. Eliminating dissident shareholders.
5. Going private, and eliminating outside shareholders.
6. Giving liquidity to stock in closely held corporations.
7. Minimizing taxes.
8. Restructuring existing debt.
9. Discouraging unionization.
10. Replacing pension plans or other employee benefit programs so as to retain cash that otherwise would be permanently invested in the other programs.
11. Recouping cash in an existing benefit plan by converting it to an ESOP which uses its assets to buy stock from the company.[6]

Also, employee-owned firms pursue two different schemes: direct and indirect ownership. As Ellerman claims, "There are no tax advantages associated particularly with direct employee ownership. The better-paid employees will usually purchase the most shares . . . so the power and profits gravitate quickly to the managerial ranks. . . . The directly employee-owned firms tend to rapidly degenerate into management-owned companies." The first case study, Standard Knapp, hints at this development despite the efforts of both management and a labor union to prevent it. In addition, even though most employee-owned firms use ESOPs where the ownership is indirect, Ellerman states, "The vast majority of ESOPs do not promote the democratic participation of the employees."[7] It is obvious that, given the numerous management or capital-based objectives behind most employee ownership methods, most worker-owned firms are best described as worker capitalism (i.e., employees by day, capitalists by night) and not as wholly participatory or democratic firms.

Since the subject of inquiry is the degree to which workplace participation spurs broader political action—that is, how does participation transform individual attitudes and efficacies—I focus on three ESOPs which claim to value participation and attempt to structure the firms to create participatory avenues. In some respects, especially at Quad/Graphics, participation represents a fundamental priority, in concert with other economic demands such as productivity, efficiency, and profit. But the case studies are not without inconsistencies. Quad/Graphics and Orange Handling's stock remains principally in a few private hands, as they move slowly from family ownership to employee ownership. Standard Knapp must negotiate with a machinist union that some believe inhibits and others believe saves the firm "from itself." With these difficulties noted, each firm has established policies and processes to promote employee involvement. Quad/Graphics is the most sophisticated, as it inculcates each worker into a participatory culture. The other firms depend more on employee initiative to take advantage of the "opportunities" to participate. As the case studies will show, the difference between Quad/Graphics' "boot camp" mentality toward creating participation and the other more "worker-dependent" approaches has a profound and ironic effect on employee efficacy and overall satisfaction.

Research on employee satisfaction and stock ownership plans generally attempts to understand the relationship between a firm's participatory structure and its effects—the more objective and, thus, supposedly more methodologically rigorous approach. Katherine J. Klein and Rosalie J. Hall, in 1987 and 1988 studies, conclude that employees view stock ownership most favorably when the following conditions are met:

1. The company makes large annual contributions to the ESOP.
2. The company maintains an extensive ESOP communications program.
3. Management is strongly committed to employee ownership.
4. The company established its ESOP for philosophical, business transfer, employee incentive, or employee benefit reasons.
5. The ESOP is an older plan.[8]

While the last four conditions reiterate the characteristics of democratic ESOPs, two significant caveats in Klein and Hall's work need discussion. First, Klein and Hall conclude that an individual's status in an ESOP firm—which is, by their definition, according to one's financial status as determined by salary, tenure, and vesting—is positively correlated with an employee's satisfaction with the ESOP. Since most ESOPs are structured to return profit or dividends based on shares held, it seems likely that the more shares one holds, the more pleased with the ESOP one will be. However, this legal structure is not labor based; rather it remains capital based. The structure does not conform to the definition of democracy that participationists prefer. Certainly, money and profit are driving motivations for all individuals, but participationists and, to some extent, the "leaders" of the three case studies in this reasearch believe that they remain one of several motivations in devising and maintaining the structure and interaction in employee ownership plans.

The second consideration is Klein and Hall's hypothesis, which their findings support, that those employees who expect a greater degree of influence in the firm's decision making are less satisfied with the ESOP than those employees who do not expect such a role. They arrive at this conclusion because their work studies the typical ESOP structure. The typical structure grants few opportunities for employees to either vote their stock shares or, if they can vote, have an equal voice in decision making. Again, this conclusion is based on capitalist incentives, incentives based on a capital outlay and not based on labor commitment or any philosophical notion of equality.

It seems that if we study truly democratic ESOPs, or perhaps fully participatory firms as the next best arrangement, employees who expect greater decision-making power will be satisfied by definition. These firms exist, in part, to promote greater decision-making power among its employees, as well as the customary profit motive. As we will see with Quad/Graphics, immediate decision-making influence and company trust are two of the firm's fundamental philosophies. Thus, Klein and Hall's apparently odd finding that ownership does not breed satisfied employees if they seek decision-making control results from the worker capitalist ESOP models they study rather than from employee participation or control in general.

The repeated criticism that most ESOPs remain capital based does not shun all capitalist demands and principles outright. In a democratic ESOP private ownership still exists. Capital remains in the hands of individuals or firms. The three firms in this study are subject to the market system where profit, efficiency, and productivity are prime considerations. However, despite the limits of the present cases, I attempt to define workplace democracy to replicate the definition that participatory theory advances. To differentiate capital-based and labor-based designs recognizes that, in the latter cases, membership rights—to vote and to receive profits and dividends—are not tied to capital. By severing the relationship between capital and membership, a worker's rights in a democratic firm are linked to his or her labor, thereby reducing the inequalities created by unequal shares, higher salaries, or longer tenure. Capitalist principles guide the behavior of democratic firms, but the democratic firm establishes the processes that participatory theory claims will encourage efficacious workers and public-minded citizens. Again, while labor-based ESOPs are the participatory ideal, none of the three firms meet all of the maximal definitional standards. Yet all three, taken together, reveal consistent patterns of participation's influence.

Given the questions about participatory theory's expectations, this study's assertions contrast with participatory theory's two main claims:

1. *Individual identities will reduce the educative effects of participatory interaction.* The individual identities and motivations that each worker brings to the work environment and assigns to his or her role in the firm negatively influence the educative and transformative effects of participation. Individuals who downplay work's significance as a fundamental part of their identity, or who have other priorities that constitute their identity, less likely will enjoy educative benefits.

2. *The worker efficacy engendered by workplace participation does not transfer to broader public action.* Participatory workplaces do not generate public activity and greater citizenship. Market forces can be an intervening factor, but most likely, cultural forces sever

the link that participatory theory makes between efficacious workers and public-minded activity. Workers may be more efficacious in their work environment and in their private lives due to workplace participation, but their participation at work will not transform them into active citizens.

The first proposition seems intuitively false if we adhere to the definition of democracy that excludes participatory workplaces—which have been created without the input of the employees and with the diminished importance of capital interests. It seems that, by the nature of their decision for employee ownership and control, workers would be favorably predisposed to the educative benefits. However, the proposition questions whether workers themselves, given their initial agreement to workplace participation, display any educative effects, especially after a healthy period of experience with participation. Also, the educative and transformative benefits that participatory theorists claim workplace democracy creates must manifest themselves in behavior. It seems reasonable to assume that behavioral changes are necessary, which are defined as political awareness and activity and not mere thoughts of action or change.

To capture these attitudes and actions, I surveyed employees of three employee-owned and participatory workplaces (see Appendix A). I selected the cases based on their degree of worker participation in comparison to other employee-owned firms throughout the country. Often times, employee ownership does not translate to employee participation in decision making. The following three cases provide at least a modicum of worker involvement, though management typically controls the degree of participation.

Also, the case studies contain characteristics that are common to the participatory debate. For instance, the first case has implemented participatory changes, while it has also grappled with the power of a labor union. The role of a labor union in the participatory literature has modified over time, from initially being viewed as a traditional component of the labor process that worker participation attempts to overcome to possibly playing an important role in advocating employee's interests as the participatory changes occur. Another case addresses the role of size in a participatory environment, as it implements participatory changes in a relatively small, face-to-face context. In comparison to the two larger firms, this smaller case seeks to clarify whether size affects the kind and quality of participation at the firm. The remaining case is often lauded as the most participatory example in the workplace participatory literature, and my examination focuses on whether the kind of participation at this firm is the kind of participation that will encourage democratic citizenship.

The surveys attempt to capture a general collection of employee attitudes about their participatory experiences. The surveys contain four categories of questions: One asks for views on the firm's structure, its participatory nature, and the degree of control and influence in decision making; a second asks for the employees' general satisfaction with the participatory experience, its benefits in terms of informing and clarifying issues, and the workers' perceptions of the educative effects of participation; a third asks for the sense of empowerment workers feel, given the participatory avenues in the workplace and its extension to the workers' affairs both at work and in their private lives; and the fourth asks for information on the workers' activities with their families, with their friends, and in their communities to assess the transformative nature of the participatory experience to encourage active citizenship. Together, these questions allow me to examine the workers' general attitudes toward their workplace and their participatory experiences. In addition, the survey allows for an initial insight into the relationship between worker attitudes and worker actions.

While surveys provide initial insights into general attitudes, subsequent interviews provide in-depth reviews of the themes the surveys suggest. Critics may suggest that these methods are subject to an uncharacteristic amount of self-selection problems (see Appendix A for self-selection discussion). Disgruntled employees or overzealous advocates for participatory plans may be more motivated to voice their opinions than those who have less "extreme" attitudes or experiences. However, what gives my research confidence is the variety of sources from which patterns of behavior emerge. Interviews expand on and clarify possible implications from the survey results. Also, insight into a firm's history, its organizational structure, and its management–labor relations adds further clarification of possible relationships. Certainly, definitive generalizations cannot be drawn from these methods; but, taken as a whole, these sources of insight and information do present a robust understanding of each firm. In turn, a better understanding of each firm allows me to offer an exploration and elaboration of themes that either support or undermine participatory theory's propositions.

With these methodological limitations in mind—or methodological advantages given one's perspective—the examination of each firm follows a specific route. Each case study includes a brief but detailed account of the change to a participatory workplace and a historical sketch of the firm both before and after participatory and ownership changes occurred (if appropriate to the firm). I also look at each firm's decision-making structure and its hierarchical or "flattening" characteristics. Of great importance, the relations between management and labor, both before and after the participatory and ownership changes, also add pertinent information from which to assess participation's effects. With this information, along with the intimations that the surveys first suggest, employee interviews were conducted with those who marked off responses in their survey that they would agree to an interview. The interviews are the backbone of this research, as they help to clarify what the survey responses alone leave in some doubt. But the research methodology in total—which includes a historical, an anthropological, and, most likely to mixed reviews, an empirical component—offers a more complete and thorough examination of the case studies and, in turn, of participatory theory's claims.

I hesitate to state flatly that this study is a case study approach. The definition of democracy, with its at least minimal participatory requirements, reduces the influence of structural discrepancies between firms, which, if they exist, would make attitudes case-specific. To believe all institutional differences are methodologically resolved is folly, but to write off implications from the research as firm dependent would be to disregard the features the firms share. Again, my task is to clarify and examine the behavior that participatory theory assumes will occur given certain changes in the workplace. I recognize that falsifiable generalizations cannot emerge from my chosen methodolgical approach, but I believe a clearer understanding of the problems associated with participation's influence can emerge.

To reiterate, the "real world" cases all display some inconsistencies with the maximum participatory standards. But while they all reduce the amount of employee control over the firm, they do provide basic participatory elements. This discrepancy between what participationists envision and what is actually operating should not take away from today's participatory endeavors. With well-documented requirements and with numerous successful examples, employee ownership and participation are well beyond a "growing pains" stage. Despite their drawbacks, which for some will remain the focus of attention, the following firms continue to receive credit as some of the most democratic, most participatory examples in the study of employee ownership and worker involvement. The task, then, is to see if they encourage the changes participatory theory argues they will, given that they satisfy certain essential if not maximal conditions for democracy in the workplace.

NOTES

1. Peter Bachrach and Aryeh Botwinick, *Power and Empowerment: A Radical Theory of Participatory Democracy* (Philadelphia: Temple University Press, 1992), 121–124.

2. Bachrach and Botwinick, *Power and Empowerment*, 123.

3. David P. Ellerman, "Worker Ownership: Economic Democracy or Worker Capitalism?" Research paper for The Industrial Cooperative Association Group, Boston, April 1986, 6.

4. John L. Cotton, *Employee Involvement: Methods for Improving Performance and Work Attitudes* (Newbury Park, Calif.: Sage Publications, 1993), 21–22.

5. J. Maxwell Elden, "Political Efficacy at Work: The Connection between More Autonomous Forms of Workplace Organization and a More Participatory Politics," *American Political Science Review* 75 (1981): 43.

6. Peter Pitegoff, "The Democratic ESOP." Research paper for The Industrial Cooperative Association Group, Boston, 1987, 4.

7. Ellerman, "Worker Ownership," 8.

8. Katherine J. Klein and Rosalie J. Hall, "Correlates of Employee Satisfaction with Stock Ownership: Who Likes an ESOP the Most?" *Journal of Applied Psychology* 73, no. 4 (1988): 636.

Chapter 3   # THE FRUSTRATION AT STANDARD KNAPP

My first case study centers on the ambiguous role of a labor union. At first glance, a labor union appears antithetical to workplace participation objectives. Traditionally, unions bargain against management to improve wages and working conditions. They seek to improve the market value of labor. A union's goals conflict with management concerns over rising labor costs that reduce competitiveness and profitability. Conversely, advocates of workplace participation attempt to make employees the decision makers, if not the owners, of what becomes their firm. In a sense, worker control alters the fundamental relations of production which unions accepted and where unions once operated. With employee ownership and participation, the union, once the protector of labor's interests, appears as a confused middleman between the workers, whom they once represented, and the firm, which the empowered workers now come to control. Or, this scenario presents the most obvious relationship given the histories of the two sides.

Union supporters argue that when employees become stock owners and begin to participate in management decisions, management interests co-opt labor interests.[1] As part owners, workers have concerns that expand from working conditions and justifiable benefits to include the managerial interest in maximizing profit at the expense of other concerns. If this is so, the initiation of employee ownership still allows for, if not calls for, union activity.[2] As union officials point out, one of the main reasons for ESOP growth in the 1980s and 1990s—in fact, the main reason the president of my second case study states why he started strong participatory measures in his firm—lies in the corporation's intention of inhibiting unions from organizing and growing. Given the dramatic downturn in union membership, this corporate strategy effectively stifles any possibility of a union resurgence by pursuing participatory plans and stock buy-ins.

Whether one supports the view of a union as historically outdated or the view of a union as a countervailing force against an ingenious, oppressive management strategy, a recent third view finds a role for union activity in the changing age of worker participation. Because the change to workplace participation and/or control remains incremental, complex, and uneven, a union often maintains its traditional employee concerns but acts more as an ombudsman and information source than as the employee's representative voice. For some, this represents one more diminution of power in the face of declining memberships and corporate domination. For others, this minimal role and minimal power represents a realistic and enlightened role from which to build membership from both the traditional proletariat and the burgeoning white-collar and service sectors.[3] Because participatory plans today offer inconsistent results, the exact nature of the "new" union's role remains unclear. Most likely, if employees come to control a firm's decision making, the union acts as a forum for policy directives which were once dictated by management. Most likely, though, since workplace participation often does not extend to investment and employment decisions, a union must still perform the task of preventing harmful management policies.

No matter the view one takes, the fundamental cause for the union's changing role centers on the changing roles that employees must consider under participatory and ownership plans. Not only does a worker-owned firm attempt to shift ownership to the employees, but it may attempt—sometimes unsuccessfully, sometimes in name only—to also shift control of the firm to the employees. If control shifts to the employees, then the union's role becomes unclear. Traditionally, unions speak for employees and solely express employee interests. Management focuses on the firm's ability to compete most effectively by implementing the most efficient processes. A somewhat competitive balance between partial interests results, depending on their respective market power. From Rousseau's perspective, their agreements do not recognize a common agenda for all to benefit; they only reveal the capitalist battle between adversaries who unwittingly rely on each other. The firm's traditional structure, pitting antagonistic interests against each other, offers little opportunity for creating a contract based on a general good. It offers only a negotiated compromise.

But the change to employee ownership and participation supposedly broadens the worker's partial interests to include co-workers' interests and the firm's general health. If employees become truly equal in their decision-making power, then, in Rousseauean fashion, workers can shake free of their partial concerns to determine in concert what benefits the collectivity. Views may differ on how to achieve these benefits; but as long as the employees continually ask what benefits all, then a common agenda develops and socializes each worker. With the complexity of a union's presence, Standard Knapp's employees reveal whether the firm's participatory design encourages them to relinquish their partial interests.

In addition, the union's presence adds complexity for workers in how they choose to express their participatory voice. To some degree, a union's presence seems to collectivize employee attitudes and interests. But if the union squashes different voices and ideas as it attempts to offer a united work force, then its role as an agent for employee participation seems nothing more than "voice without true choice." Staughton Lynd makes the same argument when discussing the role of unions and community development. He states, "If we build labor-community coalitions that include and make their peace with the bureaucratic, top-down, undemocratic structure of existing national unions, then the economic enterprises created by such coalitions will also be bureaucratic, top-down, and undemocratic."[4] Employee ownership and participation, then, present changing relations between workers and management and between workers and unions, in which all parties must reexamine their traditional roles.

In general, Standard Knapp employees' views of the firm's successes and shortcomings center on each employee's interests at work. In one sense, to recognize that diverse interests prevail casts a shadow over the claim that employee ownership will build a common agenda with shared goals. However, diversity can also be the bulwark of democracy. The issues for participatory advocates become how to maintain the Rousseauean broader allegiances and how to allow differences to remain constructive. Differences can be productive, as long as they broaden perspectives and inspire creativity and full representation. But differences must not become factious internal company rifts between combative interests. At Standard Knapp, differences are generally understood by workers and management alike as combating interests rather than as productive deliberation.

Employee ownership and participation at Standard Knapp has not allowed the firm to overcome its history of management–labor turmoil. But employee involvement changes how the general unrest develops, and it may in fact exacerbate the unrest by providing a forum for its expression. The surveys and interviews suggest that there is a palpable distrust and a mounting frustration in the firm, and it extends beyond the management–labor dichotomy. Workers with some history in the company reveal that the twelve-year employee ownership experience repeatedly creates expectations that ultimately produce partial grievances. From this, the question arises whether Standard Knapp's employee ownership and participation solves more issues than it creates. Also, should we expect participation to overcome the historical, labor–management divisions? Participatory theory expects some change in employee attitudes, but the employees' attitudes at Standard Knapp contain a history of conflict and partiality that may interfere with change.

THE EMPLOYEE BUYOUT AND THE PARTICIPATORY DESIGN

By nearly every measure, Standard Knapp succeeds in a highly competitive arena. The firm makes machinery that takes filled containers, like beer or soft drink bottles and soup and tomato paste cans, and places them into shipping cases.

The firm services leading producers such as Anheuser-Busch, Miller, Coca-Cola, Procter & Gamble, and Campbell's. It employs a host of skilled machinists who belong to the International Association of Machinists labor union. Also, the firm consists of product engineers, salespeople, office staff, and management experts who are not represented by any union. This distinction between union and nonunion people is the firm's most obvious internal distinction, as the union workers primarily function in either one of two buildings, called Plant 1 and Plant 2, while the nonunion people operate in adjacent office space. While the company downsized during the 1991 recession from 210 to 165–170 employees, and experienced a 10 percent decline in its overall business, by 1994, total shipments rebounded to record the largest contract year ever. In turn, the number of employees has increased to 191 total—105 union workers and 86 nonunion workers who are mainly office personnel.

While the manufacturing community in central Connecticut has been devastated by closings and layoffs during the last decade, Standard Knapp provides decent paying jobs. Management believes it treats its employees better than the average employers, given characteristics like an open-door policy with the president, no suits, a first-name interaction throughout the firm, and radios at workstations. Management establishes employee participation through several methods: an actively-used bulletin board, department meetings, and quarterly meetings, all of which attempt to increase the availability of information and the number of decision makers. While these meetings are open to any topic, including the company's general policies, more often than not the issues involve more day-to-day issues and problems. Of additional interest, productivity incentives offer opportunities for bonuses and/or time off, and, since 1993, overtime has become a common feature of each factory work week. In fact, factory workers have averaged fifty to sixty hours per week since 1993, significantly boosting their salaries but limiting their outside activities and perhaps their work performance.

In the years 1982–1983, when the domestic economy was weak and the dollar was strong, Standard Knapp's European competitors made less-expensive equipment. As the firm downsized, management believed the firm survived the new conditions reasonably well. The parent company at the time, Anderson Brothers, out of Rockford, Illinois, was less positive. When Anderson Brothers sought deep concessions from the union, concessions management knew were not feasible, a group of five top-managment officials, led by President Art Tanner, offered to buy the firm from Anderson Brothers. Toward the end of 1984, as the deal was being struck, the union contract was about to expire. Management explained to the union that a wage freeze was necessary, with only modest increases later, and that the cradle-to-grave group insurance plan was no longer possible. While the national union, the International Association of Machinists, rejected the proposals, the local union accepted them.

The 1984 employee buyout amounted to $7 million. Equity from the employees amounted to $900,000; $350,000 of which came from the five top-management officials. Equity from the hourly employees' pension plan amounted to roughly $600,000. At first, employees purchased stock on a volunteer basis except for top management. As perhaps an indicator of subsequent employee attitudes, 85 percent of the office staff bought the firm's stock initially, but only 10 percent of the union members participated. Perhaps the union members believed that their acceptance of the reduced wages and benefits was a clear indication of their support of the buyout, and the additional "burden or benefit" of buying the firm's stock was a step they were unwilling to take. Subseqently, recognizing the need to broaden ownership in 1987, purchasing stock became mandatory for all new employees. Today, each union member is required to purchase at least twenty-five shares. Each worker's stock purchase, whether a union or nonunion employee, is based on a percentage of his or her starting wage or salary.

Once a year, employees vote their stock allocations in choosing a board of directors. Eight people comprise the board: five members from management, two members elected from the employee or union ranks without management's involvement, and one outside official. The board reviews and decides on the business direction and on the major projects for the firm. Except for the two board members chosen without management involvement, this structure mirrors any conventional, capital-owned enterprise. Top management meets bimonthly. Quarterly meetings, which include about fifty-five total people, gather members of production teams, development teams, senior- and middle-management officials, union officials, and five to ten other employees to assess ongoing policies and disseminate information. These people report to the larger body of workers. Quarterly meetings are made up of the main factions and the principal leaders of the firm. Without involving the entire work force, these meetings offer the opportunity for the airing of any problem or development. Here, then, the firm in theory has a process in which participation from any employee can occur. Finally, department meetings, which meet four or five times a year but are slated to meet bimonthly, include top management discussing issues with department people.

In nearly every respect, capital underwrites the employee ownership structure. The significant differences in financial commitment reflect significant degrees of influence and power in the firm. Although most everyone owns stock, most employees are not true worker–owners because of the unequal distribution of stock. While these differences lead to vast inequalities, the inequalities are, for the most part, accepted. Certainly, employees complain about these differences, and a change in decision-making power based on simple employment in the firm (one member, one vote) could dramatically change the firm's direction. By no means should these differences be underestimated as part of the long-standing tension between company factions. In fact, a plausible argument can be made that the animosity that employees voice ultimately traces back to the basic inequalities that the stock structure, and its effect on the decision-making process, establishes. Just as Hirschman and participatory theorists recognize the benefits of a participatory voice, the lack of that voice in practice, because of the unequal distribution of shares, leads to employee attitudes that question the firm's design, its leadership, and the legitimacy of its decision making.

To be clear, employee anger or disgust does not center on participation itself, nor on the firm's attempt to include workers in decision making. In general, these ideas receive favorable responses. But most Standard Knapp employees criticize how the firm implements its participatory aims. Interestingly, though, while most employees do not agree with how the firm carries out its decision making, they do little to change the unequal distributions of power. In a sense, the workers, whom the firm supposedly grants the participatory power to act, do not openly dispute the firm's decision-making power or participatory processes because they appear beyond dispute. To be sure, employees question management's direction, but little effort is expended on offering an alternative vision. Despite the participatory opportunities, whether real or only in name, it seems that the employees accept and act as if they have no control over the firm's decisions.

Where workers focus their efforts to influence the situation—if they exert any effort at all—is at their immediate area of work. Some of this reaction may be that employees feel more comfortable detailing what is wrong and what can be improved in their immediate environments. They have less experience in conceptualizing and directing the firm as a whole than they do in those areas in which they interact on a daily basis. But if participation is to build a Rousseauean commonality, workers must become more comfortable with forming a common agenda and then deciding to carry it out. A general will demands generalists; however, it seems that the firm and its management profit from specific tasks from specialized workers.

In a general sense, whether employees accept the system as fair or not, whether they acknowledge the large financial outlay of some management people as a legitimate rationale for greater amounts of decision-making control or not, most employees limit their assessments to the processes and decisions to which they have access and experience. Certainly, they often generalize from their experiences, but they do not question these broader, elemental inequalities as much as they commend or reject particular policies. From this, two different conclusions emerge. One is that participatory theory's propositions that participation transforms workers finds little support in this case, where workers focus on their immediate work relations. But participatory advocates would argue that a second conclusion is more accurate: Workers make a relatively quick and accurate appraisal of management's poorly implemented processes and decide that it is in their immediate work relations—especially since workers know these areas best—that their efforts of voice will find a hearing. In short, given the workers' perception of participation's ineffectiveness over company decisions, their efforts at voice will go unheard. The result is not the earlier described "voice without choice," which means that employee responses are dictated by their environment and other actors. Rather, while employees rationally abstain from pursuing broader issues of control and power, and, thus, remain to some extent directed toward their immediate environment, employees also exercise a "choice not to voice" their displeasure with participation and the firm. In either analysis of employee actions, though, participation does not live up to the workers' expectations. The question becomes whether it is the firm's implementation of participation or participation itself that fails the workers.

If we concentrate on the individual level and focus on those participatory mechanisms that include workers in decisions, if we hone in on those activities that immediately affect an employee's attitudes about Standard Knapp, we discover that a profound mistrust exists on all sides. From the interviews, the company president explains that, after countless meetings with union officials to bargain, the larger union membership feels full disclosure is lacking. A union official believes that more tension exists now than ever before, that management decides company policy and then tries to appease the membership, that management's subordinates are less than "true-blue" (i.e., honest) and that the president should be more involved in day-to-day management than he presently is. One employee claims that "information leading to a decision is kept quiet, and they can't tell us, but afterwards, management is very open."[5]

A union member adds that the firm sets up programs and then does not sustain them. An employee-of-the-month plan died after one month. The adopt-a-machine initiative quickly expired. Problem-logs exist for employees to record difficulties they have in working with the equipment. In the first ten months of the program, the union member states no one responded to the lists of troubles. Now that the firm has someone interested in responding, the employees no longer fill out the logs. The president claims that a company newsletter expired because employees did not sustain interest. One senior-management official recognizes what employees are thinking and questions whether managment can ever relent in its power over information and in decision making. He writes, "Often, at meetings, when top management asks for opinions or comments, I feel that some employees are very reluctant to speak up. I believe that even though we are 'employee owners,' there is a feeling that top management would retaliate if you would ask questions contradicting to [sic] their way of thinking. Also, the question in most employees' minds seems to be: are they [top management] telling us everything? As part owners, shouldn't we see a financial report that is more detailed—such as salary stuctures [sic] and bonuses?"[6]

In interview after interview, employees cite trust as the crucial and missing element at Standard Knapp. The reason why tensions may be more heated now than ever before is that before trust or commitment was never an issue. Perhaps with the expectations that worker ownership and participation would change the structure and decision making of the firm also came the expectations that established differences between union and management interests would diminish. When the differences do not abate, when the differences inhibit potential change and, thus, fail to meet expectations, the workers' anticipation of trust turns to frustrated tension.

We can add a third element to the question asked. Participation fails to transform workers' attitudes (1) because of the firm's poor design, (2) because of participation itself, and (3) because the participation's effects do not meet the workers' expectations. As Aristotle argued before him, Tocqueville wrote that customs, mores, and habits were more important in creating democratic trust than mere rules or processes. When workers fail to see any significant changes spawned by their decision-making input or nominal influence, they may abstain from participation, as they view it as another empty strategy made for appearances rather than legitimate change. Participation becomes an expression of an empty voice. To exercise it is to exercise a voice with no choice. Workers recognize the difference between its stated intentions and its actual results.

FROM PARTICIPATORY DESIGN TO WORKER ATTITUDES

Despite dissatisfaction with the institutional design in which participation is realized, from the perspective of the individual employee, a general, hearty satisfaction exists with one's work and with one's immediate co-workers. Employees take pride in their efforts to create a quality product, and a sense of dedication to their jobs best describes their attitudes. In answering survey questions, 83 percent of the respondents strongly agreed that they cared about the fate of Standard Knapp, over half claimed they would volunteer extra time for the overall good of the firm, and just about half agreed that they did not mind doing more for the firm than is required by their job description. Despite the ambivalence employees show toward the firm in other areas, these results begin to reveal what the ownership and participatory experience seeks to establish: a committed work force that can distinguish between narrow, personal interests and larger objectives. It seems that Standard Knapp has survived tough economic times in the Connecticut Valley. Also, the firm appears to create a work environment that attempts to unite its employees to each other, as well as to the firm's future. One management interviewee explains these appearances as "a greater sense of belonging [in the firm], of congeniality, of control for me [because] I am more involved in a wider variety of procedures. I know I have a different feeling now [under employee ownership] than before I owned shares. I made a commitment. I don't mind telling you, before, at 3:30 P.M., I was gone. Not now! [The president] has got us in groups participating. It is more personal now—[we are] more involved in decision making."[7]

However, while it is common to hear people applauding the ownership and participatory changes, it is equally common to hear people expressing reservations about or downright dismissals of the firm's structure and policies. One union member, who has as much experience at the firm as the quoted management official, states:

I can't see any difference between pre- or post-employee ownership. This company is not any different than any other corporation. The company only wants "yes-men." Those [people] with their own mind don't last long. People are not willing to voice their opinions because they still need jobs. [In terms of rules], management wants to have the ideal, but that's not what they do. Some people are treated better than others. And this is not just between the union and the company, but between the employees and those who run the company. . . . The firm exists to put a product out. It is not really maximizing money or helping employees. . . . At Standard Knapp, I don't see [commonalities] happening. Guys come to work, and they leave. . . . Without a union, I honestly don't believe Standard Knapp would change.[8]

The last comment reveals that, despite the attempts at ownership and at building an informed, engaged work force and despite the efforts to create a sense of common purpose, deep, often traditional divisions persist. More important, though, the interviewee notes that, despite management's participatory efforts, an implicit "favoritism" exists. The recognition of the firm seeking "yes-men" confirms the "voice without choice" characteristic. For some, to benefit from the firm's design and the firm's goals means that a worker must adhere to the firm's agenda, which is not an agenda commonly agreed to by all. The union worker blames management for creating participatory objectives that it fails to sustain or pursue. To a limited extent, the employee accurately recognizes that management does not meet all of its participatory aspirations. But management also takes the blame for disgruntled workers who reject the idea that management would attempt any significant alteration in its power and, thus, do not experiment with the participatory changes.

Given management's hollow changes, the union employee depends not on the power of employee participation to build a common voice, but on the power of the union to protect its members' interests against a distrustful management. The union retains power as an escape valve for employee dissatisfaction with management's participatory implementation. In this sense, the union interferes with the common contract that participationists believe can develop between worker and management, as few substantial changes in decision-making control and direction exist. Given the workers' distrust of management's implementation, both sides need to rethink their relationship. Perhaps management needs a greater commitment to employee participation, and workers need to work with management to achieve this commitment. As it stands now, mistrust can never lead to mutuality.

The antagonisms extend beyond different labor and management agendas. One senior nonunion worker claims:

This is a terrific company, run as fair as it can be given who you are dealing with. . . . It is interesting to work for an employee-owned company, but it is secretive here. . . . I am not willing to invest any more [in the firm] because the union controls the company, maybe even the profit. They resent top management making a profit. [The union] feels like they [management] aren't telling the truth. *I feel that way too!* People resent buying into the company, [but buying in] does give me a sense of belonging. [In terms of control over the company's profit,] *I resent the union having that kind of control over my . . . money.*[9]

These comments, though, reveal the difficulty management addresses in commiting to a participatory plan. It seems that rifts exist, not only between labor and management, but also between groups of workers. Nonunion workers resent the power of the union to dictate employee policy—a power the nonunion people feel they lack—and, thus, they feel they must follow the interests of the unionized segment of the firm. But even the nonunion workers recognize management's secrecy or duplicity; and perhaps the deeper problem may be that management does little to reconcile employee factions, as the infighting keeps employee wrath directed away from management's control.

In addition, the first interviewee who noted the increased decision-making control and sensed a greater personal commitment also maintains reservations about top management and company policy. He states, "I have a sense of trust, but it is not blind. Questions are there, human nature being what it is [I am] more involved in decision making—but again, decision making to what extent! . . . Sometimes I question the feedback [the president's] getting."[10] A union official extends the blame further and apparently repudiates much of what the employee involvement endeavor has attempted by claiming, "Management is just going through the motions. [Management] just appeases you [with your involvement]. Decisions are already made. [There are] a lot of meetings, but the company never followed or listened to employees' suggestions. The supervisors only do what the top people want to hear."[11]

These representative views constitute a well-defined reality. Employees have established reasons for what they perceive as the firm's problems, and those reasons divide workers into specific categories—sometimes based on education and/or experience—and continue to maintain permanent distinctions between employees. Obviously, these divisions mirror distinct interests, often along union–nonunion lines and management–union lines. But even with nonunion employees who interact regularly with top management, an undercurrent of doubt about a lack of information or a lack of decision-making influence persists.

In fact, the survey responses send clear messages about employee involvement. Over 90 percent of the respondents strongly agree that employee participation is a good idea, and to varying degrees 77 percent agree that it is beneficial to Standard Knapp. However, 83 percent of the respondents agree that most employees feel they do not have much power over decision making, 87 percent agree that employee participation does not breed open access to all the firm's workings, and three out of five do not feel a sense of ownership in the firm. At least one-half the respondents—sometimes increasingly larger majorities—feel that their input is not important in the company's decision making, that the company is not committed to listening and responding to their interests. Consequently, they do not feel a sense of control and influence at work.

Employees, then, wholeheartedly support the concept of worker participation, but they remain dissatisfied with how the firm implements the concept. Some employees equate these troubles to the occassional battles of any happy family. Others are less sanguine, and they state that, given the established divisions and loyalties, employee ownership and participation cannot change—in fact, may only exacerbate—these animosities. Most often, but not exclusively, union members claim that no participatory changes can alter the more fundamental divisions at the firm. If they are correct, and it seems Standard Knapp struggles with numerous workers who scoff at the participatory attempts, then participatory theory's transformative proposition is questionable. It may be true that full and equal participation may render workplace citizens more attentive to the common good, but a partial realization may in fact intensify existing conflicts.

It seems, then, that the outward appearance of Standard Knapp's economic success misses the firm's internal struggles with contradictory forces. One force originates in a long, historical narrative based on the conventional antagonistic relations between groups with different interests, like management and labor. The other force emerges from a recent attempt to overcome these antagonisms through greater interaction and greater employee control. While a look at the firm's decision-making process shows that an established, hostile environment best characterizes internal employee relations, what also nurses worker frustration has to do with the unfulfilled expectations that the change in ownership and the changes in participation creates.

These contradictory forces represent the standard employee attitudes toward the union: Either it is seen as limiting the move toward worker participation, or it is seen as a necessary presence for this to occur. However, a third view clarifies their relationship by recognizing how employees use the firm's newly created participatory avenues to exercise a form of voice that, historically, was articulated through membership in the union. While participationists argue that involvement will, to cite Tocqueville, "recruit feelings and opinions, enlarge the heart, and develop the mind,"[12] these changes find little expression as employees press partial or factious concerns. The power of the culture or of the employees' attitudes of partiality, rather than the union, undercuts participation's power. According to this view, the attitudes that employees bring to the workplace may stifle any possible participatory effects. Standard Knapp's president confirms this view when he states, "[I feel] that our attempts are a lot better than anything else. The struggle we have today, and ideas I naively held ten years ago when we started, is that employee ownership would solve all the negative attitudes here.... There is a huge resistance to change [at Standard Knapp]."[13]

Despite the stifling effects of employee attitudes, the president claims that the firm is better off than before employee participation began. Sometimes the recognition of problems is a first step toward resolving those problems, and the fact that employees can quickly cite what those problems are indicates their engagement and interest in improving work life. With this meager sign, participationists claim that this "negative" interest reflects "an enlarging of the workers' hearts and minds." Two interpretations can be drawn from Standard Knapp's actions: One is that participation does not change the worker as much as allow the historical antagonisms new expression; the second argues that even the employee voice of hostility reflects a noticeable change, as employees, and not the union, are now the actors who seek to establish what they believe satisfies their participatory contract. While the latter interpretation contains a modest element of optimism for participatory changes, both views recognize the conflictual nature of work relations at the firm. Conflict may be what management thought participation would control if it were introduced, and, thus, it would benefit management's agenda. However, conflict may be an essential element of any democratic endeavor. Thus, the frustration and conflict at Standard Knapp may represent the inexact and difficult extension of democratic reform.

A LANGUAGE OF DIVISION, POINTS OF FRUSTRATION

The president's subtle remarks, and much of the common, abrasive wisdom that emanates from the employees, speak to the different agendas of management and labor. But to state flatly that the firm's troubles center on these groups is to ignore some crucial information. Without reservation, almost all respondents agree employee participation can benefit a firm. In addition, almost all respondents, especially when interviewed, express satisfaction—often enthusiastically—about the work they do and with those who work with them. It seems differences begin either when decisions about how to extend job satisfaction to a broader level or when decisions about how to implement the theory of worker participation are taken. Agreement in principle exists but breaks down quickly when words change to action.

As principles are put into practice, workers slide easily into the language of us versus them, of management versus the union. This apparent "natural" tension creates and maintains a hostile, or at least a reserved and not open, dialogue that undermines almost all attempts at accomplishing common goals. Remarks develop like "the union controls this company" or "management only pays lip-service to us." Yet a wealth of comments exist that reveal a willingness to see beyond immediate group interests and show an astute awareness of the firm's common agenda. One loyal union supporter claims, "We don't need control, but [we] have to feel that what we say is going to be listened to."[14] Another union member described the present mindset of the union membership as "Looking back, giving up much of what we had in the early 1980s was worth it, . . . but [the president] kept saying, when the mortgage was paid off, when this or that was paid off, it would be the union's turn, now in 1994 the [union] membership was looking for some of the benefits they gave up."[15] It seems that two related concerns are affecting employees' views here. One union concern reiterates the sacrifices that the union had to make in order that the employees could buyout the firm from the original owners. The other issue is the employees' assessment of the efficacy of the participatory structures. It seems that the latter issue cannot compensate for the former concern. If the former had been adequately addressed, it seems that the increased participation may have had more legitimacy.

What the union membership nearly decided to do in 1994 was strike. By a close 54 to 47 vote, the membership avoided that ultimate statement of different interests. Interestingly, top union officials pressed members to vote against it. Even within the union, differences emerged. In the 1994 contract negotiations between the union and management, a general consensus noted that the "old-timers" showed more trust in management than the younger, more vocal members. A union official admits that "The new, young people [began] right away [to make] arguments on wage structure." But the official adds that "The only time when the union is at odds with management, when the two sides lock horns, is over a lack of information when decisions are being made."[16]

The point is that the language of union–management antagonism signals rather neatly that relations within the firm are more intricate. For the most part, even the so-called combatants accept these simple divisions. Often, the divisions obscure the ability to solve differences: Differences which, in the union official's view, simply call for greater access to information; or, according to other officials, call for greater initiative to take advantage of information sources. To clarify, the workers' call for informational access shows the ineffectiveness of management's participatory design. However, management's response is that employees most often do not avail themselves to the information. Again, historical roles, often based on antagonistic and competitive interests like the union's role in providing the information to its membership, seem to interfere with the ability of workers and management to reach trusting relations. These outside forces, like the workers' suspicious attitudes and distrustful natures given their experiences with hierarchical firms, greatly determine the ability of workers to develop their minds or enlarge their hearts when they interact with management in a more participatory model.

Perhaps a more beneficial and, for the firm, more productive method of responding to these interests is to recognize their diversity. For example, one employee stated that while "The company has a need for workers to work overtime every week, some work extra all the time for their Social Security benefits, but others are happy with just eight hours a day, five days a week."[17] While he thought most people would put in the extra effort most of the time, the pressure or stress to work overtime, whether it is mandatory or not, has become perhaps Standard Knapp's most volatile issue. Management, under the strain of increasing efficiency and delivering a quality product at a competitive price, typically views overtime as an employee benefit. Workers do too, to a point. The point when employees question overtime is when, as one union member states, "The company gives carte blanche overtime. Certain departments don't warrant overtime."[18] Or, a point of frustration exists when employees feel "Something is wrong if we have to work this much and still not get anything from it [in terms of dividends or other benefits]."[19]

I have hinted that the rancor between management and labor, between union and nonunion, between Plant 1 and Plant 2, and between each plant and the office underscores the more elemental frustration, not just with the unfulfilled promises of employee participation, but also with general economic difficulties as funneled through the structure of employee ownership at Standard Knapp. The firm's participatory design, then, takes the brunt of criticism for problems it does not always create. In a sense, participation through employee voice exhibits what participationists do not expect. Participation becomes a means to press partial grievances and not a means to bridge partiality. Voice becomes an opportunity to enunciate special interests and not to find common interests. However, the alternative stresses that the fundamental conflicts result from management retaining the power and prerogatives that count. Management determines wages and overtime levels, not the employees, and what frustrates the workers is their lack of participatory voice over the issues that affect their day-to-day lives. The firm responds that it has little control over the market's demands, that the firm's wages are quite high in relation to other operations, and that overtime is generally viewed as an employee benefit. In the end, both sides state that their respective options are limited by forces outside their control. Management explains that the external market requires additional employee effort, while workers explain that the internal participatory processes do not allow them to express their interests. At Standard Knapp, the issue is how to have each side address the other's concern.

THE NUMBER FOUR QUANDARY

When Standard Knapp workers responded to the survey questions, they had the option of choosing whether they agreed or disagreed to a statement based on a seven-point scale. The selection of a number between the two extremes of one ("I agree with the statement") and seven ("I disagree"), such as four, could mean one of two possibilities. One reason is that perhaps the workers had a profound ambivalence about the statement. Given their responses to other questions, and given the subsequent interviews which displayed a vocal, engaged work force, another explanation appears necessary. A second possibility is that a midpoint response reveals a thoughtful, intelligent choice of mixed attitudes about the statements. In fact, what at first appears as a methodological quandary actually captures the attitudinal quandary that the workers show toward the firm. The employees repeatedly express a dilemma they share toward Standard Knapp's procedures and structure by expressing neither support for nor disagreement with a host of survey questions.

For instance, just over one-half the respondents chose a middling number to the statement that "Employee participation is not well-developed at my firm." While 27 percent agree and 22 percent disagree to the statement—which indicates that distinct factions exist at the firm—most respondents are aware of both the benefits and troubles associated with participation. The majority response seems to say that "I cannot fully endorse or dismiss employee participation because I am aware of examples where participation could be improved; however I also realize participation could be diminished from what exists now." Similar responses exist for the statements "Employee ownership means the welfare of workers is more often taken into account when decisions are made than would be true in a traditionally-owned firm" and "The firm educates its employees really well about company decisions." Factions of at least 20 percent both fully agree and disagree to these statements, and either a sizable plurality or a majority expresses the

"Number four quandary." The quandary reiterates the theme that, in general, Standard Knapp employees welcome the opportunities that employee ownership can create. At the same time, they express skepticism about whether these opportunities can be realized, given the present lack of accessibility to the firm's management and the resistance to employee control.

An important consequence of the "Number four quandary" is that management confronts a difficulty itself when it must decide on company policy. If significant minority factions line up at opposite ends of a company initiative, and a sizable portion of the work force recognizes the ongoing difficulties or discrepancies the firm produces in connecting participatory plans with participatory expectations, employees send rather confusing messages to the firm. Worker participation, then, produces a democratic dilemma. If management decides to assuage the minor, more extreme factions by fixing a company position somewhere between the two extremes, neither extreme faction finds satisfaction with the "middling" compromise. Also, the compromise does not satisfy the larger percentage of respondents because their middling answers reflect their collective experiences, not what they believe on any particular policy. In fact, a middling response only shows awareness of discrepancies between principle and practice, it is not a choice that defines a clear position.

For example, in response to the statement, "The company creates an atmosphere that makes it easy to be informed," 22.5 percent agree, 37.5 percent disagree, and 40 percent chose the "Number four quandary." In addition, no significant differences in responses exist between management workers and shop-floor employees for this question. Thus, groups of diverse workers hold opposite views about the same issue, and a plurality of workers believe that the firm sometimes allows information to be accessible, other times it does not. In this case, it seems that the firm should take action to open up the flow of information. However, when the firm's workers split nearly in half, or even in distinct thirds or fourths, in response to how the company operates, it is not always clear how the company should respond. In essence, if worker ownership and participation does not build and maintain a common agenda, and interests remain narrowly focused and distinct, any decision made will produce a vocal opposition.

To some extent, at Standard Knapp, separate interests result from the differences between union members and management employees. Over one-half of those workers who label themselves as members of management do feel that the company belongs to them in a meaningful way. Thirty-six percent of the total respondents do not feel this way. Management workers make up a greater percentage of the respondents who believe that participation helps them be more informed. Most important, a vast majority of management people who responded believe that their input is important in the company's decision making, although 40 percent of the total respondents disagree and 37.5 percent choose the middling numbers. Also, a vast majority of management people who responded feel empowered by their control and input, whereas 52.5 percent of the total respondents disagree that they feel empowered. Finally, while 42.5 percent disagree and 40 percent choose a middling number, 60 percent of the management respondents agree that the company is committed to listening and responding to a worker's opinions.

But to claim that Standard Knapp divides neatly along management and union lines is misleading. In response to the statements that the firm well educates its employees about company decisions and that the firm provides an atmosphere that makes it easy to be informed, management responses roughly mirror the overall negative or questionable results. Also, management workers display reservations about whether participation is well developed and whether they can participate in decision making. The results suggest that management workers are more likely to view the firm's efforts to develop participation, to open up decision-making processes, and to disseminate information in a favorable light in comparison to the unionized plant workers. These favorable views, though, also come with a substantial amount of questioning and doubt. The workers' general attitudes can be best described as varying degrees of a careful, cautious ambivalence. How company policy that has even healthy support could come from such an environment is not clear.

TESTING PARTICIPATORY THEORY'S ACTIVITY HYPOTHESIS

An important argument in participatory democratic theory claims that a sense of control and empowerment at work will cause workers to attempt to extend their empowerment to the political arena. In a sense, people are problem-solvers; and once the problems at work are resolved through participation, people will then turn to the larger and more ambiguous arena of political interaction. However, it is my argument that individualized agendas and cultural forces frustrate any possibility of workplace participation transforming even an empowered worker into an active citizen. We live in a society that clearly divides our private work lives from public issues. In fact, what ought to be seen as *our* public issues are usually referred to as quite removed from our immediate interests.

Given the decision-making structure and the questioning attitudes of the employees, it is no surprise that few workers note any connection between their activities at work and their activities beyond work. If anything, the frustrations that exist at Standard Knapp cause workers to separate their private activities—time with family, for instance—from their work lives. Even those management workers who report a sense of commitment, belonging, and empowerment through their participation at Standard Knapp do not transfer these feelings to the public arena. Sixty percent of the total respondents stated that they do not participate in any form of association. Seventy percent disagreed that their participation at work encouraged their participation in other groups.

Participatory theory argues that, through interaction to solve common problems, people will recognize the benefits of working in concert, not just for the collectivity, but for each person individually. Perhaps an example that refutes this idea is the union member who truly values his job and sympathizes with management's participatory attempts but states that management needs to recognize that different workers have different interests in seeking or not seeking overtime. The worker feels pressure to submit to overtime work although he prefers to pursue other interests, perhaps the quintessential example of a "choice" to make extra money without the "voice" to explain his desire not to always have to commit to overtime work. The company, though, feels pressure to fulfill its contracts and offers overtime as an employee benefit. What appears to the company as an employee benefit is, for the worker, a cause of dissatisfaction. No language of a common ground exists; in turn, workers speak mainly of individual concerns. The worker believes the firm does not consider his interests and learns to accept the imposed choice, and the firm believes that, with the lack of employee voice, the workers understand the policy and value the extra money.

Though nearly 60 percent of the respondents disagree with the statement that "The demands of my work do not allow me to spend time involved with other activities," those other activities rarely involve common or public issues. Seventy-eight percent agree that, outside of work, they are active in private rather than public issues. In fact, when asked directly, nearly as many respondents agree as disagree that political concerns appear remote from my daily interests or necessities. What workers do believe is that a participatory firm demands sacrifices from its employees. While 51 percent agree to some extent that an employee must sacrifice some of his or her private life interests to participate in the workplace, the same percentage disagree that a participatory workplace creates more opportunities than it demands sacrifices. It seems that, not only do workers attempt to differentiate their work lives from their private lives, they also believe the participatory process, at least at their firm, is not worth the time it demands.

These results begin to question participatory theory's expectations. In theory, participatory workers will master their environments and extend their efforts into broader realms. Participatory workers at Standard Knapp exhibit a vigorous questioning of the firm's participatory plan and draw a clear distinction between private activities and public works. To be sure, Standard Knapp does not meet the maximum definitions of a healthy, mature participatory firm, but the firm does meet minimal participatory expectations. The question becomes can the firm's decision-making processes assume complete responsibility for all the workers' complaints? Even under the minimal conditions for establishing a participatory environment, the employee mistrust and suspicion shows that the firm does not create an effective situation to measure participation's influence. But to conclude that the firm's participatory plan fails misses the subtlety of several other relationships that help to determine the firm's ineffectiveness. Specifically, the workers' factious natures, and the reinforcement of these differences with the union's presence, restrains management's ability to foster change. Also, unfulfilled employee expectations, perhaps some reasonable and others impossible, of participation contribute to different attitudes that affect what the president cites as too much "negativity" in the firm.

Given the firm's participatory failures and these critical attitudes toward work life, the one moment in every interview where the conversation immediately grew silent, as if the question just asked had no bearing—in fact, had no meaning—to the preceeding discussion was when I asked if an individual's participation at work affected other areas of their life. The common answer was that overtime ate into their private activities. Most accept the intrusion as a necessary evil, others resent the intrusion. For those few workers who are active in civic groups, their experiences at Standard Knapp cause them to cherish their civic work and the good it does, given the lack of a collective feeling and a common good that they experience at work. One employee said that employee ownership and participation gave the employee a "good sense of what politics is like, and that is something I would want to avoid."[20] The firm bears the brunt of criticism for its ineffective participatiory environment, but the power of individual attitudes, with preconceived notions of only the negative effects of politics and, in essence, of voice activity, limits what the firm can accomplish.

CONCLUSION

A theme of this chapter is that the categories of "a union employee" and "management" are long established and call to mind certain negative characteristics for many workers. It is through these categories that much of the frustration with the employee ownership and participatory experience, along with more general economic insecurities, finds expression. Standard Knapp has many union workers with careers at the firm that date well before the employee buyout. They may carry a host of established ideas that make change difficult, and a union official does claim that "There are too many old philosophies in the union."[21] But the president singled out the older union workers as displaying the most trust in the firm during the 1994 contract negotiations. It appears that the younger union members exhibit greater hostility and clamor for increased benefits because of their greater insecurity in the market. Also, union people claim management cannot simply decree change. They must educate first, and perhaps allow the union the leeway to lead its members. But such insights still adhere to the established, antagonistic categories that create more tension than cohesion. What results from this rhetoric are employee forecasts that claim "I'm pessimistic about the future of this company. . . . I'm not willing to invest any more. . . . You can't put your heart and soul in a company."[22]

To overcome the history of antagonism, management is beginning to divide the company into suborganizations based on distinct product lines. Each facet of the work force with responsibilities to the particular product line, from office and sales staff to the plant floor, is tied together. Seeing oneself as a component of a product line reduces the prominence of divisions such as union and nonunion and management and union. It also allows the worker to witness the totality of the work endeavor, from inception to completion, and to recognize the importance of each person's efforts in completing a project. But again, changing the focus of work may not necessarily change the employee attitude of partiality. While workers may begin to reconceptualize work relations and to understand the numerous efforts needed to create a product, workers may, in turn, simply shift allegiances from their union's interests to their product line's interests. In fact, that change may be management's relatively obvious intention, as the union's power weakens and allows management greater decision-making leeway, thus undermining participation in favor of management's agenda.

Also, the firm claims that it is beginning to target specific work needs and requirements. After broad-based gain-sharing inducements produced relatively minor improvements, management now believes more pointed questions about productivity needs demand attention. These efforts can take two routes. One route is that, without the open dialogue and, most likely, a measure of control in the process that the union seeks, these changes will increase the already rising tensions in the firm. The other route would be for management to introduce the proposed changes for discussion and perhaps minor modification, and not merely dictate them. Perhaps an updated series of notebooks about general company strategies and technical product information, strategically placed throughout the firm, could provide better access.

However, the changes most necessary for employees to accept even the potential for participatory benefits extend beyond the decision-making structures at Standard Knapp. The changes involve how we differentiate our private lives from our work lives and public lives and how we view our individual identities in relation to not just work, but to each other. Standard Knapp's most important lesson is not about the negative effects of a poorly structured or underused decision-making apparatus. Instead, its lesson is about our inability to employ democratic skills: to enunciate a common agenda, to recognize and accommodate, if possible, different views, and to facilitate ongoing communication.

To reiterate, though, what Standard Knapp also reveals is that, without any recognizable decision-making control, the employees' participatory voice focuses on their inability to participate and to control their workplace. Participation becomes a forum for expressing their perceived powerlessness. Their voice, then, does not have the ability to transform or to educate. Participation becomes the ability to express negative attitudes and not the ability to develop or change personally. It seems, then, at Standard Knapp, participation fails to satisfy participation's minimal definition.

Participatory advocates would argue that the firm's structure and, perhaps, the union's presence mediate participation's potential. Only with greater voice and control would workers begin to change. Participationists would claim that management expects changes from its work force, while it simultaneously inhibits those changes. As with the next case studies, employees then remain reluctant to exercise their opportunities or feel that management's participatory changes do not fundamentally alter their relationship. In turn, workers use the minor changes to call for greater change.

While Standard Knapp is not the best example of a successful participatory firm, my argument points to other causes that detract from the firm's potential. Certainly, management and worker roles have not changed dramatically. A union–management dichotomy divides employees. An unwillingness to trust one another pervades the firm, and employee interviews reveal nearly lethal doses of suspicion, doubt, uncertainty, and secrecy. But while these attitudes exist within the firm, they also are the attitudes that workers bring to the workplace from their previous experiences and generalized understanding of work relations. Just as participation does not change these attitudes, participation does not produce these attitudes.

For participation to change these established attitudes and understandings of how to interact with others and what to expect from employers means that the employee must be willing to accept change. Interestingly, while the older union workers had more trust in management's participatory changes, the younger union workers were more reluctant to accept those changes. Perhaps the younger workers depend on established economic relations to ensure economic security more so than the older workers. Thus because their youth translates into economic insecurity, perhaps with more outstanding bills and lower wages to pay those bills, they will not accept significant changes at work, no matter the potential for gain. Also, they may not be planning on staying with the firm for as long as the older workers have, whether of their own choosing or from the changing economy; and, in turn, they lack the loyalty that older workers have in the firm. The historical relations of capitalism and the subsequent worker commitment to its structures thus frustrate the potential for participation to change individuals.

Along a similar line, the individual's socialized conception of what Robert Lane recognizes as the differences between politics and economics influences whether a worker willingly adjusts to a participatory workplace.[23] In a culture where politics asks ambiguous questions and political action receives uncertain results, economics, because of its necessity, remains an arena of certainty. If you work, you will be paid; politics does not always offer such a straightforward equation. Also, though work may be necessary for most, politics and its uncertainty is seen as avoidable. The attempt, then, to instill a participatory voice and politics into individuals who interact primarily for the certitude of economic relations may result in problems that Standard Knapp exhibits: confused expectations, uncertainty, voice without choice, and contempt with compliance.

NOTES

1. For example, see Thomas A. Kochan, Harry C. Katz, and Nancy R. Mower, *Worker Participation and American Unions: Threat or Opportunity?* (Kalamazoo, Mich.: UpJohn Institute for Employment Research, 1984).

2. For a discussion of the objections and some practical examples of union activity in employee-owned firms, see Raymond Russell, *Sharing Ownership in the Workplace* (Albany: State University of New York Press, 1985). See also Staughton Lynd, "From Protest to Economic Democracy: Labor-Community Ownership and Management of the Economy," in *Building Bridges*, ed. Jeremy Brecher and Tim Costello (New York: Monthly Review Press, 1990).

3. See Joseph Raphael Blasi, *Employee Ownership: Revolution or Ripoff?* (Cambridge, Mass.: Ballinger Publishing, 1988); and Robert Jackall and Henry M. Levin, ed., *Worker Cooperatives in America* (Berkeley and Los Angeles: University of California Press, 1984), 252–253.

4. Staughton Lynd, "Economic Democracy," 271.

5. Employee interview, Standard Knapp, Middletown, Conn., 21 January 1995.

6. Employee survey response, Standard Knapp, 20 December 1994.

7. Employee interview, Meriden, Conn., 20 January 1995.

8. Employee interview, Middletown, Conn., 21 January 1995.

9. Employee interview, Middletown, Conn., 21 January 1995. Italics added.

10. Employee interview, Meriden, Conn., 20 January 1995.

11. Employee interview, Middletown, Conn., 21 January 1995.

12. Alexis de Tocqueville, *Democracy in America*, ed. Richard D. Heffner (New York: New American Library, 1956), 200.

13. Telephone interview with president of Standard Knapp, 10 February 1995.

14. Employee interview, Middletown, Conn., 21 January 1995.

15. Employee interview, Middletown, Conn., 21 January 1995.

16. Employee interview, Middletown, Conn., 21 January 1995.

17. Employee interview, Middletown, Conn., 21 January 1995.

18. Employee interview, Middletown, Conn., 21 January 1995.

19. Employee interview, Middletown, Conn., 21 January 1995.

20. Employee interview, Middletown, Conn., 21 January 1995.

21. Employee interview, Middletown, Conn., 21 January 1995.

22. Employee interview, Middletown, Conn., 21 January 1995.

23. Robert E. Lane, "Market Justice, Political Justice," *American Political Science Review* 80, no. 2 (1986): 383–402.

Chapter 4   EMPLOYEE PARTICIPATION IN
             THE QUAD/GRAPHICS CULTURE

Because Standard Knapp fails to create a participatory design and atmosphere that the employees recognize as effective, the firm does not offer a strong test for participatory theory's transformative claims. The history of conflict in the firm prior to the participatory changes, and the intermediary role of the labor union, contribute to a difficult assessment of participation's effects. Quad/Graphics represents a more potent example for participatory theory. This firm has a twenty-five-year history of participatory management and lacks the uncertain influence of a labor union. But as Standard Knapp's experience centers on its inability to bridge the partial interests Rousseau believes undermines any social contract, Quad/Graphics must address the opposite concern: That is, does the firm permit its workers to express views and interests that differ from its "Quad culture"? Even though reviewers often hail Quad/Graphics as an exemplar of employee involvement and worker satisfaction, it is an open question whether workers freely submit to Quad/Graphics' management style or whether they exercise a voice without choice. To better understand Quad/Graphics' participatory culture and how employees perceive that culture, I briefly review Rousseau's prescription for a republic.

ROUSSEAU'S GENERAL WILL AND THE "QUAD" CULTURE

Is Rousseau's general will a form of social control and indoctrination? Rousseau argues that if all first agree to submit to the general will's conditions, and if all agree to "submit to such convenants alone, they obey nobody but their own will."[1] Individuals give up a precarious independence from each other for a stable, secure, and, thus, more promising capacity to find "true" freedom with each other.

The answer for Rousseau, then, is that the question is poorly worded. If the people acknowledge a general will, what is "controlled" is only natural liberty. What people gain is civil liberty, to live with each other without fear of injustice, and moral liberty, to live under laws that people will upon themselves. The social compact controls arbitrary actions, and this control allows humans to attain freely both personal and social goals.

However, a discrepancy exists between the preeminence of the general will and how one expresses one's freedom under the general will's authority. Rousseau claims that for the will to be general, it need not always be unanimous. Differences can and will exist. Also, he writes, "If a people promises simply and solely to obey, it dissolves itself by that very pledge; it ceases to be a people; for once there is a master, there is no longer a sovereign."[2] Thus, the general will is the agreement of and to first principles. The people must will the laws that they will obey. Only with the continual deliberation of the people in assessing those principles can the will persist.

A problem begins when differences—the diversity that liberty spawns—appear. Rousseau argues that, in the declaration of the general will, "When . . . the opinion contrary to my own prevails, this proves only that I have made a mistake, and that what I believed to be the General Will was not so."[3] Again, on one hand, if the general will need not be unanimous, differences can exist. On the other hand, differences in the general will cannot exist. For Rousseau, differences emerge when partial interests take precedence over the first principles; they emerge when first principles are neglected. The appearance of diversity is not the expression of true freedom but of partiality, perhaps even of independence. This discrepancy between viewing diversity as the expression of freedom and diversity as the neglect of first principles leads Rousseau's critics, who adhere to the former view, to argue that the general will eradicates individual diversity in the name of an omnipresent state. In this critique, Rousseau's words come to mean "be afraid of lawless man, but embrace the accepted and powerful state."

The question becomes, can the general will ever be misguided? Rousseau replies, "The General Will is always rightful, but the judgment which guides it is not always enlightened. It must be brought to see things as they are, and sometimes as they should be seen."[4] But if the will is not always enlightened, how or from whom can the will be seen as it should be seen? Without a modern day lawgiver, it appears that the general will can err, that differences need protection as well as expression, and that what determines our collective will ought to be more than our submission to what amounts to mere majority rule.

However, the conclusion that Rousseau's views culminate in a form of totalitarian control is a rather crude though popular interpretation. Rousseau is as much interested in creating a form of face-to-face, deliberative citizenship as he is interested in ensuring a commitment to the common will. Critics view this commitment as a potentially consuming force on the individual. Instead, though, a more sophisticated treatment of Rousseau understands this commitment as a component of active citizenship and not as a total self-surrender to the dictates of the general will. Active citizenship entails that each individual participates with others, and that all recognize the value of and are involved in addressing the principles that guide their interaction. Rousseau's views do not call for a submission to abstract laws or the absence of private life, only that citizens continually engage in deliberating their understanding of what is in everyone's interests. With this more subtle understanding, the view of Rousseau as advocating totalitarianism seems simple minded.

The questions we ask of Rousseau's general will, or any democratic political system, apply to the employee participation program at Quad/Graphics. One of the country's preeminent printing firms, Quad/Graphics employs over 9,000 people at eight production and twelve sales locations. The company averaged a 30 to 40 percent per-year growth rate throughout the 1980s. Yearly sales estimates stand at the $800 million mark today. As *Forbes* reports, Harry Quadracci "and a few of his original employees still own around 60 percent of a company with a probable value of $800 million; an employee stock ownership plan owns 30 percent, and a few early backers about 10 percent."[5] What distinguishes Quad/Graphics' success—what, in fact, the principal private owner, Harry Quadracci, heralds as the underpinning of the firm's success—is employee participation.

But Quad/Graphics' participation exemplifies the troubles of Rousseau's well-structured republic translated into the workplace. Management and participatory researchers view the firm's participative management style as the solution to several potential ills. It reduces the growth of middle management, it rewards initiative, responsibility, and effort, and it encourages long-range thinking by those employees who tend not to think long-term. In short, the firm benefits because the employees see and feel the benefits of their efforts. As one manager stated, "[Here at Quad/Graphics,] if you want to go [in a certain direction], you can do it. If that's reality or not, I believe it. It may not be 100 percent true, but I believe it."[6]

However, an alternative view of the firm's employee participation questions its methods and effects. Just as the general will is often viewed as totalitarian, Harry Quadracci, who is also sometimes called Larry, claims that new employees enter a form of "boot camp. You are assigned a mentor, a more senior employee who helps you acculturate into the company, and over the next two years you and the company decide whether you are right for the Quad/Graphics family." In the unsophisticated view of Rousseau's views, Quadracci's participatory methods point to similar questions about the consuming aspects of the firm's general will. Quadracci states that employees "get indoctrinated, brainwashed—theirs is not to reason why. It's authoritarianism all the way, until they've proven they're adult enough to handle a participative management style."[7] But the more sophisticated view of Rousseau reveals the participatory faults at Quad/Graphics: The employees do not establish a "contract" with all other employees as equal participants of a decision-making body. In the initial acculturation to Quad/Graphics, much like the establishment of first principles, management dictates what employees come to believe. In this sense, management exhibits the totalitarian characteristics for which Rousseau is commonly criticized.

Perhaps equating the construction of a political body to the development of a firm's management style misses important differences. After all, the firm exists to make a profit; the republic exists for safety, freedom, and justice. If one is unhappy with the firm's methods and one's treatment under those methods, the employee often leaves. This option is more difficult at the state level. However, employees at participatory firms like Quad/Graphics speak of the values—such as safety and security in the form of 401(k) plans and profit sharing, such as individual freedom and control of their immediate work environment, and such as the opportunity to express themselves via e-mail to President Quadracci—that comprise the essentials of political bodies. For Rousseau, although e-mail does not compare to the deliberation necessary to make judgments in the common good, e-mail is a small step toward flattening hierarchy and making decision makers accessible to all levels of a firm.

Also, employees many times recognize economically what citizens never question politically. As one employee wrote, "The bottom line for most of us I'm sure is that employment opportunities in this area are scarce. Quad pays our bills. I do not have the time or money for further education/training and must stay in the area because of family. Quad has pretty much 'got me.' The fact that it is a 'participatory workplace' is just an interesting and lucky bonus for me."[8] As citizens, we rarely consider the option of leaving the country because of its policies. In the economic arena and as employees, a difference in policy often produces exit. But even at Quad/Graphics, where Lane and Hirschman would note that the firm benefits from the replacement of exit with voice, the employee attitude that the firm "has got me" reveals a voice without choice and a loyalty driven by self-interest. The choice is to accept the participatory plan or exit, a choice that allows the firm to decide the kind and amount of employee freedom. From this, Rousseau's notion of citizenship, even participatory actions within the firm, are smothered by Quad/Grahpics' ability to control how employees act.

The problem that participation at Quad/Graphics raises centers on whether the beneficial ends for both the employees and the firm justify the means employed to attain them. The simple-minded interpretation of Rousseau's thought argues that true freedom develops only after one willingly submits to a possibly all-powerful collective authority. However, the more subtle treatment of Rousseau notes that true freedom develops when an individual is an active citizen and a subject. Rousseau is explicit that submission to a sovereign without gaining membership in a self-legislating body is illegitimate. At Quad/Graphics, the firm seeks to establish an environment that nurtures creativity, intelligence, ingenuity, fraternity, and far-thinking by way of first establishing control and discipline over its employees. Employees marvel at the on-the-job freedom Quad/Graphics bestows, but the firm grants freedom only after employees accept the firm's general employment rules and its participatory culture. In short, Quad freedom comes from

Quad life; that is, since the firm does not allow its workers membership in the firm's "first principle" decisions, the firm as a democratic body remains illegitimate. In short, Quad/Graphics' actions resemble the kind of totalitarian control for which many mistakenly criticize Rousseau's views. However, a more sophisticated understanding of what Rousseau argues offers insight into why Quad/Graphics produces a lack of true freedom.

In the political realm, some argue that the solution to citizen apathy and to apolitical attitudes is to do as Quad/Graphics does. Establish rules, communicate their relevance, agree to a compact with clear responsibilities for and from all involved, and then, after an initial trial period, accept people who accept the system. But a democratic political system cannot be as exclusive as an individual firm. It must incorporate a wider degree of diversity. In fact, one can argue that a democratic political system gains strength and legitimacy from its inclusivity, whereas an individual firm based on democratic principles often gains strength from its exclusivity.

These discrepancies will become clearer as we explore the Quad culture through the eyes of two of its employees: one a manager who recognizes and accepts the culture and works toward his and the firm's goals; the other who recognizes but still questions the culture, who cannot resolve the questionable company methods. In the democratic political realm, both people receive equal treatment and opportunity, albeit with a thinner concept of citizenship. At Quad/Graphics, the value the firm puts on democratic participation and involvement are signs of success, but its tendency to discourage the democratic questioning of policy and principles are signs of struggle and discontent. Such signs often lead to dismissal or exit-behavior in economic activity in general, actions that have few equivalent political counterparts.

QUAD/GRAPHICS' PARTICIPATORY DESIGN

After struggling for several years after its 1971 incorporation, Quad/Graphics in the late 1970s began and today continues to grow at dizzying rates. The firm now claims it is the largest family-owned printer in North America with over 500 clients, some of which include *Time, Newsweek, People, Sports Illustrated, Outside,* and *Mad*. At its fifteen-year-old Saratoga Springs, New York production plant, which is one of Quad/Graphics' eight plants with a ninth near completion, over 900 employees work in four buildings covering over 325,000 square feet—and a 100,000-square-foot expansion project nears completion. At this location alone, nine presses, each at a cost of $6 to $8 million, print more than 2.4 million magazines weekly, the largest output of any facility in the country. Every day the Saratoga plant ships more than twenty trailer loads of freight for distribution and receives more than 60,000 pounds of cards and inserts for placement in magazines and catalogs printed on-site.[9]

At the Saratoga plant, employees fill several departments related to the printing process: imaging, plate-room, press, finishing, and distribution. But every employee, no matter what his or her job or background, undergoes exposure to the Quad culture. As *Lithoweek* reports, "The first two days with the company are spent on a 'new hire' course which tells them about the company's history, development, and values."[10] New hires are recommended a few courses to develop not only their expertise, but also their communication, leadership, and other human resource skills, typically taught by an in-house host of experts and employees. Quad tries to avoid people with printing experience because most have difficulty adapting to Quad's philosophies. Employees are young, often with minimal education, often fresh from one of the armed services. The average age of an employee is twenty-nine. The production jobs work twelve-hour shifts three days one week (7 A.M. to 7 P.M.), then four days the next. Company policy dictates that each year the night shift employees move to days and the day shift moves to nights. Quad lavishes its employees and their families with a state-of-the-art fitness facility and a medical staff as well. Each plant has a cafeteria, almost every employee has a vax (similar to e-mail) account from which the employee can write directly to Quad's president, and the medical and dental benefits outshine those of the competition.

The Quad culture initiation and educational courses are requisite introductions to the sometimes startling management structure and style. With the always attendant concern of controlling management layers, Harry Quadracci believes in a flat management structure where "nothing should ever be someone else's responsibility."[11] Similarly, devolving responsibility to the truckers who haul Quad's output, to the pressmen who operate their own presses, to each employee over his or her own work environment, epitomizes Quad's "walk away" management philosophy. In sharp contrast to the pervasive mistrust that marks Standard Knapp's operations, the employees recognize the trust management places in their hands. In turn, over 60 percent of the survey respondents give some degree of assent to the statements that they feel their input is important in the company's decision making, that they feel empowered by the control they have in their positions, and that they feel the firm is committed to listening to individual opinions and interests. At Standard Knapp, 43 percent of the respondents agree that they feel their input is important in the firm's decision making, and, even worse, only 30 percent feel empowered by their positions and feel the firm is committed to listening. It seems, then, that given the structure of the two firms and the employee responses, Standard Knapp appears both more democratic and more conflictual.

While Quad/Graphics nurtures participation and responsibility for each job and department, participation does not extend to the firm's decision-making process. In contrast to the widespread but thin stock ownership by Standard Knapp employees, Harry Quadracci and a small group of investors retain about 60 percent, or a working majority of the stock. The ESOP owns 30 percent of the company, but employees do not have voting rights over their stock. All employees with at least one year of employment participate in the ESOP. They are allocated stock based in part on their salaries, and the stock vests over seven years. While the firm encourages each employee to improve or "take control" of their immediate job area, company decision making remains firmly ensconced in a Quadracci-led, eight-member board of directors. With this financial arrangement, the ESOP is less a form of ownership and more a kind of profit sharing based on company performance.

Obviously, then, Quad/Graphics fails to meet the basic requirements of a democratically controlled firm. Employees have no say over corporate policy, despite the empowerment they feel at the more immediate level. The survey responses capture the dichotomy between their immediate power and the company's influence. For instance, employees overwhelmingly embrace the avenues that Quad establishes to foster participation. Nearly 90 percent respond that employee participation helps the firm. However, in response to the statements "One could have a lot of influence on general company decisions" and "One can have a lot of say in how the firm is run," just under 40 percent of the respondents agree, while 40 percent or more disagree. Interestingly, at Standard Knapp, where workers are much more frustrated and distrustful of management, the responses to the same questions about influence are dramatically more positive than at Quad/Graphics. At Standard Knapp, 76 percent of the respondents agree that an individual could have a lot of influence and 83 percent agree that one can have a lot of say in how the firm is run. The differences in attitudes seem to underscore the differences in the degree of ownership. At Standard Knapp, where ownership is widely diffuse, employees sense a greater ability to affect decision making than at Quad/Graphics' more restricted culture. Also, while over 70 percent of the respondents at Quad/Graphics feel that the firm "belongs to them in a meaningful way," 55 percent agree that employee participation does *not* breed open access to all the firm's workings. These responses show that employees realize that participation helps the firm but that their input has little influence on the firm's "larger" decisions.

This dichotomy between the devolution of power and responsibility to the employee on the one hand and the retention of corporate direction and shares on the other raises questions of control and influence. These questions of Quad's contradictory expectations—in a sense, telling its employees to participate but only in certain areas and to limited degrees—and the firm's truly participatory nature run up against Quad culture's "indoctrination." Perhaps Quad culture's *modus operandi* is reflected in employee statements such as: "In terms of company decisions, I do not have enough knowledge. Those with all the knowledge gather it from all the different departments. . . . The power of an individual at the bottom compared to the power of an individual at the top, well, there's not the same resources."[12]

Another employee states, "We call it Quad fluff or Quad washing. . . . We joke about it around here, whether they put stuff in the popcorn or in the Kool-Aid. They tell you 'you'll feel good about this.' It's just a matter of whether you believe."[13] In contrast to the more sophisticated view of Rousseau's notion of active citizenship, where ongoing deliberation is essential, Quad employees must first accept the Quad culture to benefit from it. Acceptance, too, builds loyalty and reinforces the culture. But if the discrepancies in participation and control cause an employee not to accept Quad "fluff" or Quad "washing," if management cannot convince employees that they will feel good about their participation and their support of the culture, then the employee response changes its tone: "The bottom line is that Larry Quadracci makes the final decision.... Management benefits from the participation, workers are simply looking long-term. Participation is a propaganda scheme.... Larry is an egomaniac. He has to be right. He wants everyone to be his slave. This place is Larry-land."[14] Whereas one employee accepts the Quad culture and thus can talk lightly of it, perhaps as a defense of one's submissiveness to the culture, another who does not as readily accept the culture feels oppressed by it.

Let me not overstate the issue. Quad/Graphics effectively promotes participatory decision making at each person's immediate work environment. Given that participatory theory needs to establish step-by-step measures, emanating out from the individual, to encourage further experimentation, Quad/Graphics presents evidence for the efficacious effects of rather limited participation. However, for any organization that attempts to employ democratic methods—in this case decentralizing power, broadening responsibility, and creating interaction—the discrepancies that exist between what the firm promotes and what employees practice and feel also reveals the limits of this "success."

TWO VIEWS OF QUAD/GRAPHICS

Whether one employee views Quad/Graphics as the expression of an egomaniac, while another sees the firm as satisfying personal and career goals, hinges on one's belief in the Quad culture. Reconciliation solves none of the firm's discrepancies here, nor does one resign oneself to a certain fate. Acceptance of the firm's message allows one to deemphasize the inconsistencies that Quad/Graphics produces. As one manager succinctly states, "It is manipulation of the mind ... but if you start believing it [the Quad message], it will improve your life. If you fight it, it will [stink]!"[15]

But acceptance does not mean blindness. The just-quoted manager labels Quadracci a "bizarre individual," while others simply refer to him as a "character." In terms of the firm's participatory methods, a female employee claims that "it allowed me to recognize that if an issue bothers me enough, I know I can change it if I put forth the effort and get involved."[16] The manager claims that because of the flat management structure, "managers may look [roughly equal in power], but they don't have the same perceived power. It is up to the person's initiative—networking, what are they trying to get out of this [job]?"[17] In a sense, then, the employees come to see the value of participation if and only if it is accompanied with their efforts to make participation valuable. The emphasis remains on the employees' initiative, and participation is a tool for workers to use to further their interests.

From these comments, we can question the belief of some participatory theorists that participation is a good in and of itself. For it is not simply participation that is the key ingredient to foster engaged, satisfied employees. The key ingredient is the efficacy that *successful* participation engenders. Employees need to see a positive return to their participatory investment. And belief in their efforts and their activity's influence is easier to attain and agree to when success is apparent. Without that return, employees reject participation; as one employee claims, "Nothing ever came out of my participation. Management is more worried about where the money is going to come from than what I had to offer. . . . I used to get involved on my days off, but I never saw anything happen."[18] Being part of a decision-making process does not appear to be enough for employees. A concrete, measurable contribution put into action is necessary for employees to report favorably on their participation. Against participatory theory's expectations, employees assess participation in market terms. If the costs involved in participating, most notably time, outweigh the perceived benefits, it remains uncertain how employees will respond. Moreover, even if worker participation extended to all decision-making control, it seems that those employees who are not always successful may judge participation as ineffectual.

A belief in the firm's goals and in the participatory process itself need not remain distinct from developing successful experiences in the process. The participatory environment encourages inclusion, which means being a member of several teams at the plant, and encourages the responsibility to feel such bonds. Without hesitation, employees at Quad/Graphics recognize the control they have and feel in their jobs, the freedom and leeway the firm provides, and the sense of responsibility these demands create. As the manager reports, "From day one [when he was not a manager but a new hire], the trust is so apparent. I was put in front of a $600,000-to-$700,000 machine and told to "run it."[19] The demands of the inclusiveness and of the delegated responsibility include pressure, whether self-imposed or from one's peers. The manager states, "At one time, I felt I wasn't living up to expectations. I felt I got to keep striving. Whether it [the pressure] was there or not, I felt the pressure because of the small group I was in. . . . Now, after I've been a manager for several years, the pressure to move ahead, it's not there anymore."[20] Another employee claims, "Because each and every one of us represents our company, if someone who is put in that position and doesn't do the 'right' kind of job, it reflects poorly. . . . Someone who doesn't handle it, sure there's group pressure. I feel it's lifting the individual up to the group's standards. For someone who cares, they come up to par."[21]

But if we return to the employees who do not first accept the Quad "washing," group pressure reinforces not teamwork, but management objectives or oversight. One employee states, "There's group pressure to do the job. It comes from above. And when you first hire on, when the rewards are really not immediate, it [makes you wonder]. Teamwork and participation are management devices. Sure, it works to everyone's advantage, but it helps management [the most]. People are happy really because there's a sense of security."[22] Though there is a clear distinction between those who believe in and those who question the Quad culture, this does not mean that factions exist in the firm. Those who question the Quad culture are aware of some of its benefits. One questioning employee claims, "At times, yes I'm negative [about this company] because I'm tired of the hype. . . . It's a big show, a big front [in some ways] like when we first started, when we had no customers, we worked anyway just to get the customers. But when I see the big picture, it's not bad. . . . It boils down to if you do your job the way Quad wants you to, you get a part of it [the benefits] in the end."[23] These comments note the conflicting feelings some employees express. Perhaps to justify their lack of exit, despite their dissatisfaction with the firm, their voice without choice, employees do note the economic rewards that loyalty to Quad/Graphics brings. But this economic reward is far less than the advantages that the firm claims participation will generate. Tired of the hype, some employees simply want the firm to eliminate the facade of inclusion and tell its employees that it operates like any other hierarchical firm. Ironically, though, the facade nurtures efficacy; and if efficacy increases productivity, then ultimately the disgruntled employees benefit from the very hype they disdain. This means, though, that the employees benefit economically from pseudo-participation, not that they benefit from participation itself.

Another worker writes of the individualistic nature of the participatory process and its benefits: "The employee creates as much participation as s/he wants which in turn allows more opportunities for the employee. There are as many 'deadbeat' managers as there are 'deadbeat' employees. . . . Some [managers] just sit back and wait for things to happen—others go 'gung ho' with their job. The same is true with employees. You are what you are—some are here just for a paycheck—others want to pursue a career to the limit." On the other hand, the writer also reveals how departments control whether individuals participate or not. The employee writes, "In our department—each department has their own criteria of what employees can/cannot do to participate [even though it's not suppose to be] some employees can speak up for changes in their department—others fear loss of job if they speak up. . . . So even though we are employee-owned and have a participatory workplace, too many employees still will not speak up for changes."[24]

This employee argues that even if the firm allows for participation and growth opportunities, those features can be controlled by middle management. It seems that Quad/Graphics' participatory experience depends, not only on initiative, but on access. A simple questioning of a process and/or its implementation may be enough to limit access. As another critical employee comments, "Unfortunately in most cases, the system is designed to help those who designed it,"[25] or those who accept it and implement it. While this employee speaks to problems at Quad/Graphics, the analysis applies to Rousseau's general will as well. For while Rousseau believes that the ongoing participation in addressing first principles insures the necessary commitment to the social contract, the commitment may be less than secure if the voice in theory means a voice with little choice in practice. Moreover, the lack of decision-making control of the firm by the employees shows that any possible debate over the firm's "first principles" is unlikely. Rousseau states that private interests will take precedence if people are left to decide partial concerns. At Quad/Graphics, though, employees have decision-making control over exactly those areas (i.e., immediate work areas) that Rousseau argues foster partial interests and not the general will.

TRANSFORMATION AND POLITICAL ACTIVITY: QUAD/GRAPHICS EVIDENCE

The central hypotheses of this research state that individual identities and interests resist the transformational or educational effects of workplace participation and that the anticipated political action that workplace involvement generates does not occur. Employee reports from Standard Knapp and from Quad/Graphics show that the individual identities of the employees override any participatory benefits. At Standard Knapp, a union member emphasizes the need for management to recognize and accommodate different employee work motivations. He notes that while some prefer overtime work for the added income and its effect on retirement pay, he prefers to pursue other activities that overtime limits.[26] At Quad/Graphics, the recognition that some employees seek only a paycheck while others seek a rising career affects how each employee participates and how each employee views participation. Involvement for one is the requisite avenue to "get ahead"; involvement for another becomes a necessary job requirement, or worse, a waste of time because decisions are predetermined.

What, then, causes workers to emphasize individual pursuits or interests over the potential participatory benefits at work? Participatory theorists would argue that the firms in these case studies fail to provide an adequate participatory decision-making structure that allows for a participatory environment to flourish. But this structural approach misses some equally important factors. One is the historical legacy of individualism that all Americans bring to work. By this I do not mean that workers are reluctant to join together because, as Tocqueville recognizes, Americans are, by nature, associational or "joiners." What individualism encourages, especially after Americans came together to accept discipline and direction in building the modern corporation, is a healthy questioning of or a vigilant disregard for authority and hierarchy. Because employees still recognize hierarchy at these firms, many feel that little change has or will occur. This attitude creates great inertia for even meager changes. Workplace participation today grows only incrementally and inconsistently because a cautious, conservative mentality inhibits participation's possibilities.

Participationists would respond that, because neither firm offers significant changes from corporate hierarchies, participation's effects on individual attitudes and behavior can only be minimal. The strong individualism is reinforced by the accepted wisdom and behavior inherent in the market system. The labor market presents individuals with clear and rather simple choices. The basic understanding of most workers is that, for their labor, they are compensated with a set wage.

For the most part, the arrangement frustrates any sense of protest; and if the employee becomes dissatisfied with the arrangement, the traditional employee response is to exit the firm.

As Hirschman claims, exit is not always an efficient mechanism for expressing attitudes. At times, voice can be more economically efficient, but the labor market's power rests on exit behavior. He states, "Customer-members will ordinarily base their decision on past experience with the cost and effectiveness of voice even though the possible discovery of lower cost and greater effectiveness is of the very essence of voice. The presence of the exit alternative can therefore tend to atrophy the development of the art of voice."[27] Participation at work, then, is atypical for most employees; and when presented with a less than ideal structure that sends conflicting messages about the employee's involvement—as these firms do—most likely the worker relies on past experience and favors exit behavior. Though employees may prefer voice behavior at their firm, voice must overcome the accepted history of exit relations, especially when participation produces inconsistent results.

Given the tension and rancor at Standard Knapp, it is reasonable to assume that employees avoid the participatory process and the collective interaction because of the highly-charged, conflictual atmosphere. At Quad/Graphics, though, where employee support for the firm and its participatory endeavors approach near unanimity, Quad culture offers a strong chance of at least challenging the power of individual interests. After a cursory review, it appears that survey responses bear this out. In response to the statement that they are more involved in other interests after work because of their involvement at work, 38 percent agree, 34 percent disagree, and the remainder are apparently uncertain. However, the apparent "transformative" effect remains disputable if we consider that employees involve themselves with private activities. Nearly 80 percent of the respondents claim that they are active in private interests rather than public concerns outside of work.

Participation at work leads theorists to argue that public activity will increase, but employees who participate overwhelmingly report only private activity. In fact, some employees remark that they participate more in outside activities because of their involvement at work, not because of participation's transformative effects. Because of work's intense and/or conflictual demands, work participation leads them to reassess and to value their free time. For some, devotion to outside interests increases as a form of "reaction" to work participation, not from its apparent benefits. This shows that workers tend to separate their work lives from their private or social lives no matter what work entails. Participationists claim that a democratic workplace will be the bridge to a democratic politics and society; but the power of the labor–capital mentality, where workers clearly understand work time as a necessity and nonwork time as their free time, inhibits the worker from connecting the realms.

A Quad/Graphics employee adds further insight into workplace participation's transformative effects when she explains, "I would have to say no, Quad has not transformed me. It was my personality. . . . It already existed. [But] Quad allowed it to develop. That's the way it is suppose to be—in theory. The company does not nurture you. [Quad, though,] has made me recognize the process, which is the same as outside, you become empowered by being involved."[28] From survey responses and interviews, participation's educational benefits, the idea that individuals' behavior changes because of their interactive work settings, finds little support. Participation at Quad/Graphics empowers employees—60 percent agree they feel empowered—but that empowerment is limited. It is limited by the firm's lack of employee decision-making control in decisions beyond their immediate job area. It is also limited by the employees themselves, as they in general do not recognize a correlation between work and their private lives. In turn, they generally would not press the company for greater control over decision making. If some do seek greater control, their demand remains highly individualistic and often with potentially damaging results for the agent. Why? Because the firm maintains the power to set the participatory agenda, and any attempts to push that agenda in directions unfavorable to management is met with punitive measures. In theory, this should not occur, because the firm implements participation to encourage change and creativity. But the workers' comments, such as, "The firm benefits those who design it"[29] and "Others feel the loss of a job if they speak up,"[30] point to the unequal power relations which interfere with participation's potential.

With regard to attempts at public or political action, prior individual commitments take center stage. At first glance, it seems that work participation does have an effect on political interest because 42 percent of the respondents disagree with the statement that "Political concerns appear remote from my daily interests," while 37 percent agree. However, a more telling response occurs to the statement that "My participation at work has encouraged my participation in other groups": 61 percent disagree, 21 percent have mixed feelings, and only 18 percent agree. The rough equality in responses to the statement about "One's sense of remoteness to the political process" measure preexisting and perhaps well-established displeasure with political concerns. Work participation may or may not affect this set of responses. But the decided rejection of any causal relationship between work participation and outside group participation calls into question the possibility for any "public activity" effect. In fact, the 61 percent statistic is significant because it is higher than the 54 percent of respondents who claim they disagree that they are active in any kind of associational life like political meetings, church committees, or the PTA. Not only do a majority of respondents refrain from public activity, but also an even greater number appear to state that work participation has little if no influence on their outside public or group behavior. It appears as if the employees seek to emphasize the lack of a connection between work participation and their associational life.

A manager claims, "I don't get involved in politics—in groups outside of here [Quad]. I do a lot of traveling, but that's more of an excuse [than a reason]. I'm not a big group activities-type person."[31] In addition, employees claim that their public inactivity is an off-shoot of the Quad culture. As with similar comments at Standard Knapp, the Quad manager believes, "They [the firm] want it [the firm's agenda] to invade your private life. . . . It's a family here. It's a bit incestuous, a sick interrelationship . . . but that's what the firm prefers." Whether the firm benefits from the interrelationship or not, the manager states, "It has a severe competitive advantage in the business. In my personal life, it doesn't bother me, but I know a lot of people who hate it. Spouses either love it or hate it."[32]

What results from work participation, then, is at odds with participatory theory's expectations. The theory presumes that as individuals participate at work they begin to feel empowered by their newfound ability to control their lives and to broaden their agenda from private concerns to a variety of issues. When one feels control at the workplace, the theory assumes this "success" and then targets other, more public issues to tackle. In a sense, individuals not only begin to feel they can influence public policy debates but also begin to sense an individual attachment to broader issues. One's personal identity intertwines with public issues. The two become inextricably bound, and a person succeeds and realizes success occurs *only* through participation.

However, Standard Knapp and Quad/Graphics reveal that individual identities and public-regarding behavior have no interrelationship in firms with participation in work-level decisions. Rather, they remain in well-differentiated realms, especially in the minds of the participatory workers. In these firms, the workers' participation does not cause them to look for other public avenues or issues to tackle. Instead, some workers see their firm as squashing their individual identities by imposing the firm's agenda and the firm's interests on them. These workers view the firm's agenda as an attempt to replace any outside interests they may have with a narrow, "family-style" but firm-controlled agenda. For others, work participation is a "nice benefit" for their work, but it has no effect in other areas of their lives. In the end, most employees never connect their work participation with other issues.

What replaces empowerment and a sense of community that participatory theory presupposes are individuals reacting to corporate policy. As a response, Standard Knapp's and Quad/Graphics' workers sometimes view their firm's agenda and actions as an attack on their personal lives. Employees begin to resist these "attacks" and separate work from their private lives. Instead of work participation motivating individuals to act in collective ways, work participation at these two firms at times reinforces, if not augments, the divisions people ascribe to private and public activity. In this scenario, workers view the workplace as a separate arena from their private lives and as a place with little influence on public affairs. In participatory theory, however, the workplace was to be one site where individuals found common ground to explore public affairs. Thus, while theory presumes that participatory work methods connect individuals with public issues, in practice, participation shows signs of solidifying, perhaps even exacerbating, the split between the private and the public.

ROUSSEAU'S PRESCRIPTION

The reason perhaps why participation at these firms discourages the uniting of private and public interests centers on Rousseau's "first principles." Rousseau states that individuals only experience true freedom through civil liberty when each decides for "himself" to submit to the general will. The emphasis belongs not to the submission, but to the individual choice to submit. The submission allows for the will's enactment. In turn, Rousseau claims that the will's enactment only results from individuals deliberating on general principles and not on particular issues or concerns. Particular issues evoke partial sentiments, and these immediate, perhaps personal interests cloud the individual's attention to what is general and good for all, including good for oneself. He writes:

> The general will, to be truly what it is, must be general in its purpose as well as in its nature; that it should spring from all for it to apply to all; and that it loses its natural rectitude when it is directed towards any particular and circumscribed object. . . . For, indeed, whenever we are dealing with a particular fact or right, on a matter which has not been settled by an earlier and general agreement, that question becomes contentious. It is a conflict in which private interests are ranged on one side and the public interest on the other; and I can see neither the law which is to be followed nor the judge who is to arbitrate.[33]

At Quad/Graphics, a general will does not develop because management establishes the participatory process which the employees must follow. Workers have much more influence and leeway in how they work. But because the firm decides the amount of participation and those areas in which employees may say no to management policy, the employees distinguish Quad culture "hype" from the actual practice of power. On matters of company policy, whether contentious or not, the legislative and judicial powers remain the president's domain. Participation in their immediate work areas does empower employees; but because participation does not extend to general company decision making, empowerment extends no further. These clear divisions at the workplace translate into clear divisions outside the workplace. As employees emphasize the power they have in their jobs, they focus on private activity after work. As employees lack influence over broader company decisions, they do not reflect on broader, public issues.

At Quad/Graphics, although employees hold shares, they do not vote their shares. A board of directors, for the most part picked by the president, decides the firm's direction. For those employees who accept the Quad culture, this arrangement is what they want and where they think decisions should reside. As one worker states, "I like him [the president] in charge. I feel I don't have the information. I like that he is not overly cautious, he's incredibly knowledgeable, and totally devoted. . . . I like the direction it [the company] is headed in. That is his job."[34] The power of the Quad culture, then, is twofold: First, it dictates that a limited few control the firm's decisions; and second, it allows those who are excluded from participating in company decisions not to feel excluded. In a similar vein as Bachrach and Baratz's recognition of nondecision-making power, Quad culture grants the employees a sense of empowerment over well-defined, however company-controlled, realms. In return, empowered employees—those employees who accept the firm's ideology—do not question those realms where the company gives them no influence, though many do recognize the problem. For those employees who do question the Quad culture, frustration over their participation in a particular arena but not over any general arena breeds contempt and/or resignation. Many of these workers draw their private lives more narrowly than other employees because their workplace experiences reinforce their powerlessness.

At first glance, it appears that Quad/Graphics' participatory approach turns Rousseau's theory "on its head." While Rousseau advocates that the citizenry continue to focus its attention on first principles and not on particular cases or laws, Quad/Graphics empowers its workers by allowing them latitude over their immediate, particular work environments but without any influence or say in general corporate policy. By all accounts, whether financial success or employee satisfaction, most employees applaud how the firm implements participation. We need to ask no further questions if we accept how the vast majority of employees feel about the firm. In one view, they are the final arbiters.

However, if the Quad culture induces employees to accept the system "as it is designed," then it is necessary to raise questions about the type of participation Quad seeks. For if Quad "washing" self-selects those most accepting of the firm's methods, participation becomes a method to reiterate the Quad philosophy and not a method to foster equality, self-development, or creativity. For constructing a healthy republic or a vigorous, creative business enterprise, it seems that acceptance does not always mesh with participation. For Rousseau, after the initial agreement to the first principles, participation allows citizens ongoing deliberation upon and revision of the principles. At Quad/Graphics, after the initial acceptance of the Quad culture, participation means only attention to one's immediate area and not to the general principles of the firm. Participation at Quad/Graphics, then, contradicts Rousseau and participatory theory. For while the theorist and the theory presume that participation for man allows his "faculties [to be] exercised and developed, his mind . . . enlarged, his sentiments . . . ennobled, and his whole spirit . . . elevated,"[35] participation at Quad/Graphics does not foster "enlarge and elevate" as much as it fosters "accept and comply." In Rousseau's words, because a master reigns, a sovereign cannot exist.

CONCLUSION

Under current federal tax laws, the minimum ownership requirement a firm can grant its employees through an ESOP and still receive favorable tax deductions and write-offs stands at 30 percent. Quad/Graphics' employee ownership stands at 30 percent. A 401(k) plan exists to augment an employee's number of shares, but the impetus to buy shares in this plan remains with the employees, as the firm only matches a certain percentage of what the employee buys. Quad/Graphics' employee ownership, then, appears to benefit both the employee and the firm, perhaps the latter more so than the former.

The participatory management structure seems to build trust with the workers. Participation, though, also remains a solid business investment. According to the National Center for Employee Ownership, participatory management increases productivity in an employee-owned firm anywhere from 6 to 11 percent. But if an employee-owned firm adheres to a traditional, hierarchical form of worker control, productivity suffers.[36] Against this backdrop, Quad/Graphics' participatory structures can easily be interpreted as a conscious business decision to maximize profits. The fact that the company does not allow its employees to vote their shares seems to confirm the maximization of management's interests for Quad/Graphics' future.

An advocate of Quad/Graphics' methods would ask why I focus attention on several, apparently minor contradictions and flaws when the overwhelming majority of employees embrace and benefit from the present arrangement. The most potent answer to the discussion of unfulfilled expectations and undemocratic processes is a business one. The firm has grown at double-digit rates since the mid-1970s. The yearly growth rate throughout the 1980s never dipped below 37 percent. In 1995, company job growth continued strong at 12.6 percent. While one of Harry Quadracci's catch-phrases has been for the firm and its employees to "think small," most employees express concern with the dichotomy between the philosophy and reality. Many, even some of whom accept the Quad culture, question whether the firm can implement a philosophy that seems ill suited to its role as a major player in the nation's printing industry.

In light of this, an issue worth considering is, how will the employees respond when Quad/Graphics cannot sustain such unprecedented growth rates? Employee ownership and participation appears as much a management benefit as an employee one. How, then, will the firm react to employee participation when the firm's profit margin decreases? Employees may begin to question the currently smooth-running Quad culture. Managers may begin to feel uneasy about ambitious underlings in an increasingly competitive job environment. Management may inform managers of budget constraints, and consequently, ingenuity may not be rewarded or encouraged. Management may also focus attention on participation but with the capitalist's perspective—a focus that views profit margins eaten away by employees who are allowed now to fail in order to feel the firm's trust in them. It seems, then, that employee ownership and employee participation at Quad/Graphics are running smoothly today in part due to the firm's robust health. When this health is threatened by an industry slowdown or change, employee participation will experience its first true test. Perhaps under such conditions, today's managerial and company acceptance of participation will become a new-found questioning. Perhaps under such pressures, Quad/Graphics will become more participatory and more democratic than today, or perhaps even more hierarchical.

NOTES

1. Jean-Jacques Rousseau, *The Social Contract*, trans. Maurice Cranston (New York: Penguin Books, 1968), 77.
2. Ibid., 70.
3. Ibid., 153.
4. Ibid., 83.

5. Phyllis Berman, "Harry's a Great Storyteller," *Forbes*, 27 February 1995, 113.
6. Employee interview, Quad/Graphics, Saratoga Springs, N.Y., 14 April 1995.
7. Michael Quarrey, Joseph Blasi, and Corey Rosen, *Taking Stock: Employee Ownership at Work* (Cambridge, Mass.: Ballinger, 1986), 45.
8. Employee survey response, Quad/Graphics, Saratoga Springs, N.Y., April 1995, no. 66.
9. Quad/Graphics, "Showing Off: The Saratoga Springs Plant," in-house pamphlet.
10. "Quad/Graphics: The Best Printer in the World or What?" *Lithoweek*, 28 November 1990.
11. Quoted in ibid. (reprint).
12. Employee interview, 14 April 1995.
13. Employee interview, 14 April 1995.
14. Employee interview, 12 April 1995.
15. Employee interview, 14 April 1995.
16. Employee interview, 14 April 1995.
17. Employee interview, 14 April 1995.
18. Employee interview, 12 April 1995.
19. Employee interview, 14 April 1995.
20. Ibid.
21. Employee interview, 14 April 1995.
22. Employee interview, 12 April 1995.
23. Ibid.
24. Employee survey response, April 1995, no. 47.
25. Employee survey response, no. 13.
26. Standard Knapp, employee interview, Middletown, Conn., 21 January 1995.
27. Albert O. Hirschman, *Exit, Voice, and Loyalty: Responses to Decline in Firms, Organizations, and States* (Cambridge: Harvard University Press, 1970), 43.
28. Employee interview, 14 April 1995.
29. Quad/Graphics, employee interview, 12 April 1995.
30. Employee survey response, April 1995, no. 47.
31. Employee interview, 14 April 1995.
32. Ibid.
33. Rousseau, *Social Contract*, 75.
34. Employee interview, 14 April 1995.
35. Rousseau, *Social Contract*, 65.
36. Corey Rosen, Director, ESOP Workshop, National Center for Employee Ownership, Albany, N.Y., 26 April 1995.

Chapter 5

THE ZARITSKY BROTHERS
Furthering Employee Ownership and Participation at Orange Handling

Nearly every discussion in creating a democratic polity and a democratic workplace addresses the issue of size. Participants, beyond certain limits, reduce the familiarity of citizens and their deliberative possibilities. Rousseau continues to describe other essential characteristics for democracies: simplicity of manners, equality in rank and fortune, and little or no luxury.[1] These traits lead him to conclude that democracies are the most difficult polities to sustain. They demand a list of traits that rarely occur at one time, and Rousseau states they require "so much vigilance and courage to maintain it unchanged."[2] From the two case studies, size may well play an influential role in participation's effects. The sheer number of employees at Quad/Graphics precludes any significant "town meeting" assembly to discuss openly the firm's policies. Perhaps as a consequence of size, the firm concentrates on building worker efficacy at the employee's immediate work area. If the firm were to focus on any larger scale, workers would lose a sense of influence, and perhaps management would lose a degree of control too. With nearly 200 employees at Standard Knapp, the issue of size is not as troubling as at Quad/Graphics, but the factionalization of interests—some union, some not—leads to a hardening of positions that inhibits the development of any forum for debate. Because interests have been institutionalized, workers and management find it difficult to establish dialogue and trust.

Most researchers and theorists assume that a larger size limits participation's effectiveness. In turn, my approach calls for a scaling back of participatory expectations to the individual or worker level. These assumptions, along with the realization that participation makes inconsistent inroads into an individualistic culture, calls for an examination of an even smaller worker environment. The third case study focuses on a relatively small ESOP firm, approximately seventy employees in three branch operations. Without the attendant hierarchy necessary for economic efficiency, under which Standard Knapp and Quad/Graphics operate, Orange Handling allows for greater interaction between all its employees, from the owners to the hourly workers, and, thus, perhaps a greater ability to communicate and deliberate. A smaller firm of this kind, then, allows for an examination of the participatory commitment without any supposed sacrifices to economic efficiency and any intrusions of hierarchical decision making.

ORANGE HANDLING'S ATMOSPHERE

Orange Handling's experiences with employee ownership and participation display several of the most common problems associated with participatory and ownership changes. Its ESOP plan, and the turmoil it generates, reveals hostile management–employee relations similiar to Standard Knapp's "institutionalized distrust." While one might be tempted to cast blame on one interest or another in accounting for the firm's difficulties, it may be more appropriate to recognize that the different interests within the company are testimony to the firm's failing to forge a common identity and a participatory environment. While Harry Quadracci at Quad/Graphics operates at one extreme by developing a "boot-camp" mentality to inculcate a participatory environment, Orange Handling operates at the other extreme by failing to offer any program or policy which would produce a lasting participatory commitment. In turn, accusation and condemnation have become part of the firm's discourse. But this hostile discourse cannot be the sole guide to understanding what ails Orange Handling's participatory and ownership plan. Rather, what needs explication is how and why the ESOP and the team-oriented work environment maintain divergent agendas and fail to provide a shared vision for the firm and its employees.

Orange Handling's change to an ESOP began in 1989. However, despite the good will, the owners showed that by creating the ESOP, the plan for most employees today remains insignificant and meaningless. Many recognize few real changes since the plan began and cynically view the ESOP as a method for the owners to reap tax breaks and/or create a "paper chase" to benefit their private interests. Some less-cynical workers simply express no sense of immediate attachment to the firm despite the plan's economic incentives. In general, management does inform the employees about how much they collectively "own," but, for the most part, workers remain unabashedly ignorant of what the plan means and how it benefits them. For most employees, ownership has not changed. Management still apparently rules autocratically, and, in turn, whatever promise the ESOP holds fails to create any strong employee commitment or even recognition.

Thus, an environment akin to the traditional antagonistic, labor–management tension persists. Workers often view company decisions as arbitrary and antithetical to employee ownership. Most important, the employees overwhelmingly believe that, while they may have the ability to voice opinions and make recommendations, their ideas often go unheeded if they counter management's views. Also, in such a small company, people know where, or rather with whom, their ideas hit roadblocks. Interestingly, then, small size can inhibit the full expression of ideas in a manner typically unrecognized in the democratic debate on participation. It seems that at Orange Handling, because it lacks an environment without a common vision and without inclusiveness, decisions become personal vendettas. Again, Hirschman's argument that voice can add to economic competitiveness and efficiency may be true, but the treatment of workers at Orange Handling displays a voice without choice.

To place blame wholly on the owners and management's implementation of workplace participation does not capture the complexity of the problem. Certainly, management is responsible for a fundamental lack of communication about the ESOP, about how the employees can and will benefit, about what the workers' roles are and will become, and about how the plan necessitates ongoing commitment to the firm. In turn, because of management's failings, the owners "throw up their hands" in trying to decipher why the participatory plan fails to produce employee interest or trust. Management asks, given their initial commitment to the employees, given their attention to teamwork and creating a working-family atmosphere, and given at least the plan's opportunities for employees to be heard and to "climb the company ladder"—though some believe the opportunity is merely lip-service—why do workers fail to respond to their initiatives? At the same time, though, management agrees that employee communication is a problem. Management also states that for some employees no amount of encouragement changes their negative attitudes. From these reports, the lasting images are of a management that offers several worker "perks" but remains perplexed as to why employees do not take advantage of these opportunities. For the workers, the "perks" appear to satisfy specific, primarily manager's or management, interests or appear as too illusory to commit to. In turn, while management asks workers to change their perspective on work, from concentrating on individual rewards to focusing on either a team's or the firm's health, employees do not trust the changes or management enough to alter their attitudes.

If communication is the key management failing, understanding and awareness of the ESOP's objectives are the central employee problems. In a typical scenario, which could apply to Standard Knapp as well as Orange Handling, the failure to inform employees of the firm's and the employees' changing roles in the participatory environment often translates into a defeatist employee attitude. The employee, either correctly or incorrectly, treats management as the scapegoat for either the lack of information or the employee's inability to change; in turn, management continues to provide minimal information, fueling employee distrust toward management's intentions and the participatory plans. This cycle, based increasingly on rumor and misperception, repeats itself—as employees find confirmation of their views, due to the lack of management communication, in nearly every company decision. In turn, management continues to tread uneasily between maintaining some form of leadership and direction while providing workers with information as part-owners of the firm.

By unraveling these problems at Orange Handling, we may better understand the ingredients for healthy ownership and participation for both owner and worker—if the two are in fact distinct. After a cursory description of the firm and its change to employee ownership and its participatory scheme, I examine the firm's decision-making structure and its implementation. An assessment of participatory theory's transformative and political activity hypotheses appears moot because the hypotheses depend on a participatory atmosphere that Orange Handling apparently lacks. However, the workers' recognition of the difference between participation in general and how it operates at Orange Handling in particular, along with responses to how employees spend their time outside of work, allow us to make some rough conclusions about the participatory plan's success. The task, then, given Orange Handling's attributes, is to decipher what changes are necessary to realize the minimal conditions for workplace involvement. From the initial insight of the often-repeated cycle of internal suspicion and blame, it seems that Orange Handling's problems point to fairly straightforward, simple-to-implement, and yet profound steps.

In addition, the atmosphere of mistrust that characterizes relations at the firm inhibits it from satisfying even the minimal definition of participation. Workers do have opportunities to voice their concerns, and management does listen; but the general employee attitude is not to participate because either it produces too few beneficial results for the effort involved or it creates friction with other employees or managers. In a sense, many of Orange Handling's problems point to the uneasiness that workers and managers have with change in general. Because employee involvement and ownership often create the need for new perspectives about the firm and one's work, not only from workers, but also from managers, mistrust is a common response to a new management and ownership strategy. The question becomes whether the mistrust at Orange Handling is an initial response that can be changed or whether the firm creates an atmosphere where mistrust is a reasonable attitude.

ORANGE HANDLING'S HISTORY AND PARTICIPATORY DESIGN

Herb and Stan Zaritsky own Orange Handling. Prior to 1970, the Zaritsky family operated a relatively small textile business. Given the relocation of most Northeastern textile operations to the Deep South at or around this time, the family decided to move into another line of business. Selling and servicing forklifts became the alternative line of business. The apparently incongruous change becomes more reasonable with three considerations: (1) That the Zaritskys must have been aware of how forklifts could service regional manufacturing needs given their textile business experiences; (2) that they could use the same buildings and land that the former business housed to keep their overhead and start-up costs quite low; and (3) that the forklift industry is based on distributorships with exclusive territories. Fortunately for the Zaritskys, Orange Handling sells and services the American-made Nissan line of equipment, which most people within the business consider the best forklift on the market.

Orange Handling has prospered. The owners, however, quickly point out that success in the Northeast, where a general manufacturing exodus persists, and success in New York state, where high taxes often hasten the exodus, often means simply meeting payrolls and staying in business. The owners claim that the marketplace has shrunk 30 to 40 percent in the last decade and that, in a competitive industry where the "mold is the same," what distinguishes Orange Handling is "our service and reputation. It is our warranties and our ability to try and satisfy the clients, and most of all it comes down to our people [employees] in the dealership."[3] Yet, as the economy has soured, as the taxes have skyrocketed, and as the competition has increased, Orange Handling has grown and bought out several other smaller companies. The firm today employs roughly seventy to seventy-five people with headquarters in Middletown, New York, and branches in Albany, New York, and Berlin, Connecticut.

As their thoughts turned to their retirements at or around their fiftieth birthdays, knowing that their children were pursuing professional careers, the Zaritskys sought out alternatives for Orange Handling: to retire the business by selling out to a larger firm, to auction the business off, or to start an ESOP to maintain a commitment to the employees as well as gain tax advantages. The ESOP appeared as the most favorable and least disruptive alternative for all involved. It would still provide a living for many people who had made earlier commitments to the business, and it would help the Zartiskys to plan and achieve a comfortable retirement.

The ESOP plan began in 1989, and the initial seven-year loan has been paid off. The employees own 30 percent of the firm's stock, with a gradual increase to 100 percent ownership over a fifteen-year period. All company profit returns to the ESOP and individuals benefit according to the number of shares they hold. Employees accumulate shares based on a percentage of their income, and workers are vested in the ESOP after five years of employment. But to emphasize the financial returns of the ESOP overlooks the values that the Zaritskys note make the firm profitable. The attention to customer service is necessary to be competitive, and they believe a productive workplace includes an almost familial working environment, a commitment to teamwork, education, and job training, and perhaps even to the creation of bonds that extend beyond the firm's walls. For the Zaritskys, the ESOP appears as a benevolent financial arrangement that fosters their belief in and concern for their employees.

However, worker ownership and concern have recognizable limits. While the employees own shares, they do not vote their shares. Decision making remains in a few hands, most notably with the two brothers having veto power over any decision made by the board of directors. The board consists of seven people, all of whom occupy management positions. At the branches, the branch manager meets every two weeks with the parts and operations managers to discuss their location's specifics. In turn, employees are told whether forecasts call for slow or busy work months. This hierarchy conflicts with management's claim to be easily accessible because of the small scale of the branches. If a worker has an immediate concern that affects productivity and calls for a management decision, the size of the branches, even the size of the larger Middletown plant, allows for access and resolution. This does not mean an easy, across-the-board interaction exists between, for instance, mechanics and management. Workers have a job to do and a place to perform it, as do managers. In some instances, workers report that the teamwork that the Zaritskys support extends only to workers who have similar job descriptions. Mechanics are "tight" with other mechanics, while bonds with other workers remain fractured by traditional hierarchical structures and power relationships. Thus, a true division of labor exists.

The Zaritsky brothers have made a substantial commitment to their employees. While they have also benefited financially from their commitment, the transfer of ownership underscores more than a simple cost–benefit accounting of their interests. In fact, the road toward full employee ownership, such as that taken by the Zaritskys, is usually a rocky one, certainly a path not well-worn nor without numerous pitfalls. The best intentions, for instance, the care and concern for the employees, often run into obstacles simply because the ownership and participatory changes are ground-breaking endeavors. Faced with obstacles, employees and management may revert to traditional, hierarchical methods of control and order because of the uncertainty of their new relations. But Orange Handling's success as an employee-owned firm with a participatory decision-making framework is contingent upon management and workers overcoming the us-versus-them, labor-versus-management mentality that plagues much of the firm's interaction.

The Zaritskys have begun a change in ownership. But without greater employee interaction and company communication, their initial commitment will sour the employees' expectations. In turn, better-informed employees, who begin to have the expertise to "experiment" with participation and worker decision making, find satisfaction with their work and with their company. How, then, can employee interaction overcome the cycle of suspicion and blame that categorizes much of the employee's actions and attitudes at Orange Handling? The answers center on both the employees and owners themselves pushing the initial commitment to greater levels of involvement and control. In short, the answer lies in continuing to pursue participatory reform. The problem that leads to the cycle of suspicion, mistrust, and blame is not from too much participation and democratic interaction. Rather, it is from not enough participation.

EMPLOYEE AND MANAGEMENT FRUSTRATION AT ORANGE HANDLING

Despite the reforms by the Zaritskys, workers at Orange Handling believe employee control does not exist and employee participation has little effect on company decisions. An overwhelming number of employees hold these views, and their survey and interview responses point to their unqualified displeasure. Few moderate voices exist. From the survey responses, employees express strong feelings about how management does not include workers in the decision-making process:

1. 76 percent feel that they cannot participate in decision making;
2. 69 percent believe that they do not control their workplace;
3. 76 percent disagree that they can have a lot of influence on company decisons;
4. 79 percent disagree that if they choose to, they can have a say in how the firm is run;
5. 83 percent agree that employee participation does not breed open access to all the firm's workings;
6. 79 percent do not feel a sense of ownership in the firm;
7. 76 percent believe that most employees do not feel they have much power over decision making.

These uniformly negative attitudes reflect management's inability to foster and reinforce a successful participatory environment. While it seems a change in structure has occurred, workers believe the changes benefit mainly the owners. As one employee writes that the firm promotes participation "only if it suits their [management's] needs or will help them prove a point. . . . They make decisions which directly effect the welfare of the employees without first getting our input. . . . Generally, company decisions are heard through the 'grapevine' or in memo form after the fact."[4] The frustration extends as much to immediate work rules or policies as to general company decisions. While management and the owners preach the value of employee input, ostensibly because workers have the experience and expertise, the employees remark that management neglects their input in nearly every instance. Once again, employees recognize that they have "voice without adequate choice." Their response is often resignation and withdrawal from participating and giving input, rather than anger. In interviews with employees who did not fill out surveys, many express the belief that ownership and participation have never meant a thing to the workers and have caused few changes in the company's direction and policies. To this, management simply responds that not participating guarantees that the employee's voice is not heard.

Even more disturbing for participation's prospects, some employees view the efforts at teamwork and building a family atmosphere as mere "window dressing," and they describe Orange Handling's working relations as vicious and consumed by interbranch rivalry. One employee states, "[Orange Handling] is 'do as I say, not as I do.' . . . Middletown has this 'we can do no wrong' and 'we don't want to hear what you found' attitude. It goes against the supposed family togetherness. [Management] tries to put that facade on—that team facade. . . . Teamwork stops when you enter the offices. [Management does not] want you to learn their roles. . . . Overall, not many people respect each other."[5] The employee's remarks note three distinct grievances. One is that the firm's headquarters in Middletown gives preferential treatment to its plant and its employees. Another grievance is that, no matter the location, management treats different employees differently. Specifically, some mechanics note a "double standard" between the rigorous accounting for their time and work (i.e., time cards, work orders, and duty sheets) and a less than rigorous accounting for employees in the offices who are not subject to the time clock. It appears difficult for some employees to reconcile the language of teamwork and family with the cost-accounting and productivity measures of time clocks and work sheets for only *some* workers. In comparison with Standard Knapp, where similar intraemployee hostility exists based on nonunion and union membership, both firms show employee frustration at what appears to be management's preferential treatment. It seems, then, for participatory and ownership measures to carry meaning in the employees' eyes, a greater degree of equality between all employees needs to exist. However, in a market system with a significant division of labor, equality is not a highly regarded value.

A third grievance is that, despite management's claims that it seeks to inform and educate its workers, employees argue that management guards access to information which limits worker knowledge. In behavior typical of hierarchical organizations, the firm emphasizes that "We are in this together"; in practice, some workers note that they operate under strict productivity requirements. The firm states that employees must have faith and confidence in each other to prosper; in practice, employees report that management regulates some jobs much more carefully than others. These practices may guarantee a measure of productivity and, ultimately, profit, but the attitudes they create undermine employee unity and morale.

To reiterate, the vast number of employees feel they have little say in what supposedly is their company. One employee argues, "Even with the minimal participation currently in place, we still only 'know' what headquarters wants us to know.... In our company, the information supplied to the decision makers in headquarters [sic] is usually ignored."[6] Interestingly, while management recognizes the employees' attitudes, they often do not locate the correct source of the problem. As a top official claims, "We [Orange Handling] do in fact lack employee involvement. ... It all boils down to communication ... and we have a communication problem."[7] However, at Orange Handling, a communication problem seems less troubling than the real source of trouble, which lies in the employees' lack of authority despite management's claims of worker involvement and control.

In the interim, employees accumulate examples of what the firm does wrong, and management continues to neglect employee grievances by highlighting other company measures. For instance, as the employees specify a set of concerns such as their input and control over decision making, management answers in generalities such as the firm's size does not allow it to increase its educative avenues. As one employee notes, "In my time here, there have been two training school opportunities, and both times the same two technicians got to go."[8] Management may indeed have other criteria to consider in its assessment of employees' concerns, but employees often state that it would seem appropriate, in a partially employee-owned firm that espouses "togetherness," for management to be more forthcoming in stating what the criteria are and how they affect the firm and the employees. Perhaps with this information, the workers' assessment of management and their roles would change. But perhaps what management fears is that, with this information, the workers would become even more conflictual. As it stands now, management may in fact be pleased with its participatory rhetoric and its retention of control. In management's view, the firm offered employee ownership and involvement as a benefit and an incentive to its workers. It seems that, as the workers sense they have no real control or power in the firm, they wonder what are the benefits and incentives of participation and ownership, and they now ask that the firm realize its commitment to participatory changes.

A more critical analysis of the truncated participatory efforts argues that management benefits from espousing an ideology of commitment and participation, while it still maintains the power of decision-making control. While this applies to Orange Handling's case, it does not offer a complete explanation of why participatory management fails. Another less obvious reason, one that management invokes in Orange Handling's case, is that the employees remain reluctant to change from the present labor–management relations. The employees, even if decidedly unhappy with management's present tactics, willingly opt to reject change. Perhaps in these examples, employees choose a hostile workplace in lieu of their fear of the unknown. As this research emphasizes, employees with experience and knowledge of one set of labor relations have difficulty in accepting and adjusting to a new set of relations. The consequence may well be that many workers simply do not want to change.

A third reason, one that characterizes Orange Handling's labor–management distrust as much as the other reasons mentioned, recognizes that management also remains reluctant to change despite its calls of change. A changing workplace with more employee participation leads to the management perception of a reduction in its control and power. Likewise, more involvement leads to a greater degree of access, which causes decision making to become more difficult and unwieldy. Such changes are often surreptitiously derailed by the very same voices which once supported the changes. Yet, these claims, true as they may be, are misleading. As with employees who desire more participation but have difficulty with changing work relations, management may espouse the benefits of change, may believe in the benefits of change, may be committed to all the benefits of change, and may still be incapable of changing its behavior from established work relations. The reason, then, for management's ineptitude in implementing effective participatory processes stems from its inability to wholeheartedly embrace the measures it seeks rather than from any devious tactics to maintain its power. Just as with the employees, part of this ineptitude comes from the power of accepted work relations, of work socialization and experiences, to manage in certain ways. From one history and culture of accepted labor–management relations, participatory experiments show the difficulty both "sides" have in accepting and adjusting to change.

To summarize, two explanations seem to account for why Orange Handling fails in its participatory efforts. One states that management uses the ideology of participation to hide its control over major firm decisions (i.e., investment) and its deafness to actual demands from the workers. The other explanation states that neither management nor the workers can accept change because they are habituated to conflict despite its self-defeating purposes. These explanations, in turn, may be intertwined; for it seems that management pursues the first strategy of retaining its power, despite its claims for participatory change, because management is habituated to the traditional conflictual relations between itself and labor. For both management and labor, true participatory changes call for new skills and new relations between the two that many may fear and many may adjust to only with great difficulty.

My argument asserts that the ingrained views of the traditionally hostile relations between labor and management affect how management implements such dramatic changes. These views also affect how employees view the participatory changes, whether management successfully commits itself to full employee participation. The ingrained views, then, lead to an important question. Would management be inclined to change its rhetoric of participation without full support if the employees were less distrustful? Or similarly, would employees become more trusting if management implemented more participatory and ownership benefits? In essence, these questions ask whether the two "sides" can overcome their habituation to conflict if conditions were more equal between them. Participatory theory assumes that greater equality can overcome the habituation. However, since both labor and management must continue to operate in the external market and under the influences of an individualistic culture, it seems likely that the employees and management would stick to old behaviors rather than to new promises.

ATTITUDES THE PARTICIPATORY DESIGN CREATES

Despite the employees' frustration, anger, and sometimes vitriolic attacks, workers at Orange Handling without question like their work and enjoy their co-workers. One disgruntled worker said, "This is a great company, but it could be much better. [We] clearly beat the competition, but it isn't because of what management says. There's no family, it's my internal drive."[9] Another worker differentiates in his responses between his love for his work and how management affects his view of his work. He states, "[It] has always been my nature [to do more for the firm than is required by my job description]. What irritates me is being *told* I must do more." He continues, "Of course, I must care to a degree [about the firm's fate]," but he specifically notes, "I care about my *immediate* co-workers."[10] Given the employees' disdain for management, it seems they focus their energies on nurturing their relations with co-workers. Although Orange Handling does not offer a strong test for participatory effects, these employee attitudes seem to support the argument that workers tend to have great loyalty to their ingrained views.

Much like the survey responses from Standard Knapp employees, workers at Orange Handling suggest that they care about the fate of the company (79% agree), do not mind doing more than is required by their job (71% agree), and are willing to volunteer extra time for the good of the firm (65% agree). With these favorable responses, it seems that employee anger does not center on the firm in general, does not center on immediate co-workers, and does not center on employee ownership—in fact, over 90 percent support it. Given these results, how can the workers overwhelmingly note positive attitudes toward the firm while they simultaneously report that the firm fails to measure up to its participatory objectives? Worker frustration seems to focus on how the firm enacts, or does not enact, employee involvement, rather than on the rejection of participation itself. Perhaps because the firm does not adequately explain what employee ownership and participation entails, employees then conjure up a host of individualized expectations which the firm has no possibility of satisfying.

Understanding the difference between employee anger at management for its failure to involve the workers in decision making and employee anger at management for not fulfilling a host of individualized employee expectations tranfers some responsibility for employee distrust from management to the workers. While not obvious, this distinction is noticeable from interview comments. A management official claims about the ESOP, "A lot of employees asked 'What guarantees are there?' Some made up their minds [before we did or tried anything]. In turn, [the ESOP] was sold [to the employees] almost too sweet. Many responded it was 'too good to be true,' and now they say 'I told you so.'"[11] Note that while the employees ask a legitimate structural question—"What guarantees are there?"—the manager explains that, as a consequence, employees were sold the plan with unrealistic expectations—it was "sold too sweet." In this regard, management had a plan that it was willing to try and, needing the workers' approval, did not adequately inform the workers of the entire ramifications of the participatory and ownership plan.

Also, while management remains responsible for not effectively developing a participatory and inclusive workplace environment, the workers develop either one of two viewpoints which further undermine the plan. One perspective is that some employees never give the ESOP and its associated teamwork philosophy the opportunity and necessary timeframe to succeed. In interviews, workers often state they have never participated in decision making because they view the process as challenging managers or "higher-ups." They view the process as a "feel good" management strategy that has little importance to the way they do their job, and they view the process as favoring certain employees that management prefers. Now, with the obvious reluctance of the workers to experiment, coupled with management's inertia toward change, the firm ends up espousing a plan it cannot follow. In turn, participation becomes hollow.

The other perspective is that some employees invest too heavily in the ESOP's successes and possibilities, given that management promoted the plan too carelessly.

In the first perspective, the ESOP fails because of the employee's either self-fulfilling prophecy or "one-shot experience" with participation's possibilities. In this view, any failure or inadequate level of success creates a disillusioned employee who has invested great expectations in the ESOP's future and feels disillusioned when its returns are less than expected. Given that the ESOP was sold "too sweetly," perhaps today's employee anger involves a bit of both: a habituated reluctance to change and a measure of unfulfilled expectations.

From both views, we must conclude that management bears most of the responsibility for Orange Handling's difficulties. To be sure, the firm has taken a step toward providing additional benefits and a "friendlier" work environment to its employees. But the firm needs to take the next several steps to implement a process which nurtures and educates its employees about the firm's expectations and the workers' responsibilities if it expects to benefit, both in terms of productivity and labor peace, from participation's possibilities. As Orange Handling operates now, it is clear that employees are confused about what the firm expects of them. One worker states, "[Management] wants you to make a million bucks, but then they tie your hands. . . . If I take that extra step, they yell at me. Now that I'm afraid to take that step, they want me to."[12] Such worker confusion, along with the lack of a consistent environment of interaction and greater employee involvement, leads to employee nonaction and resignation. From this, a debilitating cycle emerges, as management, in turn, simply does not consider worker input and workers withdraw their contributions. The promise of the participatory and ownership changes suffers, as both management and employees "learn" not to communicate. As a consequence, management feels justified in reasserting hierarchical control while "throwing up its hands" at the employees' lack of participation.

Employees learn that communication does not increase their control; management apparently learns that employees do not think of the other interests that the firm must consider in decision making. The irony is that what masquerades as company communication and interaction in this case reflects a kind of partiality or special interest. Without greater access and information, employees remain unaware of the firm's concerns, and they cannot assess these concerns in the manner management says it must. Given their partial knowledge, sometimes using rumor and anecdoctal evidence, employees arrive at self-interested, even unfounded conclusions. Interview stories quickly turn from the firm's decision-making process to a manager's or the owner's personal traits and purchases. In turn, management dismisses these conclusions as shortsighted. Yet management remains responsible for the employees' limited conceptions, as they limit the initial interchange of information and ideas. The plan itself will not change employee thinking; the plan must have management as its agent of change. In Orange Handling's case, management seems unwilling and incapable of being the agent of change.

The most apt example of management's inadequate understanding occurs when it seeks to explain why employees presently are disgruntled. Management, perhaps to justify its decisions and its power, repeatedly claims that the current difficult economic times limit resources which force the firm to shy away from fulfilling participatory commitments. This explanation demonstrates management's lack of commitment to a participatory workplace and to the value of employee input. It reveals that management views employee participation only as a method to augment any number of the firm's goals. In this perspective, involvement is a management strategy to boost productivity and profit and not necessarily to include employees in running the company.

In turn, employees recognize their lack of input. One worker states, "As a general rule my opinion or 'vote' is not required, i.e., purchase of stock, working Saturdays, meeting dates, insurance changes, company policies, et cetera. [I do not believe we have control because] 'control' would mean making decisions that would direct [a] department to be more productive and profitable."[13] The significance of this quotation is that the employee remains attuned to the same goals that management seeks (i.e., productivity). However, management, while espousing the importance of worker input, sets up barriers and creates rationalizations for why workers interests cannot be considered. Management basically states that employees "only see money going out, but not coming in," and, in turn, only management truly understands the economic bottom line. Given these scenarios and rationalizations, Orange Handling's employee participation produces nothing but frustrated and cynical workers. What the firm promises on one hand, the ability for workers to develop influence and control, the firm limits on the other hand because employees do not have full access and information.

In his discussion of the contradictions of bureaucratic control, Richard Edwards shows that what Orange Handling experiences is generally true in most capitalist arrangements. He claims that, by its very nature, capitalism forces owners to experiment with those arrangements—job enrichment, worker participation—that simultaneously offer a higher productivity model but also present resistance to their control and power. Edwards claims that minimal or even moderate changes can never produce the results that satisfy either the capitalist or the improved conditions of the worker. He argues, "Capitalists try to attain [a] higher output cheaply, by granting limited amounts of each of the needed components: some security within the overall capitalist context of insecurity, partial identification with work within the framework of private ownership, and limited self-government within an authoritarian enterprise."[14] At Orange Handling, it appears that Edwards's analysis captures the management strategy to improve productivity while also unexpectedly causing the workers' frustrated attitudes. Interestingly, while he recognizes the cause for Orange Handling's distrustful relations, he continues:

The trouble is that a little is never enough. . . . Some control over workplace decisions raises the demand for industrial democracy. . . . Thomas Fitzgerald, GM's director of Employee Research and Training, explained . . . that, once workers begin participating, "the subjects . . . are not necessarily restricted to those few matters that management considers to be of direct, personal interest to employees. . . . Once competence is shown in, say, rearranging the work area, and after participation has become a conscious, officially sponsored activity, . . . management's present monopoly [of control] can in itself easily become a source of contention."[15]

Edwards argues the same point as participatory theorists. A little participation breeds a newfound competency which is then "reinvested" by the worker into related work activities and issues. Because of this worker transformation, and his or her subsequent questioning of present structures of control, Edwards argues that capitalists often frustrate the growth of these productive experiments because they begin to challenge the capitalists' rights of ownership. At Orange Handling, then, management offers a participatory plan to experiment with its productivity effects but then limits the plan's effectiveness because of the potential challenges it may generate to management's prerogatives.

But Edwards's argument about participation's transformative effect is less convincing. On one hand, he sides with the argument of my research that the nature of a market economy and an individualistic culture inhibit the likelihood of a radical change in workplace relations. In fact, Edwards claims, "The extent that it remains experimental and confined to individual workplaces, [participation] will retain its stench as a management device."[16] On the other hand, Edwards implies that even limited participation breeds the type of transformative changes that challenge the capitalist agenda. To make both claims appears contradictory, but Edwards argues that such contradictions offer at least some possibility for change in the dominant capitalist agenda.

Finally, if management believes employee involvement finds employee support only when Orange Handling is profitable, management does not truly subscribe to the goals of worker participation and control because its support of participation remains conditional. The findings at Orange Handling offer little hope to be optimistic in assessing the future of worker participation at Quad/Graphics as well. While Quad/Graphics' employees have significant input and control over their immediate decision-making areas, the firm's tremendous growth rate eases the costs of the employees' errors. In effect, the firm's substantial profits allow management to incorporate a certain amount of "slack" or error to encourage what Edwards cites as a device to create more profit (i.e., building trust) and what Hirschman recognizes as a device to establish loyalty. On the contrary, as both authors note, these devices should not be seen as manipulative. In fact, the authors recognize these methods as potentially more valuable alternatives to those of existing market relations. At Orange Handling, where the economy's effects are felt more directly (i.e., less profit and tighter management control of costs), the firm uses an external or environmental explanation for the lack of employee satisfaction. Management believes that as the economy sours and less profit accrues, the workers question the participatory environment.

But employee participation is a decision-making process that a firm develops; it is an internal process that establishes how the firm operates. For management to cite the economy as the reason why employees are presently unsatisfied undervalues the employee frustration over their lack of influence and control over the workplace itself and over management's wholly inadequate attempts to develop a sound structural process to include workers in decision making. Management argues that employees mistakenly believe they withhold information or act with ulterior motives. They state some employees can find the "bad in any positive," and that employee suspicion does not allow the workers to realize that management is at times just as frustrated with nonparticipation and noncommunication as the employees are. But management has more control over how decision making occurs and who controls that decision making. For the most part, management's consternation stems from the lack of any perceived change in worker attitudes, though management perceives that it has "done everything possible" to satisfy the employees. In the end, management misperceives the extent of the changes it has introduced, and the employees perceptively recognize the limits of the changes.

In some sense, management remains aware of what frustrates workers. It claims that employees cannot see "long term," and, thus, the firm's efforts to make a commitment to its employees must fall short. Management states that employees in their twenties and thirties say they are not interested in what the ESOP means or what it can do for them. The employees believe if management introduces the concept, the employees will remain skeptical about its benefits for anyone other than management. Management reports that the employees claim the five-year vesting period is "too much of a commitment for the worker to accept."[17] Ironically, then, while employees chastise management for their lack of commitment to them in terms of control and input, management repeats the same lament because employees prefer not to accept a long-term employment perspective.

IS TESTING FOR TRANSFORMATION AND POLITICAL ACTIVITY POSSIBLE?

From the aforementioned discussion, it appears that Orange Handling's participatory scheme effectively vitiates any generalization about participatory theory's transformative and political activity hypotheses. The survey responses, though, do suggest strong employee dissatisfaction with Orange Handling's participatory scheme. From the surveys, 55 percent disagree to the statement that they feel a sense of empowerment at work from their participation. As for any personal transformation, 56 percent of the survey respondents disagree that their participation at work has made them more involved in other activities outside after work. As with the other cases, 78 percent of the respondents agree that work does not interfere with outside interests. Also in line with the responses at Standard Knapp and Quad/Graphics, those outside interests remain distinctly private and not public or political activities—86 percent agree that their activities are private and not public. Work participation, as it occurs now, appears to encourage no political activity. Nearly 72 percent disagree that their work participation encourages their participation in other groups.

A critic legitimately can claim that, given the lack of a successful participatory environment at Orange Handling or the frustration with and resignation from participation by the employees, the survey data have little bearing on the propositions.

Yet other evidence exists that suggests that participation encounters mediating variables in its effect on employees' personal beliefs and behavior. For example, management's frustration with employees who remain reluctant to think long term and commit themselves to the firm's participatory goals reveals that workers are influenced less by the participatory format than by other, external workplace concerns. Employees bring different agendas to the work environment, and their different identities mediate how successful any employee participation plan becomes. In Orange Handling's case, the fact that the participatory scheme is implemented poorly becomes the focus of the participationist's concern, when it may be that the diversity of worker interests about work and its priority in their lives will influence the degree of participatory commitment and success. Given my previous twofold explanation of why Orange Handling fails to create a participatory environment—that management uses participatory ideology to retain control and that the habituation to conflictual roles inhibits workplace change—it seems that the only attitude workers may share about the workplace concerns its conflictual nature. From the survey and interview responses, employees maintain the traditional views of a conflictual workplace.

The point is that, while a firm's structure is a principal concern in the literature and in management schools and research, in most studies on participation a firm's structure remains the only concern. Given that employees in all three case studies note that some employees view their jobs as careers while others work only for a paycheck, the numerous reasons to work obviously must affect whether a participatory strategy can change workers' attitudes. As an example of how different workers approach a participatory process, the management at Orange Handling recognizes that it engages in a revolving door employment process, sometimes to its displeasure. Some employees leave the firm for "greener pastures," typically for more money; and when the workers do not find those pastures, Orange Handling has often rehired them. Consequently, management states that the rehires develop one of two work personalities. Either they come back with more maturity and appreciation for Orange Handling's participatory attempts, or they come back with a "chip on their shoulder," embarrassed and angry that their "escape" failed. These different employee attitudes offer insight into the variety of expectations that management must recognize to build any lasting participatory process. In short, one employee's sympathy with the firm's participatory process may be another's resentment and anger. Certainly the plan itself demands attention; so too, though, do the attitudes that will make the plan fail or succeed.

Not only do different employee interests affect participation, but employees also undermine participation's effects by judging participation in strict cost–benefit terms. As the employees and management use efficiency and productivity as measures of participation's success, the concomitant values of unity and commitment go unnoticed. Though Jon Elster believes democratic values such as commitment and communication can only be by-products of some other mutually recognized objective like a production quota, to incorporate such values aids in accomplishing the objective.[18] Communication, for example, is less a by-product of the firm's process and more an integral component of the firm's success. Or, given that Orange Handling has been profitable despite its lack of communication, better information and some semblance of management trust could create the even more productive alternative that Edwards and Hirschman discuss. At Orange Handling, given the employee awareness of noncommitment and apparent management duplicity, these values never take hold. In the end, without management's commitment to a participatory process, and also without an employee understanding of participation's value, when the firm suffers economically, employees view participation as either "lip-service" or as poorly implemented. In short, with a lack of commitment to participation's value, both management and the workers easily dismiss its effects and its potential.

As for the lack of any political activity following from workplace participation, it seems that employees distinguish their work lives from their private or social lives whatever the degree of participation at the firm. Almost all of the survey respondents agree that their activities after work involve private and not public pursuits. Whether employees note that they tried to participate but "ran into brick walls" or that if they were to participate more than they do, interviewees claim that their priorities lie with their private, usually familial commitments. Of greater importance, employees at Orange Handling clearly differentiate their actions from their understanding of participation. For example, 72 percent of the survey respondents disagree with the statement that "A participatory workplace means that I spend more time on work-related issues in my 'spare' time than I would in a traditionally owned firm." However, 24 percent fewer of the respondents, or 48 percent, disagree with the more general statement that "An employee must sacrifice some of his/her private life interests to participate in the workplace." Employees, then, are cautious about whether worker participation necessitates greater sacrifices from them. Employees report that, for the most part, they do not sacrifice nonwork time for job-related issues. Employees appear unwilling to commit themselves to the practices and to the sacrifices that at least one-half of them report are necessary. Again, because of participation's structural defects at Orange Handling, these insights cannot contradict the participatory propositions; but they do provide mounting evidence for the importance of considering how worker attitudes affect any participatory scheme.

If the workers' actions do not conform to their understanding of a participatory plan's requirements, it seems then no plan can succeed. Employees are frustrated because management speaks of participation's value but does little to nurture it. Management is frustrated because, even when the firm achieves a collective goal, some workers find a particular, often petty detail over which to divide themselves and to squabble.[19] Confusion results from these management and employee attitudes. Employees do not know whether to believe management's and the owners' participatory attempt and, consequently, fall back into the more familiar understanding of labor–management relations. But to fall back to antagonistic relations when confronted with difficult, changing circumstances means that employees also accept established inequities. Also, management feels that its participatory attempts, albeit sporadic, have little influence on a group of workers who apparently will not change. While management realizes its potential advantages, it writes off worker participation as unsuccessful because of employee reluctance.

Given this atmosphere of distrust and anxiety at work, the significant transformation workers sense in themselves centers on their awareness and protection of their time. One employee claims, "The more I'm asked to participate at work, the anxiety I feel about not doing the things I want to accomplish [i.e., spending time with family or hobbies] becomes greater."[20] Participation at work, or rather the employees' frustration with unrealized participation, produces employees who cautiously guard against the intrusion of work into their social lives. This result contradicts participatory theory's expectations that participation enlarges views and encourages greater interaction. Instead, employees maintain clear distinctions between work activities and their social lives. As 45 percent of the survey respondents agree with the statement that a participatory workplace demands sacrifices from its employees, another 21 percent respond with mixed assent while the remaining 33 percent disagree. For Orange Handling, these numbers continue to point out the confusion over participation's value.

THE ABILITY FOR CHANGE, THE ABILITY TO CHANGE

To insure the permanence of democratic processes and institutions, Robert Putnam argues that "social capital," such as trust and commitment, are vital attributes that demand nurturance to establish and maintain healthy economic systems.[21] He equates social capital with Albert Hirschman's "moral resources." For Hirschman, moral resources are unique from other capital resources, in that they increase with use and decrease with neglect. Participation is a resource whose value increases with its use. At Orange Handling, the firm recognizes the need for social capital but does not create it. Consequently, both the workers and the management remain confused about the motives of the other and, thus, fail to build social capital. Hirschman's description of an environment that lacks social capital aptly summarizes the relations at Orange Handling: "Deep distrust is very difficult to invalidate through experience, for either it prevents people from engaging in the appropriate kind of social experiment, or, worse, it leads to behavior which bolsters the validity of distrust itself.... Once distrust has set in it soon becomes impossible to know if it was ever in fact justified, for it has the capacity to be self-fulfilling."[22]

Orange Handling has reached the stage where distrust has set in, and the participants use clichés to describe employee–management relations. As management hears employees' self-fulfilling claim "I told you so" about participation's problems, management states that there are "bad apples in every bunch." Employees say that management tries to hand out a lot of "att'a boys" to the workers, but management's tactics force employees to put trust in the acronym CYOA (cover your own ass). The question becomes, How can a firm like Orange Handling overcome this distrust?

Interestingly, the answer lies not in pursuing typical market strategies, but in building social capital. As Corey Rosen states,

> Employee ownership, on its own, has little impact on corporate performance.... But get employees to join in idea generation and planning, and the effect on corporate growth is dramatic.... An ESOP with a participative management style grows 6 to 11% a year faster than an ESOP with a traditional management style ... because cynicism grows in the latter organization. [But employee ownership] is not an explanation of the ESOP; it isn't an annual dinner. Instead, it is about everyday involvement by employees in decisions affecting their work.... The key is to make communication flow easily within the organization, so that ideas for boosting productivity don't fall by the wayside.[23]

The answer appears straightforward. A participatory management style that allows employees decision-making access creates the kind of social capital that increases productivity. Orange Handling must recognize that involved employees will make the firm more productive and profitable. Involvement, though, means a form of participation to which Orange Handling has not, in fact, committed itself. A definitive process must occur. Only when the firm first commits itself to building and maintaining social capital will its market measures, in essence the more customary definition of capital, improve. In turn, employees may begin to accept management's social capital endeavors and overcome their skeptical or defeatist attitudes. But as I have argued, the habituation to conflict retains a powerful hold on worker attitudes and behavior, especially in the absense of management's commitment to social capital.

Can both management and employees change? Despite the commitment and interest in participatory plans and employee involvement, it seems that a host of variables affect participation's success. Participation at work calls for change from all parties. It calls for change in a firm's values, from concentrating on the quarterly profit margin to focusing on building social capital. Perhaps the numerous problems that plague most participatory plans, including the three case studies here, come from the inability to change ingrained attitudes and behavior to at least participatory attempts. Management authorizes a change that it is unwilling to fully endorse, and the consequence is that this new management strategy fails because the employees see no reason to submit to its changes. The employees, too, remain skeptical of any change which alters their conception of corporate self-interest. The creation of social capital, given the perceptions of the participants, appears as a management strategy to dupe employees into accepting unknown consequences. The employees rational response, it seems, is to remain distrustful. Under these conditions, the ability of the participants to change looks doubtful.

However, despite the obstacles which inhibit participation's success, the following decision-making alterations offer the opportunity to build the social capital that employees claim they seek and management states they desire.

1. Develop both formal and informal methods of communication. An open-door policy and an active bulletin board are easy first steps, but information must remain accessible and quickly disseminated.
2. Loosen hierarchy. Much of the attitudes at Orange Handling fall too neatly into labor–management categories. Refocus interaction to work lines where layers of employees must interact to succeed.
3. Demand input before—a formal requirement perhaps—and give details immediately after decisions affecting the firm's welfare.
4. Expand not only employee control of their immediate work areas, but begin to include them in company direction. If they are to be the eventual owners, allow them to control the firm's decision making.
5. Commit greater resources to disseminating information and educating the employees as to what the ESOP is and what the firm expects of the employees. As it exists now, it is not clear that the firm knows what to demand of the employees, and, in turn, the employees do not know what to expect from management.

These changes remain vague and, therefore, raise questions, such as what decisions must be accessible and call for input and what decisions remain the privy of the board of directors or the owners? However, the Zaritsky's efforts to resolve these questions will show their level of commitment to employee participation and control. The present frustration shows that both management and the employees seek a more satisfying work environment than the present operation. Frustration shows concern for the firm and belief that participation can benefit the firm, but only if management establishes and supports social capital and workers act collectively to pursue these alternative objectives. Ironically, management and worker frustration is a sign of concern and interest in the firm's future. The objective now is to address the concern before deep distrust turns to ingrained antagonism.

NOTES

1. Jean-Jacques Rousseau, *The Social Contract*, trans. Maurice Cranston (New York: Penguin, 1968), 113.
2. Ibid.
3. Interview with Stanley Zaritsky, Orange Handling's co-President, Albany, N.Y., 19 April 1995.
4. Employee survey response, Orange Handling, April 1995, no. 29.
5. Employee interview, Orange Handling, Albany, N.Y., 18 May 1995.
6. Employee survey response, no. 29.
7. Employee interview, Middletown, N.Y., 24 May 1995.
8. Employee interview, Albany, N.Y., 18 May 1995.
9. Ibid.
10. Employee survey response, no. 29. Italics added.
11. Employee interview, Middletown, N.Y., 24 May 1995.
12. Employee interview, Albany, N.Y., 18 May 1995.
13. Employee survey response, no. 29.

14. Richard Edwards, *Contested Terrain: The Transformation of the Workplace in the Twentieth Century* (New York: Basic Books, 1979), 155.

15. Ibid., 155–156.

16. Ibid., 156.

17. Interview with Stanley Zaritsky and management official, Albany, N.Y., May 1995.

18. Jon Elster, *Sour Grapes: Studies in the Subversion of Rationality* (New York: Cambridge University Press, 1983), 91–100.

19. Management relates the episode—which for them has become symbolic of their "no-win" efforts at participatory management—that after a branch had met and far exceeded some production and sales quotas for a given period, management would satisfy a previous "bet" and pay for a branch dinner. While at first pleased by management's efforts, the employees could not agree on where to eat or what to eat; and management reports that employees were, in the end, generally upset with the entire dinner reward.

20. Employee survey response, no. 29.

21. Robert D. Putnam, *Making Democracy Work: Civic Traditions in Modern Italy* (Princeton, N.J.: Princeton University Press, 1993), 167.

22. Ibid., 169–170.

23. Jay McCormick, "Taking Stock of Employee Ownership Plans," *USA Today*, 30 May 1989, 3B. Also, statistics and general ideas repeated at ESOP Workshop, National Center for Employee Ownership Workshop, Albany, N.Y., 26 April 1995.

Chapter 6   **THE CONTRADICTIONS OF PARTICIPATORY DEMOCRATIC THEORY**

Up to this point, I have described more than explained behavior. Or more accurately, where I offer explanations, it seems alternative views at least demand consideration. In addition, given the varying conditions at the three employee-owned firms, it remains difficult to formulate generalizations and to offer reliable conclusions. Perhaps, then, it is necessary to reiterate my initial contentions and explain how the examination of the present cases adds some qualifications to the expectations of participatory theory. However, my task has never been to disparage participatory theory. The research attempts to clarify and expand the theory's assumptions, given the limits of today's firms, in order to better understand whether workers undergo attitudinal and behavioral changes. Obviously, the cases in this study do not match up to the strong definitions that participatory theory advocates. But simply to dismiss the cases as poor examples is to miss factors which affect both weak and strong participatory firms alike. In short, participatory theory offers a causal path to advance a number of democratic ideals—participation and citizenship to name just two. Given the constraints under which many participatory firms operate, my research seeks to clarify what occurs along the path.

Some may argue that the case studies reviewed cannot be the basis for adequately assessing participatory theory's propositions. Each firm has either a significant structural barrier to employee control, such as the lack of complete employee ownership and, thus, decision-making control, or a host of historical impediments, like vitriolic labor–management relations, that unduly influence how workers participate. Participatory theorists would claim that what these case studies in fact reveal is how, without specific structural requirements such as full decision-making involvement, participation has little effect. Without employee ownership and involvement, without complete dissemination of information, and without strong lines of communication, participation becomes either another corporate tool to maintain its power or an empty promise no one truly supports.

However, to expect such dramatic changes in ownership, control, and behavior neglects the transition between capitalist control and worker control. If society is presently in this transition, which itself is questionable, an evaluation of how management adopts workplace participation allows us to understand what initial problems develop. Also, an evaluation informs us as to what initial expectations are more complex than first hypothesized. To expect every firm, and society in general, to simultaneously and unequivocally adopt workplace reforms seems folly. In fact, many participatory theorists themselves claim that, in reality, workplace changes will occur piecemeal. If a piecemeal approach is at once less radical but somewhat more feasible, despite the protests of the far left, the propositions that participatory theory advances need scrutiny and clarification, as workplaces move in an incremental but not dramatic participatory direction. Because this movement occurs at times with unexpected results, the complexity of the effects provide useful information to guide present understanding. While we cannot expect drastic, wholesale societal changes overnight, we can approach workplace change with the practical knowledge from the participatory experiences of firms undergoing workplace changes. At this point, the fact that management embraces workplace participation in some firms and with some employees produces a host of questions that demand scrutiny. The case studies here underscore how worker participation finds limited expression despite management's purported support for these changes.

My research attempts to recognize some potential obstacles to participatory practices that have not been noted and to temper generalizations about participation's effects from present examples. For example, many studies of employee-owned firms at first focused on employee buyouts of economically troubled, privately held firms. When the employee ownership venture soon went bankrupt, researchers often overlooked the workers' insurmountable assumed debt or the firm's declining economic environment and concluded that employee ownership could not succeed. The lesson was not to write off employee ownership nor to wait for ideal circumstances to experiment with its possibilities. Rather, after more research and a wider sampling of firms, the lesson learned was to measure a participatory and ownership experiment with an eye toward a firm's structural makeup.

Despite the problems that prevent firms from achieving the strong definition of participation and providing strong tests of participatory theory's propositions, enough participatory features exist in the structural design of the firms to make reasonable insights about how workers approach and respond to participation. In assessing participatory opportunities, Standard Knapp appears as the firm with the most potential for realizing deliberation and interaction throughout the firm. Precisely because of this potential, the firm is the one with the most distrust and frustration—as expressed by both workers and management. Quad/Graphics' workers report more efficacious attitudes from their participation, but their involvement does not extend to as large a decision-making field as does potentially Standard Knapp. Orange Handling has even greater potential than Standard Knapp given its small size, easy accessibility, less hierarchy, and lack of a union. But all three cases show that management restricts worker participation, either by design or unconsciously by learned behavior that it finds difficult to overcome. As a consequence, management's actions undermine an easy analysis of participatory theory.

Moreover, the cases reveal that a firm's structure is not the sole condition for ensuring the aims of worker participation, even if the aims focus only on increasing economic productivity. As Quad/Graphics reveals, the workers to a large degree accept their limited participation and still report a sense of empowerment through their work. Is it a feigned acceptance as employees remain internally hostile, as in the case of General Motors where Thomas Fitzgerald reports that participation sweeps all issues of control to the workers' agenda? The interviewees' responses reject this view, as employees remain on the whole positive about the firm's different management style and the trust that it shows its employees. Not all the employees, however, respond to the "hype" that surrounds the worker involvement, and these different worker responses reveal the necessity for a variety of management programs. Often, what bothers Quad/Graphics' workers is the Rousseauean dilemma of "guiding people to their freedom" or a kind of psuedo-participation where employees decide on specifics without participating in the firm's "general will." Anthony Sampson reports that GE's Jack Welsh "persuaded [Boeing's people] that people must be taught to 'control their own destiny.'"[1] Some workers are repelled by this paternal guidance; perhaps those workers need more participation and less teaching. As it is, they either opt to leave the firm or remain at their job with disgruntled attitudes from their lack of influence.

The other conditions that build a strong participatory work force center on what Putnam labels as social capital. Even if a firm commits itself to a participatory structure, the endeavor can be frustrated by managers who feel their power diminish as their roles change. Sampson writes that, as Boeing brought Japanese methods to its Seattle plant, many managers "weren't interested. . . . They said, 'I don't ask people—I tell 'em what to do.'"[2] What distinguishes Quad/Graphics from the other case studies are the employee reports of trust that the firm shows in its employees and the commitment the employees feel in return. These feelings do not emerge merely from the firm's participatory design. They emerge from theory put into practice, from interaction and deliberation. In fact, what workers at Standard Knapp and Orange Handling concentrate on when assessing their firms is the lack of social capital, of trust and openness. A successful participatory firm, then, encompasses more than just attention to a specific structural arrangement. It requires the ability to change management's and workers' thinking, attitudes, and behavior.

As the case studies have shown, and what this research argues, is that cultural and market influences affect these attitudes and affect whether workers are receptive to the participatory changes. Participatory theory states that greater participation educates and transforms workers. The cases reveal that, not only must the design exist, but social capital must develop; and that the workers and management must "fight through" competing attitudes and experiences to become participatory. Participatory theory, then, may be an accurate although overly simplistic accounting of a process that is more complex, more involved, and more difficult to achieve than the initial "causation" indicates.

THEORETICAL EXPECTATIONS AND PRACTICAL CONCERNS

As we have seen, advocates of workplace participation define and employ it differently. As Greenberg noted twenty years ago, management uses participation as a means to the ends of productivity, efficiency, and increasing profit.[3] As Ronald M. Mason notes, though, that while participatory democrats "realize that participation will potentially lead to a plethora of benefits, they, more than any other group, pursue workplace participation as an end in itself. Participatory democrats, by and large, want little more of participation than more participation. Democracy conceived in terms of participation comes close to defining the good life."[4] But participatory democrats, like all other groups that advocate workplace participation, forecast specific ends from participatory experiences. At the individual level, participation educates, transforms, and develops one's beliefs and opinions. Participation builds a greater sense of one's purpose, of one's value, and of one's connection with others. Because work today often lacks any intrinsic value—for instance, work is reduced to labor—participation can encourage an individual's ability to sense the intrinsic values of human development and creativity.

The growth of efficacy in one's workplace through interaction with others reinforces participation's value and expands the individual's scope of problem solving. In essence, participation's effects at the individual level create social and political benefits also. For democratic theorists, participation empowers people to act in and to change social and public arenas. Thus, as a consequence of participation's effects at the individual level, political action occurs as empowered individuals expand their interests to public issues and begin to resolve problems. For participatory theorists, participation ultimately encourages individuals to act as citizens.

Participatory theory, then, bases its expectations on a process of rational action and interaction: Individuals, through deliberative interaction, transform themselves through a kind of mutual self-education; in turn, their increased efficacy encourages them to act on public–political issues. My study critically addresses two aspects of this causal process. The first centers on the raw material of the participatory process, which is the individual, and questions whether participatory theorists can rely on the individual always acting with rational intent in his or her deliberative and interactive choices. My second issue focuses on whether the processes or systems that socialize people into thinking and acting in individualistic ways, such as the market system and liberal democracy itself, undermine the effects of any participatory endeavor. These concerns add nuance to participatory theory, first, by analyzing how individuals react to participation given their particular interests and desires and, second, by recognizing that workplace participation remains one of several factors that account for an individual's development.

Guided by the assumption that individuals will act in predictable, mutually reinforcing ways, much of the workplace participation research centers on discovering the structures that promote individual efficacy, empowerment, and development. Participation, through the creation of efficacy and empowerment, apparently becomes the "rational variable" that changes individual motivations into civic involvement. This assumption overlooks the fact that, in some contexts, participation does not foster rational, other-regarding thinking. Rather, participation may solidify individual biases that tend to isolate groups within firms and/or develop a company "groupthink" mentality against outside interests or firms. Rothschild and Whitt note that some researchers believe that "unilateral, defensive, closed, mutually protective, non-risk-taking behavior . . . is nearly universal. It permeates not only Western bureaucracies but also counter-bureaucracies such as alternative schools. . . . Change in organizational behavior, then, cannot be expected to follow from fundamental change in the mode of production."[5] Though not ideal participatory formats, workers at both Standard Knapp and Orange Handling exhibit suspicious and defeatist attitudes despite the efforts of management to create some form of a participatory environment.

Participatory theorists grant participation significant power to alter individual behavior. Pateman's conception of participatory democracy bases its power on the educative effects of interaction. I ask whether participation directs individuals toward public awareness or whether participation turns individuals toward seeking various ends of their own rational or irrational choosing. It seems participatory theory attributes too much power to participation's transformative effect. Individuals apparently have established goals that limit participation's effects, as workers remain primarily motivated to earn a wage, care for a family, or meet certain payments before they choose to enter into a participatory process. In this sense, the public-regarding effects of participation can develop, but they develop as "by-products" of the individual's principal individualized motivation to participate in the first place.[6] To assume that participation has the ability to override these other motivations underestimates their power to influence behavior and their persistence even under strong democratic circumstances. Participationists may be correct in assuming that a participatory politics would emerge from a participatory education and upbringing, but the reality is that individuals are socialized and educated in a hierarchical, bureaucratic culture. To assume that participatory changes will dramatically alter behavior, given a person's hierarchical socialization, misses the educative effects of the latter.

Participatory theory leads us to a search for those structural arrangements, whether in the workplace or in the community, that promote ongoing participation. Often, though, it seems the answers beg the questions. Studies regularly conclude that a participatory politics or an engaged work force depend on a history or tradition of involvement. For instance, Putnam concludes that, today, Northern Italy's successful democratic governance has its roots in its tradition of civic community. In a sense, the study argues that the most advantageous precondition for democratic rule is a history of democratic interaction. Summarizing his thesis, Putnam states, "This is one lesson gleaned from our research: social context and history profoundly condition the effectiveness of institutions."[7] For today's American workplace or for contemporary American politics, with its history of hierarchical, bureaucratic market relations and rights-based individualism, the possibility for a profound behavioral change toward democratic interaction seems remote.

Because such societal changes appear unlikely, my research examines and elaborates on participatory theory's expectations. My argument adds two behavioral considerations to participatory theory's model. One consideration calls attention to the variety of individual motivations toward work, politics, and participation. The second concern notes the effects of a mediating, if not determining, history and culture on individual behavior. Whereas participatory theory believes that participation is the fulcrum for change, I argue simply that it is participation by particular individuals with different desires within a specific cultural context that affect a participatory group's dynamic. Participation can and does build commonalities from different agendas; but I believe it also necessary, given the social context and the belief in individualism, to account for the power of different attitudes to affect participation's implementation.

Specifically, I argue that structural mechanisms in or of society—by this I mean the market system and the traditions of individualism—play a major role in determining a firm's participatory structure. As Joyce Rothschild and J. Allen Whitt write,

The basic contradiction within democratic organizations is between the logic of substantive rationality, in which the democratic process is of value in itself, and instrumental rationality, which is directed toward a product. All organizations are concerted actions toward some end and, as such, must be instrumental. One may begin by making shoes because one gets pleasure form the act of creating them. But what begins as a vehicle for self-expression must also sell on a market. It is impossible to live in a market economy, dominated by exchange-for-profit maximization, and not be touched by this concern.[8]

For most workers today, there is little sense of substantive meaning for the work they do. Rothschild and Whitt note that, "Researchers find that both the working class and the petty bourgeoisie have significantly lower job satisfaction than any other class. Workers are less satisfied because they work in jobs that are less intrinsically rewarding."[9] Overlooking the effects of class, for most workplace participatory experiments today, what remains elusive is the development of substantive rational objectives, such as personal interaction and growth or building a sense of worker control, to augment the instrumental rational goals of production and profit. Moreover, it is not only the market system that forces a participatory workplace to adhere to instrumentally rational decisions to the exclusion of substantive and perhaps more rewarding rational behavior. It is also the ability to commit to and fully experience the effects of participatory processes, and civic activity seems unlikely given the "natural" tendency toward private interest and activity. In a culture socialized on a "freedom from" mentality, interaction of any kind for people often translates into a thinking of lost freedom.

However, Francis Fukuyama claims that Americans are less individualistic than we believe we are. He believes that two currents, one of individualism and one of communitarianism, run throughout American history. While the former may be the dominant belief, he ironically cites the growth of corporations as an example of our sociability. He states, "From the moment of its founding up through its rise at the time of World War I as the world's premier industrial power, the United States was anything but an individualistic society. It was, in fact, a society with a high propensity for spontaneous sociability, which enjoyed a widespread degree of social trust and could therefore create large economic organizations in which nonkin could cooperate easily for common economic ends."[10] He also employs Tocqueville's observations about the numerous civil associations and the American proclivity to join together to solve its problems as examples of our sociability. But do these observations hold true today, do they accurately depict economic relations and attitudes? For one, Tocqueville excluded manufacturing from his notion of sociability. Also, it seems that to use the growth of the modern corporation as an example of communitarianism misses the changing economic times. With capital's power to dictate economic relations, by this I mean that the mom-and-pop stores were victims of the Industrial Revolution and the concentration of capital and capitalist's desire to control those relations by employing hierarchical and bureaucratic methods, the worker had few options other than to follow the newly emerging mechanisms of economic control.

While Tocqueville noted that any decline in civil associations would give rise to rampant selfishness, he also thought that our associational life would check, almost by nature, the possibility of a "aristocracy" emerging from manufacturing. Obviously, capital's power and the decline of associational interaction meant the rise of Carnegie, Mellon, Rockefeller, and Morgan.[11] In addition, bureaucracy and hierarchy made social trust superfluous, and to believe that workers and capitalists were engaged in some common objective misses the hostility and conflict that plagued the growth of the American corporation. A more adequate interpretation of the emergence of the American corporation would understand it as an expression of individualism, first by the powerful capitalist and second by all the corporate workers who mistrust, not just the capitalist, but the hierarchical and bureaucratic design that, in turn, reduces access, limits information, and controls employees.

If American sociability is less obvious today and hierarchy builds mistrust instead of trust, it seems likely that the beliefs and motivations that each brings to the participatory workplace affects how the collective experience operates. Again, participatory theory believes that interaction is the central variable. But a participatory workplace comprises a variety of individuals who often have different definitions of what participation means. Whether participation itself can reconcile these differences depends as much on the individuals themselves as it does on the form of participation and the deliberative process. Moreover, while it may be a theoretical necessity for participatory theory to assume individuals act rationally, a theory that rests on building efficacy and empowerment must consider the varying attitudes and expectations individuals bring to the participatory endeavor because, for the most part, the workers and management do not commit themselves to any common will when they begin their interaction. At the very least, an analysis of the individualized measures of participation's effects is needed to assess participation's success. Individual desires and expectations oftentimes produce rational behavior, but they also are based on irrational hopes, beliefs, and expectations.

THE CAUSAL PATH ANALYZED

To posit the possibility of workers exhibiting irrational behavior as a response to participatory processes begins to recognize the complexity of workplace involvement. But workers' actions do not have to be solely irrational to recognize the complexity. Rather, participatory theory provides too simplistic an account of how employees undergo any degree of transformation because the theory does not account for the attitudes and actions that employees bring to their workplace. Participatory theorists argue two causal events occur: Workplace participation produces efficacious workers; and in turn, empowered workers seek out other arenas, like politics, in which to participate or from which participation effects their judgments on national politics. As argued, these propositions need revision. First, because different individuals bring different expectations to the participatory experiment. Second, and at a more fundamental structural and behavioral level, these participatory expectations seek to bridge two arenas that often remain inherently conflictual for most people. As Robert Lane claims, people evaluate and act in the market arena with different criteria than they evaluate and act within the political arena. He argues that there are different measures of justice for the two arenas, as people view market rewards as somehow more fair than the political demands of fairness and equality.[12]

Workplace democracy, then, attempts to encourage or socialize people into thinking of the two worlds as connected, if only in the apparently reasonable sense that efficacy in one's immediate environment causes one to resolve issues in other areas of one's life. But if people view these arenas as wholly distinct, the ability to see any connection between efficacy at work and empowerment in any political pursuit does not occur. In addition, at the individual level of efficacy, if the participatory changes produce confusion about employee roles, employee rights, management relations, and collective commitments, the workers often project their individual expectations into the participatory process. As a result, the participatory workplace fosters workers with different agendas and different measures of success. Cliques can then form, and that undermines the objective of open communication and information flow.

These observations lead to two alternative propositions: Participation does not breed efficacious workers if clear work expectations about the goals of participation are neglected; and any subsequent political activity by empowered workers will not occur because cultural tensions between the private work arena and the public or political arena discourage individuals from linking the two. With respect to the first proposition, though the goals of participation quite often include references to creating a "family environment" with trustworthiness and attachment to the firm, these goals often show the management's ambiguity in communicating how the goals can be achieved and the workers' confusion in reconciling private behavior—trust and commitment—in a work setting. Thus, the creation of social capital encounters immediate doubt among employees unless there is either significant structural changes and/or some recognizable changes in incorporating workers into management responsibilities. The second proposition reveals a deeper tension that troubles any participatory attempt to create active citizenship. It states that, perhaps even if management communicates its expectations and requirements and then implements participatory changes, the fact that individuals are socialized to differentiate private activity, such as family concerns or hobbies, from work issues inhibits the ability of individuals to view work in more meaningful ways other than mere necessity. In fact, if workers view work neither as a private activity nor as a contribution to any common good, then it exists independent of what participatory theory assumes—as if it is an activity solely to be endured. Under such conditions, workplace participation's ability to transform ingrained attitudes meets substantial obstacles.

With these propositions laid out, I offer several implications that emerge from the case studies. I concentrate on participatory theory's assumptions that participation educates and transforms workers and that participation bridges economic and political thinking and behavior. In doing so, I employ three lines of analysis that attempt to explicate worker behavior and how this behavior affects participatory theory's hypotheses. The first line of analysis applies Hirschman's understanding of "exit, voice, and loyalty" to the participatory workplaces. My reason for employing Hirschman's views is that his economic analysis mirrors that of participatory theorists, in that they both seek to reconceptualize what counts as rational and irrational individual and firm behavior. The second line of analysis considers how formal and informal participatory power—the former means the typical participatory emphasis on structural conditions (i.e., creating the "perfect" participatory workplace), while the latter means the social capital conditions like building trust, responsibility, and commitment—either supports or rejects my alternative propositions. The third line of analysis addresses the problem brought up in regard to both Quad/Graphics' success and Orange Handling's difficulties; namely, that any participatory experience operates within the confines of instrumental rationality, or economic success. To some degree, it seems criticism of participatory activity can be traced to a firm's inability to control its economic future. Quad/Graphics is lauded as a participatory success in part, I believe, because it is first an economic success. Orange Handling, conversely, has had participatory difficulty because of its economic uncertainties.

EXIT, VOICE, AND LOYALTY

Similar to Lane's argument, Hirschman's work links "exit" behavior with economic activity and "voice" with political activity. Consumers who stop buying a firm's goods or workers who leave a firm exercise the exit option. The exit option is one of the requisite characteristics of the free market system, and the simple demand function is its most obvious example. Conversely, Hirschman defines voice as the consumer's or worker's "direct expression of dissatisfaction to management or to some authority to which management is responsible." Voice is activity to change an unacceptable state of affairs, exit attempts to remove oneself from the unacceptable state of affairs. Just as exit remains the general response for much of economic analysis, Hirschman argues that voice, or the lack thereof, grounds much of political analysis.[13]

Despite the introduction of workers' interests and perhaps the dispersion of its power, management often rationally supports workplace participation because voice increases productivity. If management can use its workers to discover production "glitches" or consumer preferences, it avoids the longer and more costly process of relying solely on consumer or worker exit. Also, as participatory theorists claim, worker interaction fulfills basic human desires that create a greater sense of satisfaction with work. Participation reduces absenteeism, theft, sickness, and associated productivity measures. Voice, then, can be viewed as management's recognition that cooperation and interaction are values worth establishing on instrumental grounds. Relying only on exit means that management feels worker involvement is not particularly important or necessary—a message disastrous for employee commitment and self-worth but wholly accepted as a central element of the free market creed.

Now, given that workplace participation establishes a "voice" option for the employees in the traditionally exit-dominated economic arena, a blurring of basic, established relations, understandings, and perceptions occurs. If management does not explicitly communicate its understanding and expectations of the voice option by its workers, the workers must attempt to sift out when exit and voice are appropriate. Also, to add greater confusion, Hirschman notes that exit and voice must operate within certain boundaries. He states, "Voice has the function of alerting a firm or organization to its failings, but it must then give management, old or new, some time to respond to the pressures that have been brought to bear on it.... The citizen [or worker] must thus be in turn influential and deferential."[14] For the worker to know when to exercise voice, when to exercise exit, and when to exercise voice and then be patient all remain exploratory adventures into unfamiliar and nontraditional terrain (i.e., into the terrain of direct democratic politics). Again, if management does not provide sound direction, these explorations easily turn into individualized activity and/or self-defeating exercises. This does not mean that management must be the sole agent of change, but today management typically holds the power to ensure change. Workers, with their specialized jobs that tend to exacerbate their individual differences, find difficulty in articulating either voice, exit, or patience.

Also, Hirschman recognizes what advocates of workplace participation note as a fundamental revision of the typical worker–owner relationship. Instead of relying on exit as the principal economic activity, participatory theorists propose voice as the activity that subsequently connects economic activity to political activity. Hirschman writes, "The relation between voice and improvement in an organization's efficiency has considerable similarity with the modus operandi of exit.... In the case of any one particular firm or organization and its deterioration, either exit or voice will ordinarily have the *dominant* reaction mode.... In the case of normally competitive business firms, for example, exit is clearly the dominant reaction to deterioration and voice is a badly underdeveloped mechanism; it is difficult to conceive of a situation in which there would be too much of it."[15] In participatory workplaces, voice replaces exit as the dominant economic mechanism. However, given that workplace participation calls for a revision of traditional economic understanding by the workers, employees ironically note instances in which there is too much voice. Standard Knapp interviewees themselves recognize that the firm suffers from "too many generals and not enough regular soldiers." Also, at times, a management that proposes participation also stumbles along with its own rethinking of economic activity and, thus, communicates its methods and goals ineffectively. In turn, the opportunity for different voices to enunciate different expectations to already-confused workers increases dramatically, and with disastrous economic consequences, especially with the more horizontal, dispersed power characteristic of employee participation and ownership. At Orange Handling, management displays as much frustration with the workers' "cliquely" participation and lack of common commitment as the workers express about management's allegedly duplicitous participatory scheme. What activity results from this "interactive confusion of voice?" Exit, the very reaction the participatory experiment seeks to diminish. One worker at Orange Handling, who thought highly of his co-workers, of the quality of the firm's service, of his role in producing good results, and of participation in general, was relieved that he was leaving the firm because he was no longer able to cope with the overall work atmosphere.

Loyalty, Hirschman's third category, combats exit as the most-valued and trustworthy customers or workers remain tied to the product or firm.[16] Building loyalty is yet another rational management strategy because it keeps the workers who—because of their commitment and interest—may be the most effective at solving the firm's problems from simply leaving. Participatory theorists claim that the exercise of voice and control by workers over decision making fosters loyalty because the employees sense the firm trusts them and, thus, they seek to return the commitment. Hirschman notes, "As a result of loyalty, these potentially most influential customers or members will stay on longer than they would ordinarily, in the hope or, rather, reasoned expectation that improvement or reform can be achieved 'from within.' Thus loyalty, far from being irrational, can serve the socially useful purpose of preventing deterioration [of the firm] from being cumulative, as it so often does when there is no barrier to exit."[17] Hirschman's point is that irrational behavior, from the point of view of a market system, does have a rational basis if other values exist. Again, replacing the value of exit with the values of voice and the development of loyalty allows for a reformulation of rational behavior and for a reappraisal of what constitutes efficient and productive firm behavior.

Standard Knapp's union vote in January 1995 over whether to strike reveals the power of loyalty. With union officials telling its membership not to vote for a strike, the no-strike decision was decided by a mere three-vote swing with over one hundred votes cast. Standard Knapp's president states that the most hostile union workers are typically younger and that the older union workers consistently side with management's ideas and decisions. Perhaps the older workers remember the commitment that management entrusted to the workers in the shift to employee ownership and evaluate their status differently given the difficult economic times in central Connecticut. It seems the younger workers, who constantly claim that if not for the union the workers would have nothing, have less regard for the mere existence of their jobs and remain more concerned about increasing wages and benefits, given the difficult economic environment in what they are told is "their" firm.

At Orange Handling, management has difficulty in generating worker interest in employee ownership because the younger workers remain suspicious—suspicious of managment's unconventional, trusting behavior and suspicious of the true rewards of the proposed plan. Workers shy away from participation because they believe the ESOP benefits only accrue to those close to retirement. They also are unwilling to commit themselves to a single firm for an extended employment period of twenty to thirty years. This lack of a long-term perspective, and the preference to have the freedom to leave the firm, epitomizes the strength of the exit option and how workers, perhaps unknowingly, employ it.

For participatory theorists, the dichotomy between younger and older union workers shows that establishing loyalty reorients attitudes toward alternative values. Participation, commitment, and trust do recast worker attitudes. However, the crucial insight from both examples is that participation does not necessarily recast attitudes toward alternative values for *all* workers. The younger workers' interests in their private benefits, and their belief that the union is the vehicle in which they trust to pursue these partial interests, shows that participation does not necessarily produce the causal process that participatory theory assumes. Again, the firm's structural participatory deficiencies detracts from the power of this conclusion, but the difference in attitudes given the same participatory experience reveals the difficulty that participation encounters in affecting attitudes. Also, the tendency for younger workers to hesitate to join long-term employment payoff plans or to invest for the long term in their present firm reveals the power of the dominant economic mechanism. Participation has the ability to change behavior and reorient thinking, but it remains more a potentiality than a likely outcome, given the motivations individuals bring to the participatory workplace and given the power of the exit option in the present economic system.

Hirschman's value is that he notes methods that are typically viewed as solely political behavior—voice, participation, and loyalty—and recognizes that they produce economically rational, socially productive results. In a sense, he argues, much as participatory theory argues, that the narrow definitional parameters created by economic analysis neglect alternative examples of individual rationality and socially useful policies. He introduces political action into economic thought and, thereby, gives support to the participatory advocates' claims that participation has beneficial consequences for workers, for firms, and for society. How then does this interaction of political and economic thinking affect participatory theory's assumptions about individual transformation and political activity?

The case studies repeatedly show that workers and firms both have difficulty in incorporating so-called political action into their economic behavior. The most common and most powerful example highlights why people tend to refrain from poilitical activity in general. Without clear measures of one's participatory impact, and without certain returns, individuals regularly decide not to "risk" the effort for the often ambiguous results. At each firm, some interviewees state that, while they once did attend meetings and contribute their experiences and information to increase productivity, they never felt that management listened or that any of their ideas were initiated. The firms, in effect, use up loyalty by ignoring the voice of the workers. To be certain, management is open to hearing more about productivity changes than about input into the firm's larger decisions—hiring and firing, forecasting, and investment. But interviewees use examples of their "lack of voice" that focus almost exclusively on their immediate work area, not on broader, company-wide concerns. They offer comments, go to several meetings, talk with their co-workers, and most likely meet with a manager or higher official. But without tangible, immediate results, they now choose not to participate. Without the typical returns associated with the economic arena, they choose to refrain from the political activity that attempts to initiate and prize alternative, "extra-economic" values. But also, workers are frustrated because they are unable to exercise the "power" that they thought they had. In either case, individuals have difficulty implementing the apparently contradictory role of being influential and deferential.

Only at Quad/Graphics does a profound groundswell of support exist for the firm's participatory procedures. The workers enthusiastically report that they feel empowered and embrace the opportunities for involvement. The firm succeeds in producing efficacious workers because it sends clear messages, with the indoctrination to the Quad culture and with in-house Quad University skill-training classes, about where and when employees exercise their participatory skills. Viewed through Hirschman's understanding, these messages establish the certain boundaries which need to exist for voice and loyalty to be effective. Employees realize that it is with their immediate co-workers and over those issues which affect their daily work routine where they feel empowerment. However, decisions concerning company direction, despite the firm's claims of employee ownership, do not involve the workers. They do not vote their shares, and the firm remains almost exclusively in the hands of one family. For many employees, though, their participatory control over immediate areas translates into the thinking that, without the adequate information (i.e., balance sheets, interest rates), they should not have a voice in company decisions at all. Ironically, though, at all three firms this information was available to any employee who asked for it. This attitude, therefore, stems from successful indoctrination into management's expertise or a rational decision given one's limited knowledge not to seek out other participatory avenues. In either case, these attitudes question participatory theory's expectation that empowered workers will rethink their political judgments or act to change political issues.

Also troubling for participatory theory is the fact that Quad workers acutely recognize the economic rewards of their participatory efforts. In all three firms, one common response to the advantages of employee ownership and participation was the opportunity for advancement and for "hiring-from-within." Quad interviewees note that those who want a career at the firm "do the things necessary."[18] If joining more committees and taking classes after work are necessary to make one's name known to the appropriate people, the interviewees in these instances equate the exercise of voice with some predetermined, rational, and exact economic reward, namely promotion. The lesson workers understand is that participation produces certain economic results. For participatory theorists who argue that participation should be valued in and of itself, Quad/Graphics appears as a participatory success, precisely because it does not promote participation as a value in and of itself. Participation is a process and a method toward achieving specific goals.

Orange Handling's decision to open up discussions with its employees over workplace and working improvements for its smaller second shift again epitomizes the difficulty workers have in developing the goals of participatory voice given the system and the history of economic exit. Management states that one of the many questions it had asked the few second shift employees was whether they felt their work could be accomplished during the day shift. Management claims it was making only preliminary inquiries and, at the same time, trying to involve its workers in decision making while exhibiting open communication. In turn, management reports that one good worker who heard of the inquiries found another job because he could not work during the day. In this case, while the continuation of the second shift was never in question, at least one worker acted without exercising voice and in keeping with the dominant exit mechanism.

Another example of exit behavior in the participatory firms is the great reluctance for many workers to answer the research surveys.[19] Interviewees at Standard Knapp and at Orange Handling, where the more hostile worker–management environments exist, often claim that many co-workers do not respond because they are too concerned about management "finding out" and introducing some sort of purge—itself an economic activity as the firm rids its undesirables. Even at Quad/Graphics, where the survey response rate was higher than the other two firms and much more enthusiastic, one notable group or job category that never responded was the firm's "runners." The job entails transferring stacks or boxes of publications from one site to another for added production or for delivery. It is typically given to new hires and is the most physically demanding of any at the firm. Given their diminished status, their lowly wages, their job's physical demands, and their uncertain status in the firm, it is clear that Quad participation means less to this group of workers than other economic concerns. In fact, their actions conform to the typical "acquiescent" economic behavior that Hirschman seeks to reevaluate with a participatory voice.

These examples raise questions about the simple causal process underlying the claim that participation creates efficacy. Workers find it difficult to overcome the dominant economic thinking that produces the exit option. But even a clear management communication process about its commitment to participation does not necessarily change worker behavior. Participatory workplace employees face the contradictory role of remaining involved in a participatory process, where recognizable results are less certain, while also acting in an economic arena where certain results are demanded. In addition, because of the contradictory nature of exercising voice within an exit-dominated arena, workers often interpret the process and merits of participation differently. These interpretations, while they appear in keeping with the goals of involvement and creative thinking and while they appear as examples of individual freedom as expressed in political discourse, produce a variety of conflicting expectations that hamper the firm's principal profit-making activity. Whether workplace participation's success demands meeting many of these employee expectations remains debatable. My point is to show that today's market system seems to spell trouble for all workplace participation schemes.

Because of these uncertain or conflictual cues, workers do not exhibit any behavior that links—nor any perception of the connection between—participation at work with any possible public or political activity. The most telling example of the lack of political activity comes less from the overwhelming survey responses that workers claim they engage in private activity after work hours and more from the uncomfortable silence and blank stares when interviewees try to determine what questions about their political activity have to do with their participation at work. In interview after interview, the most difficult questions for the interviewees dealt with the workers' reporting of their public actions. In part, their anxiousness comes from their inability to claim any political action and, thus, perhaps to satisfy the researcher and the survey.

But also, many simply did not fathom any connection between work and politics. In their minds, these realms remain distinct and produce separate evaluations. For most, politics remains an activity to be avoided, a dirty word. Lane argues that people assess economic relations as "more fair" and "more just" than political processes, and that people push the problem issues into the political debate. From this, it seems that no economic debate exists—people receive just desserts for honest effort—but that the articulation of social priorities and their financial costs produce heated debate. People view politics less as the opportunity to participate in collective decision making and more as the arena of conflict. For the most part, people tend to avoid conflict and, thus, tend to abstain from participation. This perception of politics as conflictual and filled with unintended and uncertain results is magnified in relation to the relative certainty of economic relations (i.e., supply and demand, wages come from hours worked). Perhaps, too, the underlying but unrecognized conflict at work, through hierarchical and bureaucratic relations, force workers to find a place where they perceive some self-control and some individuality. In the end, their private lives remain their only refuge.

But the point is that participatory structures attempt to reduce hierarchy and bureaucracy and open up the economic realm for greater employee participation. However, it seems that while workers can respond positively to the participatory processes, these processes do not often change the workers' perceptions of political interaction. Because they retain distinct evaluations of each arena, a change in one does not necessarily produce a change in the other—especially since the more conflictual one, namely politics, is not the arena that undergoes the initial change.

In addition, when pressed about their after-work activities, several interviewees stated they felt the firm would most likely prefer it if they had no outside interests and would just focus on work-related issues and events. Whether accurate or not, the workers view the firm as exercising an all-consuming presence or authority in their lives. In its worst form, workers see no personal identity apart from the firm, thus contemptuously seeing the firm as restricting their freedom and sense of development. Such an outcome contradicts the participatory claim that work participation empowers individuals to seek out other areas to exercise their newly discovered political attitudes and abilities.

The notion of an all-consuming firm dictating an employee's life reiterates the underlying power relations that workers perhaps unwittingly understand as part of work life. In turn, participation at work meets some resistance because employees seek to escape work's control. In general, participation appears as a voluntary activity with good intentions and predictable results. But with the controls in the workplace, with its hierarchical design and its distinct lines of authority, participation in this arena seems less voluntary—a matter of Hirschman's choice of voice, a much more imposed or enforced voice without true choice. It is of great importance to note that despite the many ESOP and participatory plans in operation today, very few firms first asked their employees what kind of participatory scheme would appeal to them. From their inception, participatory plans lack employee input and, thus, reinforce who controls their work lives.

Interviewees, especially at Quad/Graphics with its indoctrination program and pervasive Quad culture that allows for complete immersion into a "company lifestyle," recognize a firm's ability to comprise or "invade" all aspects of a worker's life and the life of that worker's family. In response, workers and their families respond either with disdain or with resignation. While one Quad/Graphics employee responds that "Yes, I do get negative, but . . . it's a big show, a big front. You can get molded real fast here."[20] Another worker claims that "[Management] wants it [the firm] to invade your private life, . . . and some people can't stand it."[21] With either attitude, the employees consciously seek to separate themselves and their activities from the firm. As a result, work participation does not foster outside, political participation. Rather, it creates a work force adamant in maintaining a clear division between work activities and private interests, an attitude that undermines participatory theory's expectations.

INTERNAL STRUCTURAL EFFECTS ON PARTICIPATION AND EFFICACY

In the discussion of the contradictory external influences or roles that affect a participatory workplace, two variables are noted. A worker's age and the firm's communication processes play important roles in a firm's participatory success. Yet participatory advocates would argue that a worker's age should play a less influential role than the proper decision-making power and control with the necessary communication network within the firm. Creating an effective communication process where management transmits options and employees easily decipher them and respond, along with the opportunities to initiate action, appears commonsensical to those who are interested in the firm's participatory success. Also, if the firm is set to establish a participatory workplace, it must build commonalities and unity by bridging, not just hierarchical or bureaucratic differences, but also individual differences. The firm must show all employees that the ownership or participatory plan favors their interests and that their collective success—the firm's profit and growth—benefits each worker. Management experts, in the name of enhancing productivity, have offered numerous human relations changes designed to encourage participation—for instance, quality circles, total quality management, reengineering, team-based empowerment, activity-based management—to foster worker cohesion and empowerment.

Participatory advocates should recognize that workers bring different expectations and different levels of commitment to their jobs. The advocates could then claim that a variety of participatory schemes (by variety I do not mean schemes that create only pseudo-participation) can satisfy the variety of participatory interests at each workplace. Instead of searching for and then implementing "an ideal" structural arrangement that creates a united work force, a management team should explore what kinds of participation best suits its different kinds of workers. In none of the three case studies did the participatory program arise from worker ideas and interests, but all three firms could benefit from this alternative starting point. Just as Hirschman noted that the worker is confronted with the difficult task of knowing when to act and when to defer, management, too, must rethink its leadership and recalculate when to guide and when to follow.[22]

While participation at Quad/Graphics remains very much a management tool, it succeeds because it effectively communicates roles and expectations. If workers accept those responsibilities, the rewards are usually quite immediate. Although as noted, Quad is unique in its methods because the efficacy it breeds occurs under its controlled direction. For some, this sense of empowerment remains only Quad empowerment. Or, as Cohen notes, we all remain free as long as not many of us choose to exercise our conditional freedom.[23] However, in comparison to the other case studies which offer the potential for greater worker freedom of expression and control, only at Quad/Graphics does an individual feeling of employee empowerment exist. Interestingly, then, the establishment of the ideal internal firm procedures to advance participation seem to develop from the evolution of the imprecise, changing informal practices that either already exist or that participation needs to foster. In short, institutions and rules are important in deciphering participation's effects; but just as workers do not always act rationally, structures and rules are not the only essential ingredients for participatory success. In other words, social capital is a necessary ingredient in creating a participatory workplace.

Given the assertion that individual attitudes and expectations affect any participatory plan, and specifically that individuals may develop irrational expectations or behavior whether management is effective in communicating and involving workers in decision making, the importance of creating efficacious workers remains paramount in theory. Participatory democratic theorists conclude that efficacy occurs only after workers have the opportunity and take the responsibility for making the decisions that control a firm. Empowerment occurs when a firm is under the democratic control of its employees. Since none of the cases meet these strong democratic standards, from the theorists' view, individual empowerment would seem unrealized. Consequently, for strict participatory theorists, the Quad/Graphics workers' sense of efficacy, given their limited input and control of the firm, remains either partially unrealized or perhaps a form of "false consciousness" as to their actual powerlessness.

However, an alternative understanding of the workers' efficacy, one that differentiates formal versus informal structures and relations, recognizes their power and control as crucial for the firm's operation and crucial for the success of the participatory methods. In the formal financial and decision-making arrangement, Quad workers know they exert little influence on company decisions. But in their immediate work areas, where they see the effects of their efforts on a day-to-day basis, they report a sense of control and influence. Moreover, every interviewee claims that a strong co-worker rapport exists and that, in general, they feel a sense of responsibility to their work, their fellow employees, and to the firm. These efficacious attitudes may present few changes from previous and less-ambitious worker involvement practices, but they present at least a potential for participation to influence employee behavior. Given that today's participatory changes typically include a substantial commitment of private money, usually from management to the collective employee ownership endeavor, it seems that employee ownership today produces a greater management commitment, at least in theory, than previous involvement strategies.

Commitment and efficacy seem part of a cyclical process that ratchets actual empowerment to increasingly greater heights. At first, interviewees speak of the informal practices that build responsibility: the trust other workers and superiors show, the opportunities to satisfy the individual's degree of interest and motivation, and the inclusive nature of the teamwork mentality. With greater involvement in one's job activities or in company policy comes more opportunities for responsibility. The obvious example is promotion and "climbing the corporate ladder." But even "established" managers claim to enjoy the diversity of activities the firm either allows them or, more typically, that they create and to which they respond. In a sense, then, they feel efficacious because the firm relies on them to use their experiences to direct the firm. It is at this point where employee-directed participation differs from previous management school, human relations approaches to worker involvement. Here, the employees are in control, the firm remains a watchdog or an accountant. The firm's philosophy leaves much of problem solving and productivity measures to the workers who are most familiar with the daily procedures. A lesson, then, for a participatory workplace perhaps is to be found in one of Quad's trademark catch-phrases, "think small." Efficacy seems to occur when workers recognize their value in their immediate work environment.

Standard Knapp provides an example where the existence of hierarchy and established, internalized conflict makes it difficult to create a "think small" or "start small" approach for workplace participation. Standard Knapp comes closest to fulfilling some of the definitional standards of a democratic participatory workplace. But because capital still directs many relationships and hierarchy stunts others, Standard Knapp also displays the greatest amount of distrust and hostility. While the firm's formal structure grants the employees a limited amount of power to direct it—though more power than Quad/Graphics grants its employees—the firm fails to create the informal mechanisms that encourage a participatory environment. Most often, interviewees comment that the employees do not own the company and that, in the end, after all the talking, a few select people decide what the firm does. Without a sense of control and with a sense of division and rivalry, the informal characteristics of trust, commitment, and responsibility find little opportunity to emerge.

The obvious obstacle that inhibits the creation of informal bonds is the workers' union. It divides labor and management, as well as unionized skilled plant employees, from nonunionized office or "inside" personnel. From an initial inspection, it appears that the union's goals mirror those of the worker ownership and participation plan. Both management and the union claim to satisfy the workers' interests, and, in Hirschman's words, give "voice" to employees. Yet the union acts more as a mediator between workers and management, more as a protector. It is unclear whether with the union's absense a more hospitable participatory environment would exist; but it seems that without the union, the employees would have one less source of hostility between themselves and with management. In theory, a participatory workplace acts as a mechanism for workers to define for themselves and then act in pursuit of their defined interests. Ideally, the workers themselves ultimately control the process; they—and not a union—are their own protectors. Or, as I argued at the beginning of Chapter 3, in these inconsistent changes to worker ownership, a union's role must be to act less as the definitive articulation of workers' interests and more as a conduit of information.

Without the informal procedures and relations to sustain participation at Standard Knapp, the formal rights of ownership and participation suffer. Although the employees have the power of "voice," their actions are more symbolic of the exit option. At both Standard Knapp and Orange Handling, many interviewees mention that fellow workers who held similar distrustful attitudes were reluctant or hesitant to respond to the survey—despite its acknowledged confidentiality—because of the fear of reprisal. Their response was not to respond, to acquiesce. Or the few who did respond were vocal knowing that the union would protect them.[24] This acquiescence shows that simply fulfilling the formal arrangements for participation does not necessarily lead to its use or success. Formal opportunities for participation can exist; but without informal mechanisms and support, workers tend to rely still on traditional "exit" economic behavior.

At Standard Knapp, the union may be the barrier to participatory success. It remains a familiar remnant of more traditional management methods, and many employees may be reluctant to rely on new participatory methods given the hostility of past relations. But Standard Knapp's significance is that the union voice blocks the creation of the informal relations that need to evolve for participation to succeed despite the presence of the formal requirements of a participatory workplace. As an institutional design, then, a participatory workplace depends as much on the sometimes difficult nurturing process of building trust and commitment as on the firm's official recognition of the employees power and control.

On the other hand, the union may be merely symptomatic of the larger issue of formal and informal participatory relations. At Orange Handling, where no union presence exists, management remains just as frustrated and workers express just as much uncertainty as their counterparts at Standard Knapp. It seems that, while both management and workers acknowledge that participation is a good idea, management does not communicate what it means by participation, and the employees in general do not ask nor respond. Thus, implementing participation opens a Pandora's box of mixed messages. On the one hand, a participatory workplace acknowledges management's confidence in its employees and its reliance on them to take the initiative in furthering the interests of the firm. On the other hand, as the cases reveal, employees remain unsure of what participation means and look toward management for direction and leadership. Without that direction (which management often fails to provide, even though this failure seems contradictory to the aims of an employee-controlled workplace) workers opt for the traditional economic behaviors of acquiescence or exit—or they become frustrated and embittered by managment's false "promises" and their own failed expectations.

Two tentative conclusions emerge. One is that worker efficacy develops from the informal and reciprocal relations in each employee's immediate work environment. This conclusion should raise few eyebrows among researchers; however, much of participatory research devotes its attention to the proper formal decision-making mechanisms that enhance employee control. The other conclusion is that the aims of participatory theory appear in contradiction to the procedures workers either accept or unwittingly follow. Just as Hirschman noted the difficult dual role for the worker of being influential and deferential in a participatory workplace, it seems that management must be aware of similar dual functions. If either fails to fulfill these seemingly contradictory roles, as the cases reveal, both end up returning to traditional economic activity where voice remains hollow and relations remain antagonistic.

THE MISLEADING EFFECT OF ECONOMIC SUCCESS

It should be clear that not all participation generates worker efficacy. At Standard Knapp, the divisions that the union's presence maintains do not allow for a participatory culture. Conversely, the participatory culture at Quad/Graphics appears for some workers as too confining and autocratic. One employee states that Quad looks for creativity and initiative, but managment also hires young people, many just out of the military, because the firm wants discipline too.[25] At Orange Handling, no one variable or process discourages worker efficacy. Although some acknowledge that communication can improve and others argue that the firm lacks the informal reciprocal relations that build trust and commitment, management and some of the workers cite the firm's economic health as an intervening variable.

As I argued in Orange Handling's case, workers and management officials who cite bad economic times as a negative influence on the participatory process use this to deflect criticism away from the failings of the process itself. If participation seeks to create worker ownership and involve employees in decision making, the firm's health does not seem particularly relevant to these initiatives. Participation's effects cannot be assessed if they depend on a firm undergoing an economic boom. Participation must be an integral part of a firm's philosophical mission and not simply a fair-weather management device.

However, when workers and management grow increasingly frustrated with the atmosphere of negativity within the firm, then discussion usually turns to the economy and its effects. At Orange Handling, management claims that, when it implemented its ESOP plan in 1989, it also had reached a profit-making zenith. With hindsight after the early 1990s recessions and now on a small but encouraging rebound, it equates the firm's distress with worker petulance and the firm's success with worker satisfaction. But the workers take a different perspective on this causal relationship, and their words reveal the spurious relationship between economic health and participatory success. When workers at Orange Handling hear from management about economic downturns, probable layoffs, and decreasing profits at best, they seek more information and raise issues that demand more thorough cost accounting. In several interviews, workers use examples of how to control costs and cite expenditures by management that appear wasteful and sometimes frivolous. In these examples, workers try to reconcile what they are told and how much they need to sacrifice with what they see and how others do not sacrifice.[26] For the workers, this apparent contradiction between words and actions shows management's lack of concern for disseminating information and responding to employee ideas and a more general lack of management interest in its employees. The power of this perception, whether accurate or ill conceived, is that it produces and reinforces behavior that undermines the supposed benefits of the participatory process.

For instance at Standard Knapp, management responds that the workers do not "know enough" for their examples to make legitimate claims about the firm's expenditures. At Orange Handling, management states that recent profits have been reinvested in the firm's overhead and inventory. These moves make long-term economic sense, but officials claim they also tend to incite workers who would rather have the profits "in their pockets" than in the firm's equipment. But what causes the workers to lack the necessary information is management's exclusion of the employees from the decision-making process. Also, what irks employees the most, and what causes the most anger, are management's questionable—in the workers' eyes—expenditures. It seems that such questions underscore issues of equality. One Orange Handling worker wonders why "the owners drive around in Cadillacs, [another] in a new Tempo, and [another] with a new 4 x 4 . . . after a kid in Middletown had to get his face busted with a chain binder to get some material changed."[27] In a sense, if participation's success depends on a firm's profit margin, the participatory goals and processes are the measures to be cut when times get tough. Without any greater commitment, management only equates participatory opportunities and voice with economic health.

Like Orange Handling, Standard Knapp has also experienced participatory "growing pains" since the firm instituted its ESOP. These pains have coincided with difficult economic times, as employees became more vocal and more factionalized when the firm downsized in the early 1990s. Again, the power of the dominant, "exit-driven" economic system to determine employee behavior becomes clear when workers begin to break into factions when presented with a "decreasing size of the pie." Also, despite its commitment to employee ownership and participation, traditional "exit-driven" behavior determined Standard Knapp's response to an economic tailspin. Instead of involving its workers in deciding how the firm could adjust to the economic turmoil, management decided to lay off some workers with no job certainty in the future. Many skilled plant workers clearly favor the protection of their interests by the union, in the face of management's lack of concern or commitment to their needs. Given these inconsistencies, the union and the employees are not inclined to commit themselves to management's ideas for participation, and, in turn, the traditionally hostile and competitive relations between the union and management and between the worker and management persist. Interestingly, then, management continues antagonistic relations with its union counterpart by not encouraging the participatory processes. In a workplace environment that showcases employee involvement and unity, the attachment to participatory goals lacks substance when an economic downturn has workers scrambling for their individual interests. Standard Knapp's actions again reveal a "voice without true choice," as employees lack the input and control over job security to have an effective say in how the firm responds. Consequently, the social capital necessary for any participatory endeavor fails to materialize given these rather traditional economic relations.

With its meteoric growth rates and substantial yearly profits, Quad/Graphics' future appears as participation's next test case. Thus far, Quad's economic success allows it to bestow many luxuries upon its employees: education programs, generous compensation and medical benefits, a company-staffed wellness center, and day care. One of the firm's viewpoints that produces these services is the firm's commitment and trust in its workers. If a connection exists between economic success and a firm's participatory plan, then Quad's commitment to its participatory philosophy will undergo its first difficult assessment when its growth slows and its profit margins decline. If management supports the "Quad culture" methods and the workers sense its commitment to the participatory processes, the firm likely will weather a host of internecine battles.

Quad/Graphics has not experienced similar "growing pains" as the other two cases. The firm's owner has been astute and fortunate in exploiting a niche with superior technology in an aging industry. The firm also has aggressively erased competition and diversified into ancillary industries in the publishing process over the past fifteen years. The firm, then, treats its workers royally when it prospers and expands in the external marketplace. It seems that if, in its future, it faces increased competition and a diminishing market, then its aggressive history forecasts that the firm will rid itself of any unproductive measures. As its external market contracts, the firm looks to internal processes to cut costs. Now, if no strong attachment exists, or perhaps even with a strong attachment to participatory management, Quad may determine that its employee benefits eat into its competitiveness. Only with the firm's recognition that employee participation enhances worker health and company profit will the internal processes remain. But given the aforementioned economic downturn, it seems reasonable to assume many of the worker benefits now in place will be trimmed in the name of economic competition or making the firm "leaner."

This scenario underscores the contradictory nature of a firm's participatory commitments. To predict future behavior demands attention to present and prior action. Quad's behavior will change when its economic health changes. In the larger market arena, its behavior upholds traditional economic assumptions and action. Within the plant, its behavior favors an alternative participatory approach. With its present economic success, the two realms do not conflict. But given the likelihood of decreased growth and profits from today's staggering rates, the possibility of conflict between the two areas exists. When increased competition develops, it increases the likelihood that Quad will use the methods of the dominant economic system because those methods and that behavior have produced Quad's success.

Two related conclusions emerge from how firms and their workers discuss the relationship between their participatory decision-making processes and their profit-making success. First, if a firm uses profitability as the impetus for employee participation, then the firm's commitment to the participatory process is questionable. In effect, if management argues that workers participate easily when profits are comfortable but that workers tend to gripe and question the participatory process when profits decrease, then management has not adequately displayed and developed the value of participation. Management's excuses confuse the issue because management uses externally-determined criteria (i.e., profit) to evaluate an internally supported process. If participation receives internal support, which in all three firms it overwhelmingly does, then this decision-making process helps the firm be more productive. Yet management argues that when the profit-making results change, workers' attitudes toward a process that they apparently endorse changes. Usually, though, it is management's attitude that changes, and participation comes under attack. By implication, perhaps the external market system dictates internal firm relations hostile toward developing a participatory workplace. In the end, it seems the firm will most likely be more productive if it internally supports participation; but if it treats participation purely instrumentally, it will not produce the beneficial economics it expects.

The second conclusion is that, as a variety of worker attitudes affect how the participatory process proceeds and as workers have to function with contradictory roles, a firm also functions under contradictory roles. The firm, whether it remains management operated or employee operated, must compete in a system with predetermined rules that emphasize the simple economic equation of lowering costs and maximizing gain. However, the firm also operates with a participatory work force that emphasizes other goals and values that do not always or easily conform to lowering costs and maximizing gain. Given these sometimes different and conflictual agendas, the firm must decide how much "friction" is worthwhile. In its most simple terms, this equation is the tradeoff between efficiency and democracy. But a firm cannot err on the side of democracy—in economic terms this means err on the side of "slack"—because too much slack in a firm makes it less competitive and ultimately economically vulnerable. If, then, a firm experiences conflict between the preestablished, external market forces and its internal, participatory commitments, it is likely that, for the sake of survival, the latter will undergo revision. Interestingly, the necessity that dictates the second conclusion (i.e., mere existence) allows us to understand the less than complete support that the firm gives to maintaining the additional goals that make up a participatory work force. Given these possible pressures, it is little wonder that participatory plans experience substantial change and produce a variety of interpretations.

CONCLUSION

The preceding analysis discusses specific variables that affect how workers respond in a participatory workplace. At Standard Knapp, the present hostile relations between management and most union workers reveals a history of antagonism between the two groups. Perhaps, then, Standard Knapp's participatory workplace offers its own contradiction. It appears as a continuation of the hostility between the two groups, as now the unionized workers have the firm's recognition to "voice" their concerns, and it also appears as a new forum for the bridging of different interests. In pursuit of the latter goal, the firm seeks to overcome the historical divisiveness that limits competitiveness today. But, by upholding the union's power, many of the unionized workers refrain from entering into the participatory endeavor because they do not trust the firm's first steps toward building trust and mutual commitment.

If the union's presence blocks the building of trust at Standard Knapp, it is precisely the informal relations that generate trust, commitment, and attachment that Quad/Graphics' workers claim give them a sense of efficacy. Moreover, these informal relations appear most important to employees, as they seek control and influence over their immediate decision-making environments before they concern themselves with larger company decisions. Or, more accurately, if workers sense that they exercise control over their immediate job activities, then they more likely can reconcile themselves to a lack of control over the firm's direction and investments. Without any participatory effect over their immediate area, workers then tend to extend their criticisms about influence and input to all levels of the firm's control. At Orange Handling, without the important informal relations between management and the mechanics and without the codified internal structure designed to promote participation and educate the workers, employees and management stew in a pot of frustration.

Despite the individual variables that make each participatory firm distinct, my central discussion exposes the contradictory nature of the participatory firm in general. As Hirschman notes, the participatory firm attempts to initiate "voice"; but even if workers adequately adjust from "exit" behavior to voice behavior, they must know when to exercise voice and when to exercise patience and compromise. In a sense, since they disdain the political system, and since the system does not teach citizenship, workers must educate themselves as to the requirements of good citizenship, even if it remains only at the company level. This result appears as an inversion of the typical argument that participatory theory makes about the transfer of local participation to national participation. In addition, just as workers need to know when to initiate and when to obey, management must somehow adjust to the new requirement of when to lead, how to lead, and when to follow or guide. At Standard Knapp and Orange Handling especially, without clear guidelines for management and workers as to their new roles, workers begin to interpret their roles and the role of participation differently. With different views, expectations vary; and when workers define success or interaction differently, conflict and frustration result.

These problems appear resolvable with more decision-making power and better communication, clear roles and expectations, and creative experimentation that values other goals than mere profit and productivity. Yet the power of the market system overrides the alternative values that a participatory firm may seek. As Rothschild and Whitt note, given that the firm must first satisfy instrumental needs and requirements to exist, other more substantive values often undergo continual reevaluation.[28] With the firm's questioning of the values it once upheld, the workers respond by questioning the firm's commitment to the value itself. The participatory firm, then, swims against the market's tide, and the market's power often makes a participatory firm forsake, if only for a time, its substantive commitments. Owing to the market's dominant power, the lesson may be quite simply that compromise will be part of the participatory process. Without the necessary schooling for both the workers and management about how to compromise among themselves when under pressure from the market, participatory firms easily succumb to a number of contradictory procedures and so-called market "requirements."

NOTES

1. Anthony Sampson, *Company Man: The Rise and Fall of Corporate Life* (New York: Random House, 1995), 8.

2. Ibid., 7–8.

3. Edward S. Greenberg, "The Consequences of Worker Participation: A Clarification of the Theoretical Literature," *Social Science Quarterly* 56, no. 2 (1975): 191–209.

4. Ronald M. Mason, *Participatory and Workplace Democracy: A Theoretical Critique of Liberalism* (Carbondale: Southern Illinois University Press, 1982), 182.

5. See Joyce Rothschild and J. Allen Whitt, *The Cooperative Workplace: Potentials and Dilemmas of Organizational Democracy and Participation* (New York: Cambridge University Press, 1986), 66–72.

6. Jon Elster, *Sour Grapes: Studies in the Subversion of Rationality* (New York: Cambridge University Press, 1983), 33–44. Elster refers to by-products as states that can never be brought about "intelligently or intentionally." While participation can be instituted intelligently with specific purposes, it is my argument here that participation does not necessarily breed other-regarding action.

7. Robert D. Putnam, *Making Democracy Work: Civic Traditions in Modern Italy* (Princeton, N.J.: Princeton University Press, 1993), 182.

8. Rothschild and Whitt, *Cooperative Workplace*, 189.

9. Ibid., 147.

10. Francis Fukuyama, *Trust: The Social Virtues and the Creation of Prosperity* (New York: The Free Press, 1995), 281.

11. The introduction to this book discusses the possible relationship between associational life and capitalism's power.

12. Robert E. Lane, "Market Justice, Political Justice," *American Political Science Review* 80, no. 2 (1986): 383–402.

13. Albert O. Hirschman, *Exit, Voice, and Loyalty: Responses to Decline in Firms, Organizations, and States* (Cambridge: Harvard University Press, 1970), 15. See also Chapter 8.

14. Ibid., 32–33.

15. Ibid., 33. Italics his.

16. Ibid., 79–82.

17. Ibid., 79.

18. Employee interview, Quad/Graphics, Saratoga, N.Y., 12 and 14 April 1995.

19. For more information on what I claim are the noneffects of the nonrespondents, see Appendix A.

20. Employee interview, Quad/Graphics, Saratoga, N.Y., 12 April 1995.

21. Employee interview, Quad/Graphics, Saratoga, N.Y., 14 April 1995.

22. Carris Reels in Rutland, Vt., is the one firm to my knowledge that first informed its employees of the possibilities of employee ownership and participation and asked for their input as to how the firm should involve the employees in deciding all the firm's decisions. As of January 1996, the firm was in the process of becoming employee owned and operated.

23. G. A. Cohen, *History, Labour, and Freedom: Themes from Marx* (Oxford: Clarendon Press, 1988), 263.

24. The question that arises from the apparent bias in who responded in the surveys and interviews is whether the sample is representative. As Appendix A relates, and as I explained in Chapter 2, self-selection issues are possible. But, given the variety of sources that all reveal similar themes, I believe the workers who did not respond would offer similar, if not more hostile, complaints against the firm(s). Frustration and anger are apparent in the sources researched; additional examples of the same would only emphasize these themes.

25. Employee interview, Quad/Graphics, Saratoga Springs, N.Y., 12 April 1995.

26. Interviewees at Standard Knapp and Orange Handling especially gave examples of how management spoke of the need for cutting costs but then made expenditures that the employees thought excessive and inappropriate.

27. Employee interview, Orange Handling, Albany, N.Y., 17 May 1995.

28. Rothschild and Whitt, *Cooperative Workplace*, 189.

Chapter 7　　　　　THE "ROUGH MIX" OF A
　　　　　　　　　PARTICIPATORY WORKPLACE

Political theorists have extolled the educative benefits of participation since Aristotle wrote about the citizen as being intended to live in the polity. But Jane Mansbridge argues that many theorists do not explicitly claim that participation changes individual behavior. In particular, she claims that Rousseau's general will "does not entail deliberation, nor most of what we mean today by political participation. It means instead recognizing as an individual what is in the common good and acting upon that recognition."[1] However, Rousseau writes that "The passing from the state of nature to the civil society produces a remarkable change in man; . . . his faculties are so exercised and developed, his mind is so enlarged, his sentiments so enobled."[2] It seems that the different interpretations note a different emphasis for participation's effects. Aristotle and Rousseau understand political participation as the method to create virtuous citizens, whereas Mansbridge seems to value participation as a developmental end in itself. These values need not be exclusive, but Mansbridge's emphasis appears to concentrate on the benefits that accrue to the individual more so than the individual's benefit to the polity. As an example of Mansbridge's thinking, Arnold Kaufman states that participatory democracy's function "is and always has been . . . the contribution it can make to the development of human powers of thought, feeling, and action."[3] Kaufman's view of individual development, then, is more expressive than the earlier theorists' orientation toward instilling and promoting virtue.

Political theorists, though, are as interested in participation's effects on the polity as they are in its effects on the individual. Rousseau, for instance, focuses on how to build and sustain commitment to the common good. While J. S. Mill explained how participation enhances an individual's development (i.e., it creates virtue, activity, and intellectual stimulation), one of his concerns was that these traits would provide attention for the general good and for a legitimate, stable government.[4] Of recent note, it is Pateman who took the theoretical concern for the polity's welfare and made it the ultimate objective of participation. Thus, participatory theory argues that, not only does the individual develop through participation, but also this interaction creates the possibility for a democratic society.

With workplace participation, participatory theory offers one method to solve both individual and collective ills. If individuals sense that their efforts, in any number of common endeavors with others, assist in achieving a mutual goal, the theory argues that these empowered people flourish as well as over time develop a public perspective.[5] My task is to flesh out what I believe are the additional, underappreciated considerations for participatory theory. One concern focuses on the microlevel of individual attitudes and behavior, as well as how irrational expectations may affect how each person participates. The other concern focuses on the macrolevel, as each worker and each firm exist in a social context today that makes worker participation and its importance difficult to embrace and sustain. Participatory theory can offer more valuable and predictable insights if it can articulate how these concerns, both micro and macro, affect its particular assumptions for individual development and social action.

I believe the case studies reveal some of the contradictions that today's examples of workplace participation create. Participatory theory spends scant attention to the pressing practical issues that the cases reveal because the theory does not assume or consider the effects of incremental social change on the participatory experience. Given the constraints of what Hirschman calls the dominant economic ideology, the market system's inability to accommodate participatory changes limits and perverts participation's effects. The contradictory nature of today's participatory experiences is that, even if firms adopt participatory reforms, the workers often display conventional market behavior because of their inexperience with the new structures that the participatory changes create, their lack of commitment to participatory values, and perhaps from their general lack of comfort with participation's new demands on them. Moreover, given their inexperience, workers look for management's level of commitment to participation and react accordingly. Management, too, falls victim to advocating a structural change that it often does not fully support or implement.

But I want to emphasize that while critics often deride management's lack of commitment, and the employees' subsequent "voice without true choice," as an example of capitalist co-optation or accommodation, management's actions must also be viewed within the same prism as the worker's attitudes and actions. In essence, I think the case studies reveal management's retention of power, despite their claims for employee ownership and participation, for a reason other than simply to maintain control. The reason is that management often reverts to its traditional role—just as workers revert to "exit behavior" if presented with conflictual cues—given the contradictions inherent in participatory endeavors within the dominant market economy. This emphasis, then, does not unilaterally find fault with management and its inability to decentralize decision-making control. Rather, the emphasis points to the inability of all actors, both workers and management, to effectively implement participatory reforms and then act in accordance to these reforms given the power and tradition of the dominant market system.

Edwards, along with many other Marxist thinkers, claims that without a collective voice for systemic change, along with a conscious political movement, the entire project of worker participation remains more a human relations ploy by management than a radical change for worker development or action.[6] But given the power of the dominant economic system and its ability to socialize workers to its values and its conception of justice, it seems utopian to expect fundamental changes in how society perceives work and politics. In the absence of radical change, it will be within the milieu of economic individualism and capitalist control that participatory theory must assess its propositions. To simply write off participation's possibilities because of these constraints is to submit to the very attitudes and processes that participation can change. The project, then, is for participatory theory to recognize what forces, whether individual or social or governmental, limit its proposals and then work toward either overcoming or affecting those limiting forces. In turn, the project needs to assess what individual and social changes are possible given the limits of present workplace attempts at change.

Finally, in addition to these limiting conditions, the methodological constraints for evaluating participation's effects remain daunting. Mansbridge reports that, in the case of the educative effects of participation, "The postulated effects [take] subtle forms that [can]not easily be captured in empirical studies of relatively small numbers of people. First, it [is] hard to find situations in which a researcher [can] measure the qualities of people before and after participation. . . . Second, changes in people's heads are hard to measure."[7] With workplace participation, the difficulty lies in determining conclusively whether participation is the variable that dictates subsequent feelings of empowerment and political action. Perhaps any simple change from the hierarchical and bureaucratic relations typical of most workplaces to a somewhat decentralized workplace would cause changes in attitudes and behavior. Consequently, it remains a possibility that participatory workplaces exhibit changes in worker attitudes and behavior because any change in a firm's design, and not necessarily a participatory change, creates beneficial attitudinal changes.[8]

In fact, management's recognition of participation's effects has produced a host of advocates of participatory workplaces, all with different methods and different objectives. As a result, confusion reigns as similar research results lead to divergent interpretations. Standard Knapp's participatory process serves as a relevant case. If viewed from a managerial point of view, the worker's participation adversely affects economic performance, as it tends to highlight and exacerbate lasting tensions. However, a participatory theorist can argue that, while Standard Knapp suffers some economic costs from worker participation, the firm benefits in the long run from worker involvement, as employees do recognize a limited ability to influence decisions. Viewed from both points of view, the firm comes to represent the rough-and-tumble world of democratic contestation. It is an ongoing affiliation, full of compromise and frustration, yet full of small victories too.

The different perspectives center on what each approach values. Management and business-oriented research measures structural changes as they affect productivity.[9] Also, given the increasingly competitiveness in and downsizing of the1990s, business seeks methods to develop better decision makers. Participation, then, is of value, as it improves these instrumental ends. Employee empowerment may be considered an integral component in creating productivity, or it may be a corollary occurrence; but it remains primarily a by-product according to management thinking. From this perspective, democracy is primarily a form of decision making. Conversely, participatory theory views participation as the path to worker development. In turn, engaged, motivated workers, who sense their ability to control their environment, build the necessary conduits that sustain democratic citizenship. Participatory theory values participation because it generates efficacy and empowerment. They define democracy, then, as a method for empowering workers to control their lives.[10]

Ultimately, participatory theorists argue, efficacious workers do increase a firm's productivity. In general, to distinguish between the firm's concerns and the theorist's arguments is to distinguish between short-term interests versus long-range planning and how a firm's goals mesh with its employees' goals. While it appears that the distinction between short- and long-term goals should interconnect—for instance, that a firm needs a complementary short- and long-range vision—it is also true that they can conflict—for instance, that long-term goals often take a backseat when economic survival focuses attention on short-run solutions. Also, as the case studies show, management institutes a participatory plan with little employee input, as if any form of participation will increase productivity. But viewed this way, participation creates more difficulties than it solves, as in the case of Standard Knapp and Orange Handling, because vast differences exist between the firm's goals and the employees' expectations. As noted, without a clear understanding of what participation seeks to address, both management and workers remain leery of its possibilities and contemptuous of its half-baked implementation.

If management and workers have different ideas about what participation means, the confusion intensifies as the workers themselves bring different identities and expectations to the participatory experiment. The case studies reveal that workers want to maintain a recognizable dichotomy between work and other areas of their life. Work is understood as a necessity in order to have the resources to enjoy or take part in those activities that one chooses. Participatory theorists believe that work and other life pursuits interconnect, and that empowerment at work will lead to greater involvement in political matters. To be sure, political life need not absorb private life, but the theorists argue that the transformation in the workers' development will transfer to that workers' attitudes and behavior when considering public issues. However, workers' words and actions resist any connection between their work lives and political action. Because work often comes first—that is, because personal sacrifices are necessary to get ahead at work—workers tend to isolate work activity from other activities. Its necessity and its sacrifices place it in a mental category separate from family life and personal enjoyment. One worker writes, "The more I'm asked to participate at work, the anxiety I feel about not doing the things I want to accomplish becomes greater."[11] If workers maintain the distinction between their work activities and their outside life, if in fact they look at work participation as an intrusion on what they truly want to do, participation will have only negative effects on their outlook.

Participatory theorists respond that only after people engage in participating can they begin to recognize the benefits of participation for themselves and for their groups. It is only with this "leap of faith" into the practice of participation can one understand its benefits. To view participation as an intrusion on other life activities does not allow its benefits to affect oneself. But to grant participation such priority and give it such importance in a worker's life disregards other aspects of that worker's life. To believe participation changes a worker no matter what the circumstances may be devalues the beliefs and experiences that worker has had before his or her participatory experience. One Quad/Graphics worker succinctly recognizes that "Quad allowed me to develop. Has Quad changed me [with its participatory process]? No, it existed already . . . it was my personality. The way it is supposed to be, in theory? No, [the firm] does not nurture you."[12]

This quotation reveals important differences both from what Quad/Graphics participatory culture attempts to bring about and from what participatory theory argues. Despite the firm's "culture" of trust and involvement, of instilling responsibility and pushing workers to actively find ways to improve their immediate work area, this worker feels that the firm does not nurture this type of behavior. The interviewee claims that no matter what the firm's plan may be, some workers will participate more than others, and some will consistently be more involved than others. The quotation's implication is that participation does not transform workers as much as it allows participatory personalities to flourish. The difference here is that the central variable for change becomes the worker's personality and not participation itself. This leads to the troubling view that some personalities are more suited to participation than others, and perhaps deliberation and responsibility are not characteristics that all or most people can develop. If this is so, participation may be a detriment as much as an aid in democracy's development.

But to begin to label some personalities as participatory and others as not strikes at the democratic heart of participatory theory. To some degree, participationists advocate a "rough" equality of talent or capability, or perhaps of a general human ability and need for interaction. To claim that some people are better able or more likely to participate begins to undermine the universalizability of participationists' claims and of their application. In her discussion of "a democratic personality," Carol Gould lists several characteristics which seem generalizable: reciprocity, open-mindedness, flexibility, commitment, responsibility, sharing, communicativeness, and supportiveness.[13] She begins her list with initiative as the first trait, the kind of initiative that the worker exhibits in her response. However, as the case studies reveal, initiative can be stunted, not just by the participatory design, but also by the contradictory impulses that the worker feels in a participatory or "voice" firm within an "exit" market economy. As Hirschman notes, the uncertainty of when to exercise voice, when to exercise exit, and when to be patient can undermine any worker's predisposition to activity and initiative.[14] In fact, the firm may unjustly become the "brunt" of the employee's frustration over his or her difficulty in determining when to act and how to act. In several instances, interviewees voice a general disgust with the firm which may result, in part, from their inability to define what role they must play in the participatory process.

The fact that there may be distinctive participatory personalities need not be participation's deathblow. In fact, to recognize that some workers have a greater capability to benefit from participation, and not hold participatory plans in contempt, is a first step in understanding the diversity of attitudes and experiences that workers bring to any workplace. Just as Gould has done, participatory theory can begin to note individual characteristics that facilitate participatory success. The intention of participatory theory is not to select-out those participatory personalities for a firm's benefit. Though, from a management perspective, this activity already has supporters. Edward E. Lawler writes that "Both the job enrichment approach and the team approach require individuals who value internal rewards. . . . Those . . . who do not look to their work for this kind of satisfaction simply cannot be tolerated in an organization that designs work to involve employees. They are in a very real sense uncontrollable."[15]

Again, the firm and the worker find themselves caught between conflicting messages. It seems that if some personalities are better able to become participatory, then the firm should select those workers to help the firm compete effectively but with participatory means. Yet this selection process undermines the democratic objective of participatory workplaces and participatory theory in general by rewarding specific abilities, just as any workplace today rewards specific skills. For workers, if certain traits are preferable, just as certain skills are preferable, some will make themselves more "marketable" by changing their attitudes and behavior if it is at all possible. But the market dictates these self-improvement attempts, not participation itself. Moreover, another argument against a selection bias is that common deliberation among a variety of workers seems to be an important condition of democratic freedom. If participatory theory seeks ultimately to create a truly empowered citizenry, the ability to express one's views and the opportunity to interact with others who may disagree seems a fundamental aspect of a healthy, vigorous democratic culture.

It seems that the management perspective emphasizes typical exit behavior: Get rid of those who make the firm less efficient or productive. In this case, it would be those lacking some of Gould's characteristics for democratic interaction.

But the alternative response, to paraphrase Jefferson, seeks to overcome the problems of the employees' lack of democratic traits with the recognition of and the working toward developing more of those traits.[16] This rejects the notion that we must exclude some from participatory workplaces because they lack the experiences or education necessary for participatory success. To exclude people because they lack democratic personalities is truly antidemocratic. Rather, participationists and democratic workplaces need to assess what participatory traits workers exhibit and what traits the workers lack to focus on what each workplace needs for participation to succeed. In this scenario, participation is not a "cure-all," for that frustrates a firm and its workers. Employees need to recognize participation as an educational method to assist them at their job. With a less-heroic role for participation, it is less likely to become a lightning rod for most of the firm's criticism, especially in difficult times.

What are some of the characteristics of a participatory personality? From the case studies, the characteristics that the most participatory workers share are similar to the well-documented characteristics that active voters display. Age, education, and previous participatory experience are some of the variables that affect a worker's motivation to participate. But to reemphasize the democratic nature of any participatory experiment, the lack of these characteristics does not necessarily imply that participation will fail. It means only that a firm must recognize what participatory resources it has and use those resources in implementing its participatory plan. My focus is on how to incorporate the individuality of today's workers into the participatory mechanism. The solution I advocate in accepting the differences among workers and adjusting to them makes an initial attempt to deal with present participatory problems and yet accommodate the democratic objective of participatory theory. The fundamental problem of creating individual commitment to the general will, or to the firm if we reduce the scale, still persists, but the undemocratic tendency toward selecting only "participatory" people to play a part is deemphasized.

The recognition of a participatory or a democratic personality appears antithetical to participatory theory because much of current theory gives little attention to the differences people bring to participate. Aristotle, however, did argue that the masses displayed a "collective intelligence" far greater than any few rulers could. He wrote, "Each individually will be a worse judge than the experts, but when all work together, they are better, or at any rate, no worse."[17] Aristotle thought that a variety of contributions would lead to a better deliberative judgment. But it is important to note that Aristotle thought moral and intellectual virtue were essential components of good citizenship, that "The goodness of the citizen is just this—to know well how to rule and be ruled."[18] Today, though, the need for virtue to master the duties of good citizenship has been replaced by the less demanding enunciation of individual rights. Instead, current participatory theory spends its time focusing on the less contentious arena of virtue and the more "controllable" area of establishing institutional arrangements that allow participation to operate.

But as most democratic theorists from the Greeks onward agree, habits and mores are as essential as laws and constitutions.[19] Without the tradition and habits of participation, workers at best are confused about what the firm expects of them. A firm without a clear understanding of what participation means often fails to communicate consistently what it expects of its workers. When trouble erupts, participation becomes the culprit, and the workers and the firm the victims, in participatory theory's search for the "correct" structural requirements that will produce citizenship.

By noting the existence of participatory personalities we can begin to clarify what affects participation. While participatory theory focuses on the interactive dynamics of participation itself, I argue that external forces first affect any participatory endeavor. These forces are both macro and micro in nature. The macro influences come from the uncertain, often conflicting dictates of the market economy in which the individual and the firm function. The micro cues are the personal characteristics and experiences that affect one's ability and desire to participate—traits, attitudes toward work. Given these forces, any participatory attempt will involve some who are eager and energetic and some who remain hesitant to accept the participatory changes. In general, the former often become so-called leaders or simply successful participants, and the latter may follow typical exit behavior and either acquiesce or leave.

With these different attitudes and behaviors, the question becomes how to sustain participation and encourage the hesitant to participate. Democratic workplace research has isolated several determinants that promote the participatory process. Klein and Hall's 1988 study of thirty-seven ESOP firms with 2,804 employees concludes that the principal factors that determine workers' satisfaction with their ESOP involve *both* company and individual characteristics. Internally, employees "are most satisfied with stock ownership when (a) the firm makes large annual contributions, . . . (b) the company maintains an extensive communications program, (c) management is strongly committed to employee ownership [and] the ESOP is an older plan."[20] While these structural conditions have become the benchmark for participatory theory's proposals, it is interesting to note that no deliberative process is seen as important or necessary by the employees or by the researchers.

Also of interest, and apparently in contradiction to my argument about the characteristics of the democratic personality most likely to participate, Klein and Hall report that an individual's education "is negatively related to ESOP satisfaction, perhaps because more educated employees recognize the financial risks associated with employee ownership." Also, to add strength to participatory theory's emphasis on internal mechanisms overcoming individual characteristics, Klein and Hall report, "The significant interaction between education and ESOP communications suggests that an active ESOP communications program may assuage the skepticism of highly educated employees; the more active the company's ESOP communications programs, the stronger and more positive the correlation between employee education and ESOP satisfaction. Here, an ESOP characteristic may compensate for or offset an employee characteristic that typically leads to dissatisfaction with the plan."[21] These findings need not destroy my argument. Klein's and Hall's results focus on action after the firm has initiated an ESOP and the educated employees remain aware of the potential drawbacks. My argument about the influence of education applies to the time before and to the time of a plan's initiation. Educated employees, just as they remain well aware of the pitfalls, can be one segment that first recognizes the potential benefits of employee ownership and participation. In addition, the deliberative process itself must play some educative role, as workers' attitudes begin to be shaped by their interaction with others.

For any plan to gain support and take effect, employees must perceive how gains outweigh costs and must expand their notion of what counts as a "gain." At Standard Knapp and Orange Handling, a group of educated employees once did and still do believe that participation's benefits outnumber its costs. Perhaps a more insightful interpretation of Klein's and Hall's statistical conclusion would understand education as a mediating influence between undivided support and utter contempt for employee ownership. Their research recognizes that education renders some employees not wholly dissatisfied but rather "leery" of full-fledged enthusiasm, principally because of the financial risks. Only with a firm's ongoing commitment to effective company communication does this educative "accountability" begin to subside. Perhaps then a healthy degree of deliberation and questioning will keep a firm committed to its ownership and participatory endeavors.

Interestingly, when this questioning does not exist, when employees fully embrace employee ownership, some often end up disappointed. I have argued that enthusiastic proponents often project irrational expectations upon participatory arrangements. Similarly, Klein and Hall conclude that, "Employees who desire a great deal of influence in decision-making tend to be less satisfied with the ESOP than those who desire relatively little influence in decision-making."[22] Though this conclusion supports my contentions, Klein and Hall study primarily privately held firms, firms such as Orange Handling and Quad/Graphics in this study. These firms typically limit employees from voting their shares, thereby restricting employee input to their immediate decision-making environment. Without a clear company message about ownership and participation's role, or, in other words, allowing the employees to interpret the firm's participatory attempt differently, Orange Handling produces a disgruntled work force and a frustrated management who openly question the benefits of the firm's participatory practices.

Ironically, with a clearer vision of participation's limits and the knowledge that some decisons are not under their control, Quad/Graphics' employees report greater satisfaction with the firm, their job, and their degree of control and influence. Rothschild and Whitt explain this apparent irony when they note that, "Workers would register even lower levels of satisfaction [with their work than those workers in higher classes report] if it were not for the fact that . . . workers tend to scale down what they expect from the jobs."[23] In Quad/Graphics' case, their empowerment may come at the expense of their power over company decisions. In a sense, Quad/Graphics allows its workers to decide on the most immediate, particular issues and not on the most general, most common decisions. This state of affairs contradicts Rousseau's writings, as he argues that if citizens became involved in the administration of particular matters the republic would dissolve into individualized disputes. For a state of self-legislating citizens to prosper, it must focus on general issues of what binds them together and what satisfies the good of all. In addition, given my emphasis on the inherently conflictual messages that participatory firms provide when they exist in a market economy, the cases show that management is not always clear about participation's goals. In fact, communication alone cannot alleviate the contradictions, since the firm's participatory actions produce friction with the firm's external, market environment.

Standard Knapp is a better example of Klein's and Hall's conclusion that those who desire more decision-making influence are often less satisfied with the ESOP than those who desire less influence. Standard Knapp employees vote their shares, and the firm has established an accessible management and communications network. Though employees report they do not concern themselves with the "nuts and bolts" of the firm's decisions, and management notes that it is difficult to sustain employee interest in the minutiae of decision making, employees still believe that management does not fully inform the employees of all details. In every interview, every worker and official cited the lack of trust as the most pressing problem for the firm. While participatory theorists most likely would remedy Standard Knapp's situation with a greater emphasis on communication, the firm's management would most likely respond—as would Orange Handling's management—that the employees show little sustained interest in understanding the issues the firm faces. In addition, as one Standard Knapp employee remarks about "his" fellow workers, "Expectations have to be realistic. We're not all going to be instant millionaires [when we become employee owned]. Maybe they believe all owners are rich!"[24]

The internal characteristics that sustain participation and encourage the hesitant include instrumental ends. If workers recognize beneficial results—in some instances an economic return, in others the firm's satisfactory commitment, and in most a combination of both results—then employees view ownership and participation favorably. But the fact that some employees' irrational expectations muddle participation's success allows critics to wonder whether participation is at all desirable. As Jon Elster argues, "In some cases a little discussion is a dangerous thing, worse in fact than no discussion at all, . . . if it makes some but not all persons align themselves on the common ground. . . . Also, an inferior outcome may result if discussion brings about partial adherence to rationality in all participants, rather than full adherence in some and none in others."[25] In effect, Elster claims that the inadequate attempt to alter the clearly established and understood values of exit behavior in the workplace to include voice behavior leads to at least suboptimal, if not fatal, economic consequences. He also argues that the attempt to replace negotiation with pseudo-consensus can lead to greater conflict, as in Orange Handling's case. These results occur because not all employees accept or adhere to the new voice behavior, and, thus, differing methods are employed by different agents in addressing and resolving a firm's issues.

Hirschman further compounds the problem by arguing that, although exit behavior dominates American thinking, "To some extent, exit is itself responsible for the emergence of its opposite." Hirschman means that while Americans maintain a psychological commitment to exit behavior and the market economy, they can come to cherish an alternative if they choose to engage in the typical exit behavior of leaving one's group as they become "socially mobile." As an example, he argues that immigrants tend to show an undying allegiance to American principles and institutions because they commit significant efforts and money to leave their homelands. He claims that "The result [of their high price in severing ties] is a strong psychological compulsion to like that for which so large a payment has been made." While the example seems inapplicable to nonimmigrants, Hirschman states that the "United States [has] long been the country of last resort . . . exit from the country has long been peculiarly unthinkable. . . . Situations may arise, however, in which qualms can no longer be repressed." Under these questionable times, people have several options to choose. Hirschman argues that most will follow three steps: one, "Another exit may be attempted, but this time within the confines of the country"; two, "Since the country cannot be at fault, responsibility for unhappiness is assumed to lie with the person"; or three, "If the country is too obviously at fault . . . then voice will come into its own."[26] Though exit may be responsible for its opposite, it is important to note that voice occurs only as a last resort. In essence, all other options, including a psychological "self-depreciation," must occur before voice is chosen. This process shows the power of the socialization to exit behavior.

It remains uncertain whether a voice option becomes wholly beneficial for individuals who choose not to exit. Voice can become a valuable choice to replace exit behavior, but an irony is that the high costs associated with either reducing the value of exit or strenthening the value of voice can also produce workers who may "overvalue" voice's influence. The workers who often express frustration and anger, such as those employees at Orange Handling who reveal disappointment because management acknowledges it sold employee ownership "too sweetly," represent unfulfilled expectations. It may be true that management does not allow employees the control or input that the employees thought they would have, but, at the same time, the costs of choosing to become a participatory firm can create expectations that the firm cannot satisfy—expectations that may project a specific political agenda. In this sense, both employee ownership and participation become scapegoats for perhaps, as I have argued, either unrealistic or irrational expectations.

But let me emphasize that, while these possible results present an explanation for the lack of participatory success or for employees' rejection of participation, such results do not apply to all firms. I recognize that the potential for a negative critique of participation comes from the variety of attitudes and expectations that make up any workplace and from the apparent contradictions that Hirschman notes the workers must cope with to realize participatory mechanisms. My argument, in other words, is that the ability to recognize these expectations and contradictions will decrease the possibility of their unintended participatory effects. In both Hirschman's and Elster's examples, the combination of the two different mechanisms of voice and exit for prescribing and understanding behavior often produce undesirable results. A participatory workplace, which attempts to combine voice behavior with exit "realities," often confuses its participants and creates unforeseen troubles.

Elster's argument that a little discussion or voice may lead to unintended consequences attempts to raise doubt about, not just Habermas's "ideal speech situation," but the generally accepted idea in much of democratic theory that any degree of participation and/or interaction improves the outcome of the political process. He claims that "Even in the good society the process of rational discussion could be fragile, and vulnerable to individual or collective self-deception." As the case studies show, individuals bring different expectations to their participatory workplaces, and these expectations, some rational, others not, determine the individual satisfaction and collective success of the endeavor. But Elster states, "To make it [public discussion] stable there would be a need for structures—political institutions—that could easily introduce an element of domination."[27] This notion mirrors the thinking and the emphasis of participatory theory. Given that individual differences can disrupt the process of participation, participatory theorists and Elster see the need for processes or structures that transcend the destructive differences individuals exhibit.

By Elster's own logic, though, his solution seems simple minded because it attempts to resolve the fragility of public discussion by establishing institutions and procedures governed and operated by those same people who exhibit this fragility in the first place. Elster may respond that these institutions would overcome the frailties of decision making, but to add layers of procedures and structures to existing structures, or to replace one set of institutions with another, seems to encourage an instrumental misreading of the problem. The problem may not be how to control the negative effects of participation, but rather how to come to value the deliberative diversity necessary to articulate a common vision. Certainly, lawmaking and bureaucracy seek to overcome the arbitrariness that Elster believes can be inherent in public discourse, but the alternative to irrational decision making can be something less dramatic than institutional development. If nothing else, the strength of participatory theory and workplace participation comes from a citizenry that seeks a change from bureaucratic and regulatory dictates. They seek the ability to have influence, if not control, over areas where domineering institutions have come to override collective and individual initiative. To be sure, Elster astutely identifies the irrationality and arbitrariness of public discourse and how the political process suffers from such action. But to remedy this irrationality with institutions that employ these irrational individuals and that develop their own irrational organizational behaviors simply transfers the problem from one context to another.

Hirschman offers a less dramatic and, for many, a less appealing vision of the dynamics between rational and irrational behavior, between participation expectations and realizations, and between exit and voice behavior. He concludes that "Conditions are seldom favorable for the emergence of any stable and optimally effective mix of exit and voice." The reasons for this seemingly unachievable mix lies in the different expectations individuals come to internalize. He claims, "The effectiveness of the less familiar mode [voice in our case] becomes not only more uncertain, but tends to be *increasingly underestimated*. The reason is that effective use of the less familiar mechanism requires that its power be discovered or rediscovered whereas the preferred mechanism is routinely familiar; since quite properly we dare not believe in creative discoveries until they have happened, we will underestimate the effectiveness of voice when exit is dominant."[28] In effect, Hirschman argues that we can only become accustomed to voice behavior by practicing it regularly, for we have become accustomed to exit in voice's absence. Because one mechanism remains, not only dominant, but preferred by workers and citizens, the tendency to employ voice is much weaker than exit. At participatory workplaces, which must exist in an exit-dominated external arena, management and workers must exhibit an ongoing use of voice behavior to offset the preferences, the habits, and the well-worn experiences of employee exit beliefs and behavior. Any management behavior that appears exit related is fodder for workers who question the endeavor, and most workers question the participatory endeavor because of the dominant exit mechanisms. Similarly, if workers maintain exit behavior, management questions its participatory processes and its efforts to promote employee voice.

Hirschman's conclusions, then, temper the starkness of Elster's conclusions. Because of the irrationality of workers and citizens, Elster opts for greater institutional stability in determining the collective good. Yet, it seems that much of the fervor for changes toward workplace participation evolve from the dissatisfaction with the institutions we create. People today appear to seek out a measure of control in their lives that they perceive has been lost to faceless institutions and written procedures. In fact, as more and more communities seek local control of issues, individuals often claim that established procedures appear arbitrary and that the rules lack the necessary insight and expertise to warrant any legitimacy. But Hirschman's insights reveal that community or employee displeasure for a firm's actions, and the desire for change, may not be enough to challenge established institutions and norms that cause the displeasure. What Hirschman offers, though, is not only the recognition of the difficulty of change, but the possibility that despite the suboptimal results, a mix of both voice and exit can exist. This recognition appears as a crucial first step in creating any combination of the two behaviors in economic activity.

For participatory theory, the recognition of a "rough mix"—by this I mean the congruence of apparently contradictory forces such as participation within the exit market economy—means that the theory needs to assess its propositions given the power of the exit-dominated marketplace. This does not mean that participatory theory must lose sight of its final aspirations of employee empowerment and the development of democratic citizenship. Rather, Hirschman's arguments about the external environment and my claims about individual predispositions serve to narrow participatory theory's expectations in order for it to claim minor changes as successes. In the initial stages of my argument, I offered a model of concentric circles for participatory theory to measure its development. Emanating out from the individual within a participatory firm, each circle represents a step toward the goals of participatory theory. The first circle could be employee empowerment, followed by complete employee control of the firm, and the final circle could be the fulfillment of a democratic culture. While firms like Standard Knapp and Orange Handling present as many difficulties as they do promises, Quad/Graphics seems to make a first step to the most immediate circle. The Quad employees note a sense of job efficacy and feel that they have the ability to influence immediate decisions. They acknowledge the trust the firm has in them, and they typically try to reciprocate by at least staying involved.

However, these employee feelings of satisfaction and power are only a first step, as they emerge from the less than democratic methods of indoctrination or perhaps of the employees' feigned loyalty. But as Hirschman informs us, this mix of participatory voice in an exit-dominated arena generally remains less than ideal. For participatory theory to gain relevance, it must focus on understanding and accommodating the difficulties of the "rough mix" and not on the failures of measuring up to its ideals. Any attempt at a combination of exit and voice is a form of success, but to be aware of what restricts participatory attempts allows theorists and employees to better understand how to combat the restrictions and how to assess participation's effects.

Finally, let me attempt to respond to the critique that Bachrach levels at Greenberg's research on the Northwest plywood firms that could apply to my research as well. Bachrach states, "In essence, Greenberg's study can be viewed as an in-depth analysis of repressive worker participation. Indeed, he may be right that democratically controlled enterprises cannot effect social change or overcome prevalent market values. However, his study throws no light on the issue, since ... he ends up studying ... anti-democratic rather than democratic enterprises."[29] The case studies examined here reveal many characteristics that limit their participatory and democratic potential. But my argument has not been to write off participatory theory, only to make it more aware of the constraints that contemporary cases reveal. Given the societal preference for market relations and exit behavior, participatory democracy cannot and will not be implemented under ideal circumstances. If theorists and researchers understand the forces that challenge participation's proposed effects, then both a more realistic understanding of participation and a more effective strategy to fight these forces can emerge.

Certainly, employees and management may change their, at times, contradictory behavior given a change in the amount of actual control the workers come to have. My contention, though, is that within the complex milieu of exit relations, and with varying commitments and understandings of participation, there is no easily definable course that participatory changes will follow. It seems that we are left with confusion between propositions and practical examples, and the endeavor is made more difficult because there appears to be little agreement over where to focus the study of participation's influences and effects. Most of participatory research concentrates on structural changes, but I call attention to workers' individual interests. Research often concentrates on the internal workings of a firm, but I call for a consideration of external forces. Perhaps, then, the study of participation needs to mirror the implementation of participation: Both need to seek, not a resolution, but a continual reexamination of participation to better understand changing relations.

NOTES

1. Jane J. Mansbridge, "Does Participation Make Better Citizens?" *The Good Society: Committee on the Political Economy of the Good Society* 5, no. 2 (Spring 1995): 1.
2. Jean-Jacques Rousseau, *The Social Contract*, trans. Maurice Cranston (New York: Penguin Books, 1968), 64-65.
3. Arnold Kaufman, "Human Nature and Participatory Democracy," in *Responsibility: NOMOS III*, ed. Carl Friedrich (New York: Liberal Arts Press, 1960), 184.
4. J. S. Mill, "Considerations on Representative Government," in *Utilitarianism, Liberty, and Representative Government*, ed. H. B. Acton (London: Dent, 1951), 195, 239–240.
5. Pateman, Bachrach, and Mansbridge are three proponents of this perspective.
6. Richard Edwards, *Contested Terrain: The Transformation of the Workplace in the Twentieth Century* (New York: Basic Books, 1979), 153–157, 201–209.
7. Mansbridge, "Better Citizens," 6.
8. This is the conclusion of the well-known Hawthorne studies.
9. For a typical review in this field, see Edward E. Lawler, *The Ultimate Advantage: Creating the High-Involvement Organization* (San Francisco: Jossey-Bass, 1992).
10. From the earlier discussion, note the interaction between participation's educative effects and its basis for developing a democratic polity. Pateman's work emphasizes this interactive role.
11. Employee survey response, Orange Handling, Albany, N.Y., April 1995, no. 29.
12. Employee interview, Quad/Graphics, Saratoga Springs, N.Y., 14 April 1995.
13. Carol C. Gould, *Rethinking Democracy: Freedom and Social Cooperation in Politics, Economy, and Society* (New York: Cambridge University Press, 1988), 283–306.
14. Albert O. Hirschman, *Exit, Voice, and Loyalty: Responses to Decline in Firms, Organizations, and States* (Cambridge: Harvard University Press, 1970), 44–54, 120–126.
15. Lawler, *Ultimate Advantage*, 107.
16. Thomas Jefferson, "Letter to James Madison," in *The Portable Thomas Jefferson*, ed. Merrill D. Peterson (New York: Penguin Books, 1975), 417.
17. Aristotle, *The Politics*, trans. T. A. Sinclair (New York: Penguin Books, 1962), 125.
18. Aristotle, *The Politics*, 109.

19. Tocqueville's *Democracy in America* is one of the representative arguments for the influence of mores on democratic government.

20. Katherine J. Klein and Rosalie J. Hall, "Correlates of Employee Satisfaction with Stock Ownership: Who Likes an ESOP the Most?" *Journal of Applied Psychology* 73, no. 4 (1988): 636.

21. Ibid., 636–637.

22. Ibid., 636.

23. Joyce Rothschild and J. Allen Whitt, *The Cooperative Workplace: Potentials and Dilemmas of Organizational Democracy and Participation* (New York: Cambridge University Press, 1986), 147.

24. Employee interview, Standard Knapp, Middletown, Conn., 21 January 1995.

25. Jon Elster, *Sour Grapes: Studies in the Subversion of Rationality* (New York: Cambridge University Press, 1983), 38-39.

26. Hirschman, *Exit, Voice, and Loyalty*, 112–114.

27. Elster, *Sour Grapes*, 42.

28. Hirschman, *Exit, Voice, and Loyalty*, 125.

29. Peter Bachrach and Aryeh Botwinick, *Power and Empowerment: A Radical Theory of Participatory Democracy* (Philadelphia: Temple University Press, 1992), 123.

Appendix A

SURVEY AND INTERVIEW NUMBERS

The same basic procedures were followed in locating and researching all three firms. Both the National Center for Employee Ownership (NCEO) and the Industrial Cooperative Association (ICA Group) publish listings of worker-owned firms throughout the country. I located Standard Knapp through an ICA listing and Quad/Graphics through an NCEO casebook on select worker-owned and participatory firms. Orange Handling participated at a NCEO workshop on employee ownership in the Albany, New York, area.

I first wrote an explanatory letter to the designated contact, typically the firm's president, at each workplace. I outlined my theoretical research interest and also highlighted how the firm could benefit from the information I would gather about employee attitudes. In my initial letter I included a sample employee survey, which is included as Appendix B, for the contact to assess the intent and merit of my research agenda. Standard Knapp and Orange Handling quickly agreed to the project. Both sought to gauge attitudes that the president and owners had a sense were not helping the firm and wished to use the research information for both confirmation and company forecasting. Quad/Graphics agreed to the project after a lengthy delay caused principally by the firm's size and the routing of the decision from the Wisconsin headquarters to the Saratoga, New York, plant.

The survey consists of five sections, A–E, with each section containing up to seventeen statements. For most of the statements, respondents were asked to use a 1–7 point scale, one representing agreement to the statement, seven reflecting disagreement, and the numbers between representing varying degrees of agreement or disagreement. The first section asks workers about background information such as age, length of employment, and in which department they work. The next section asks of participation in general and the firm's implementation of participation and ownership rights. The third section asks respondents about their activities outside the workplace, the fourth about their perceptions concerning any changes they recognize from their participatory experience, and the last section about the workers' activities, both private and public, and their general perceptions about potential benefits of employee participation.

After the firms agreed to the research, I mailed surveys to Standard Knapp (165 total) and hand delivered surveys to Orange Handling (60 total) and Quad/Graphics (300 total). Standard Knapp and Orange Handling distributed the surveys to each employee in their respective firms. At Quad/Graphics, since 300 surveys was only one-third of the Saratoga work force, the firm's personnel manager assured me the surveys would be allocated according to the firm's representative makeup. Later, when I expressed my concern over receiving no surveys from the runners, she told me they had access to the surveys and that she would try to have the managers reiterate to the runners their opportunity to fill out the surveys. At Quad, then, the surveys were not hand delivered to each employee. Instead, the employees were told of the surveys and where they could go to pick one up, usually the manager's office. This arrangement often leads to a distribution disincentive, as the newly employed and relatively powerless runners may be reluctant to even obtain a survey since this action can be perceived as the first step in expressing some grievance.

Along similar lines, despite repeated declarations in writing about confidentiality throughout the survey, in the survey cover letter, and by the firms' presidents and owners as the surveys were distributed, workers at Standard Knapp and Orange Handling told me that some co-workers were reluctant to respond for fear of repercussion. I do not think this fear adversely affects the survey's representative character, only the volume of complaint against the firms. I do think this fear reiterates the power of the market economy, of market relations, and of market thinking to dictate even open dialogue or participatory behavior. Despite the reluctance of some employees, the general interpretations of the firms are quite apparent from those who did respond, and the interviewees who told me of others who did not respond said the nonrespondents thought as they did. Does this resolve a self-selection bias in those who agreed to an interview? Given the overwhelming themes displayed at Standard Knapp and Orange Handling, I think it does. As for Quad/Graphics, I think the difficulty in assessing employee satisfaction and empowerment comes not from the few who chose to participate in the research project, but from the diversity of opinion that the survey responses and interviewees express about the firm's definition of participation and democracy.

To further ensure confidentiality and to increase the response rate, postage-paid envelopes were included with every survey. With these assurances, the rates were at best just above average:

Standard Knapp: 41 responses / 165 total = 24.8 percent response
Quad/Graphics: 68 responses / 300 total = 22.6 percent response
Orange Handling: 29 responses / 60 total = 48.3 percent response
Total: 138 responses / 525 total = 26.3 percent response rate

At the end of each survey, respondents are asked if they would be willing to be interviewed about their attitudes and experiences at their workplaces and would they like to view the survey results. Of the 138 respondents, 25 wrote they would agree to an interview, and 25 others claimed they would like to see the results. For each firm, the numbers break down in the following manner:

Standard Knapp: 7 potential interviewees / 5 actual interviews
Quad/Graphics: 12 potential interviewees / 4 actual interviews
Orange Handling: 6 potential interviewees / 9 actual interviews

The discrepancy at Orange Handling arises because I include a group conversation with several employees on a dinner break who expressed similar attitudes, if not more dismissive and negative, about participation's effects and management's commitment besides those who I officially interviewed and compensated. In general, though, interviewees were selected based on a calculation of representative experience both with the firm and with the participatory process. Preference, then, was given to employees with more work experience in general, which means typically workers in their late thirties and forties. Interestingly, though, given Quad/Graphics' philosophy of trust and participation from an employee's first day—or, as some would argue, its philosophy of hiring young people in order to "mold their minds"—Quad interviewees were in their early thirties or younger.

The interviews themselves occurred either at an employee's home or at a common area at the firm. Standard Knapp's employee interviews all took place in residences. Quad/Graphics' employee interviews involved both residences and two different common areas at the Saratoga plant. Orange Handling employee interviews likewise involved in-home sessions and plant locations. At no time did I sense any insecurity from the interviewees about the effects of being interviewed at the workplace. In fact, the decision to choose the workplace site for an interview was made by the employee. All interviewees at first declined and then reluctantly accepted compensation for their time. Money did not seem to be a motivation for an interviewee's time, nor did I feel that respondents were eager or desirous to respond "accurately" to any question.

Each interview lasted from seventy to one hundred minutes. I took notes as interviewees responded, and they politely waited for me to "catch up" before a followup question. This process, different from just tape recording their answers, allowed the respondents time to reflect on their answers, and they repeatedly came up with additional workplace examples to highlight their arguments. The interview structure followed the survey format, with employees first addressing participation and ownership in general and then proceeding to how their firm implements those ideas. After some time discussing their work roles and their attitudes about participation and its workplace effects, only then would I ask questions about their lives outside of work and whether work affected their "outside" time. As my results note, when I began to speak about political issues or public activity, the discussion would become noticeably more "uneasy" or "difficult."

Workers easily shared their attitudes and experiences about workplace participation, but they did not make a connection between work issues and activity and their activity outside or after work. As I also indicate, if employees did note a connection, it was expressed as a negative one, such as work does interfere with outside hobbies or groups or commitments like family, but "that's the price you have to pay."

Finally, I felt no pressure from the firms to advocate a certain line of analysis or to reach specific conclusions. Given Quad/Graphics' well-documented history and successes, they were the least interested in my findings. Standard Knapp and Orange Handling sought survey results and copies of my reports. But their intentions were less to monitor my findings and more to validate general impressions they suspected of their employees. The latter two firms gave me ample time to satisfy my research requirements first before addressing their concerns. Feedback from both firms since they have had my reports has been minimal.

Appendix B

SAMPLE SURVEY QUESTIONNAIRE

Workplace Participation Survey:

Be assured your answers are confidential. Please be honest in your responses.

A. First, some background demographic questions: (remember, this is confidential information).

1. Male or female _____

2. Age _____

3. How long have you been employed at this firm _____ years _____ months

4. What job title do you presently have:

    management _____   laborer _____   other (describe) _____

    secretarial _____   technician _____   _____

5. Your education level:

    some high school _____   some college _____   graduate degree _____

    high school grad./GED _____   college degree _____   other _____

6. Your race or ethnicity _____

7. How would you describe the family in which you grew up:

    poor _____   middle class _____

    working class _____   upper middle class _____

    lower middle class _____   upper class _____

Directions: In the space provided, place the number of the response which describes how you feel about each statement. Some questions ask you to write a response, but most only require that you provide the number which comes closest to your feelings. Please remember there are no right or wrong answers.

1	2	3	4	5	6	7
Agree	<------				------>	Disagree

B. These first questions ask how you feel about the structure of and degree of employee participation at your workplace:

    1. This firm actively promotes employee participation _____

    2. In general, I think employee participation is a practice that helps this firm _____

    3. Employee participation is a good idea _____

    4. Employee participation is not well-developed in my workplace _____

    5. As employees, we can participate in decision-making _____

    6. I do NOT believe we as employees control our workplace _____

    7. I have a lot of influence on general company decisions _____

    8. If I choose to, I can have a lot of say in how my firm is run _____

    9. Employee participation improves productivity _____

    10. Employee ownership and participation implies the welfare of workers is more often taken into account when decisions are made than would be true in a traditionally-owned firm _____

    11. I feel a real sense of ownership in this firm _____

    12. I do not mind doing more for this organization than is required by my job description _____

    13. I care about the fate of this firm _____

    14. I do not feel this company belongs to me in any meaningful way _____

    15. I am willing to volunteer some extra time for the overall good of the firm _____

    16. In general most employees do NOT feel they have much power over decision-making _____

1	2	3	4	5	6	7
Agree	<------				------>	Disagree

C. These next questions ask about your activities outside the workplace: **For #1 you can answer Yes/No.**

    1. I have some outside interests _____

    Some of my interests include: (please check)

        sports _____ ; do you primarily watch or participate _____

        reading _____

        listening to music or playing a musical instrument _____

        television _____

        arts and crafts _____

        group affiliations _____

        other (please name) _____

Please use the 1-7 scale for the following questions:

2. Work takes up most of my time so I have little time for outside interests _____
3. My family (or other important responsibility) takes precedence over my participation activities at work _____
4. I think that because of my work participation, I enjoy more activities after work hours _____
5. I prefer few demands at work because they can interfere with other aspects of my life _____
6. Work is important to me _____
7. I have other interests and demands that limit the time I can devote to work issues _____
8. Because of my firm's participatory opportunities, I often feel pulled in different directions _____
9. The conflict between personal goals and commitments and work goals and commitments is greater for participatory firms than for traditionally-owned and operated firms _____
10. For the most part, my work does not interfere with my outside interests _____
11. My outside interests are more important to me than my participation at work _____
12. I feel I would like to participate more at work than I do _____
13. Other responsibilities prevent me from participating at work _____
14. Outside interests have become LESS important to me as I participate MORE at work _____
15. Outside interests have become MORE important to me as I participate MORE at work _____
16. I think a relative balance exists between the demands at work and the interests/ commitments/responsibilities that I have and that I take on outside of work _____
17. If I did not have to work as much as I do now, I would: (please explain)

D. This section asks how you feel about and whether you perceive any changes in yourself from your involvement in the workplace: **(Please use the scale)**

1. Because of my participation at work, I feel MORE informed about my job _____
2. I think participation helps me be informed about the company in general _____
3. I think the firm educates its employees really well about company decisions _____
4. I could be better informed about the company's principles and decisions by the firm or its designated committees or groups _____
5. If I participate MORE in acquiring information and making decisions, then I will be better informed about my job and about the company _____
6. The participatory structures do NOT affect how knowledgeable I am about my job _____

1	2	3	4	5	6	7
Agree	<------			------>	**Disagree**	

7. The company has created an atmosphere that makes it easy to be informed about company decisions _____
8. Employee participation does not breed open access to all the firm's workings _____

9. Employee participation is beneficial to the firm in which I work _____

   If you agree with # 9, explain how it is beneficial, or who it benefits:

10. I make an effort to be informed on company decisions _____
11. I feel the participatory nature of the firm allows for more interaction between workers and between management and workers _____
12. I feel that my input is important in the company's decision-making process _____
13. I have enough control and input in my job that I feel a sense of empowerment _____
14. I think the company is committed to listening and responding to my opinions and interests _____

E. These questions ask you about your activities with your family, with your friends, and in your community:

(Again, please use the scale to respond.)

1. I spend most of my free time with my family _____
2. I am active in associations such as church committees, local political concerns, or the PTA _____
3. My participation at work has encouraged my participation in other groups _____
4. The demands of my work do NOT allow me to spend time involved with other issues _____
5. Political concerns appear remote from my daily interests or necessities _____
6. Outside of work I am active in personal or private interests rather than public issues _____
7. A participatory workplace means that I spend more time on work-related issues in my "spare" time than I would in a traditionally-owned business _____
8. A participatory workplace needs a specific kind of individual to work in it, one who is more committed and motivated than typical _____
9. A participatory workplace is a MORE demanding workplace for the employee _____
10. The rewards of a participatory firm are GREATER than those of non-participatory firms _____
11. A participatory workplace requires sacrifices from its employees _____
12. An employee must sacrifice some of his/her private life interests to participate in the workplace _____
13. A participatory workplace creates MORE opportunities than it demands sacrifices _____

   If you agree with # 13, please explain what opportunities:

If you would like to add to your answers from any section, or if you would like to address issues you feel I have missed, I welcome your comments: (If you would like to see the survey results, please list your name and address. If you would welcome the opportunity to be interviewed, please include, in addition to your name and address, a telephone number and a time that I can most likely reach you.)

SELECTED BIBLIOGRAPHY

Albelda, Randy, Christopher Eaton Gunn, and William Waller, eds. *Alternatives to Economic Orthodoxy*. Armonk, N.Y.: M. E. Sharpe, 1987.
Alchian, Armen A., and Harold Demsetz. "Production, Information Costs, and Economic Organization." *American Economic Review* 62 (1972) 777–795.
Aristotle. *The Politics*. Translated by T. A. Sinclair. Baltimore, Md.: Penguin Books, 1962.
Bachrach, Peter. *The Theory of Democratic Elitism*. Boston, Mass.: Little, Brown, 1967.
Bachrach, Peter, and Aryeh Botwinick. *Power and Empowerment: A Radical Theory of Participatory Democracy*. Philadelphia: Temple University Press, 1992.
Barber, Benjamin. *Strong Democracy: Participatory Politics for a New Age*. Berkeley and Los Angeles: University of California Press, 1984.
Baumann, Fred E., ed. *Democratic Capitalism? Essays in Search of a Concept*. Charlottesville: University Press of Virginia, 1986.
Bernstein, Paul. *Workplace Democratization: Its Internal Dynamics*. Kent, Ohio: Kent State University Press, 1976.
Berry, Christopher J. *The Idea of a Democratic Community*. New York: St. Martin's Press, 1989.
Blasi, Joseph Raphael. *Employee Ownership: Revolution or Ripoff?* Cambridge, Mass.: Ballinger, 1988.
Blinder, Alan S., ed. *Paying for Productivity: A Look at the Evidence*. Washington, D.C.: Brookings Institution, 1990.
Bowles, Samuel, and Herbert Gintis. *Democracy and Capitalism: Property, Community, and the Contradictions of Modern Social Thought*. New York: Basic Books, 1986.
Brecher, Jeremy, and Tim Costello, eds. *Building Bridges: The Emerging Grassroots Coalition of Labor and Community*. New York: Monthly Review Press, 1990.
Burawoy, Michael. *Manufacturing Consent: Changes in the Labor Process under Monopoly Capitalism*. Chicago: University of Chicago Press, 1979.
Byrne, Edmund F. *Work, Inc.: A Philosophical Inquiry*. Philadelphia: Temple University Press, 1990.

Cohen, G. A. *History, Labour, and Freedom: Themes from Marx*. Oxford: Clarendon Press, 1988.
Cotton, John L. *Employee Involvement: Methods for Improving Performance and Work Attitudes*. Newbury Park, Calif.: Sage Publications, 1993.
Dahl, Robert A. *A Preface to Economic Democracy*. Berkeley and Los Angeles: University of California Press, 1985.
Darwall, Stephen, ed. *Equal Freedom: Selected Tanner Lectures on Human Values*. Ann Arbor: University of Michigan Press, 1995.
Derber, Milton. *The American Idea of Industrial Democracy, 1865–1965*. Urbana: University of Illinois Press, 1970.
Edwards, Richard. *Contested Terrain: The Transformation of the Workplace in the Twentieth Century*. New York: Basic Books, 1979.
Ellerman, David P. "The Legitimate Opposition at Work: the Union's Role in Large Democratic Firms." *Economic and Industrial Democracy* 9 (1988): 437–453.
———. "Worker Ownership: Economic Democracy of Worker Capitalism?" Research paper for The Industrial Cooperation Association Group, Boston, Mass., April 1986.
Elshtain, Jean Bethke. *Democracy on Trial*. New York: Basic Books, 1995.
Elster, Jon. *Political Psychology*. New York: Cambridge University Press, 1993.
———. *Solomonic Judgements: Studies in the Limitations of Rationality*. New York: Cambridge University Press, 1989.
———. *Sour Grapes: Studies in the Subversion of Rationality*. New York: Cambridge University Press, 1983.
Elster, Jon, and Karl Ove Moene, eds. *Alternatives to Capitalism*. New York: Cambridge University Press, 1989.
Erikson, Kai, and Steven Peter Vallas, eds. *The Nature of Work: Sociological Perspectives*. New Haven: Yale University Press, 1990.
Espinosa, Juan G., and Andrew S. Zimbalist. *Economic Democracy: Workers' Participation in Chilean Industry, 1970–1973*. New York: Academic Press, 1978.
Foy, Nancy. *Empowering People at Work*. Brookfield, Vt.: Gower Publishing, 1994.
Fukuyama, Francis. *Trust: The Social Virtues and the Creation of Prosperity*. New York: The Free Press, 1995.
Garfield, Charles. *Second to None: How Our Smartest Companies Put People First*. Homewood, Ill.: Business One Irwin, 1992.
Grady, Robert C. "Workplace Democracy and Possessive Individualism." *Journal of Politics* 52, no. 1 (1990): 146–166.
Greenberg, Edward S. "The Consequences of Worker Participation: A Clarification of the Theoretical Literature." *Social Science Quarterly* 56, no. 2 (1975): 191–209.
———. *Workplace Participation: The Political Effects of Participation*. Ithaca: Cornell University Press, 1986.
Gould, Carol C. *Rethinking Democracy: Freedom and Social Cooperation in Politics, Economy, and Society*. New York: Cambridge University Press, 1988.
Gunn, Christopher Eaton. *Workers' Self-Management in the United States*. Ithaca: Cornell University Press, 1984.
Gunn, Christopher Eaton, and Hazel Dayton Gunn. *Reclaiming Capital: Democratic Initiatives and Community Development*. Ithaca: Cornell Universtiy Press, 1991.
Habermas, Jurgen. *Legitimation Crisis*. Translated by T. McCarthy. London: Heinemann, 1976.

Harrison, Bennett. "The Failure of Worker Participation." *Technology Review* 94 (January 1991): 74.

Hirschman, Albert O. *Exit, Voice, and Loyalty: Responses to Decline in Firms, Organizations, and States.* Cambridge: Harvard University Press, 1970.

Hirst, Paul. *Associative Democracy: New Forms of Economic and Social Governance.* Amherst: University of Massachusetts Press, 1994.

Holden, Barry. *Understanding Liberal Democracy.* Atlantic Highlands, N.J.: Philip Alan, 1988.

Jackall, Robert, and Henry M. Levin, eds. *Worker Cooperatives in America.* Berkeley and Los Angeles: University of California Press, 1984.

Joseph, Martin. *Sociology for Business: A Practical Approach.* New York: Polity Press, 1989.

Kanter, Donald L., and Philip H. Mirvis. *The Cynical Americans: Living and Working in an Age of Discontent and Disillusion.* San Francisco: Jossey-Bass, 1989.

Karasek, Robert, and Tores Theorell. *Healthy Work: Stress, Productivity, and the Reconstruction of Working Life.* New York: Basic Books, 1990.

Kelso, Louis O., and Patricia Hetter Kelso. *Democracy and Economic Power: Extending the ESOP Revolution.* Cambridge, Mass.: Ballinger, 1986.

Klein, Katherine J., and Rosalie J. Hall. "Correlates of Employee Satisfaction with Stock Ownership: Who Likes an ESOP the Most?" *Journal of Applied Psychology* 73, no. 4 (1988): 630–638.

Lamberti, Jean-Claude. *Tocqueville and the Two Democracies.* Cambridge: Harvard University Press, 1989.

Lane, Robert E. "Market Justice, Political Justice." *American Political Science Review* 80, no. 2 (1986): 383–402.

Lawler, Edward E. *The Ultimate Advantage: Creating the High-Involvement Organization.* San Francisco: Jossey-Bass, 1992.

Lichtenstein, Nelson, and Howell John Harris, eds. *Industrial Democracy in America: The Ambiguous Promise.* New York: Woodrow Wilson Center Press, 1993.

MacPherson, C. B. *The Political Theory of Possessive Individualism.* Oxford: Clarendon Press, 1962.

Macy, Barry A., Mark F. Peterson, and Larry W. Norton. "A Test of Participation Theory in a Work Re-Design Field Setting: Degree of Participation and Comparison Site Contrasts." *Human Relations* 42, no. 12 (1989): 1095–1165.

Mansbridge, Jane J. *Beyond Adversary Democracy.* New York: Basic Books, 1980.

———. "Does Participation Make Better Citizens?" *The Good Society: Committee on the Political Economy of the Good Society* 5, no. 2 (1995): 1–7.

Mason, Ronald M. *Participatory and Workplace Democracy: A Theoretical Development in the Critique of Liberalism.* Carbondale: Southern Illinois University Press, 1982.

Mathews, David. *Politics for People: Finding a Responsible Public Voice.* Urbana: University of Illinois Press, 1994.

Nolla, Eduardo. *Liberty, Equality, and Democracy.* New York: NYU Press, 1992.

Oakeshott, Robert. *The Case for Workers' Co-ops.* Boston: Routledge & Kegan Paul, 1978.

Pateman, Carole. *Participation and Democratic Theory.* New York: Cambridge University Press, 1970.

Pitegoff, Peter. "The Democratic ESOP." Research paper for the Industrial Cooperative Association Group, Boston, January 1987.

Putnam, Robert D. *Making Democracy Work: Civic Traditions in Modern Italy.* Princeton, N.J.: Princeton University Press, 1993.

Quarrey, Michael, Joseph Blasi, and Corey Rosen. *Taking Stock: Employee Ownership at Work.* Cambridge, Mass.: Ballinger, 1986.

Rosen, Corey, and Karen M. Young, eds. *Understanding Employee Ownership.* Ithaca: Industrial and Labor Relations Press, Cornell University, 1991.

Rothschild, Joyce, and J. Allen Whitt. *The Cooperative Workplace: Potentials and Dilemmas of Organizational Democracy and Participation.* New York: Cambridge University Press, 1986.

Rousseau, Jean-Jacques. *The Social Contract.* Translated by Maurice Cranston. New York: Penguin Books, 1968.

Rubinstein, Sidney P., ed. *Participative Systems at Work: Creating Quality and Employment Security.* New York: Human Sciences Press, 1987.

Russell, Raymond. *Sharing Ownership in the Workplace.* Albany: State University of New York Press, 1985.

Sampson, Anthony. *Company Man: The Rise and Fall of Corporate Life.* New York: Random House, 1995.

Schecter, Darrow. *Gramsci and the Theory of Industrial Democracy.* Brookfield, Vt.: Gower Publishing, 1991.

Schuller, Tom. *Democracy at Work.* New York: Oxford University Press, 1985.

Simmons, John, and William Mares. *Working Together.* New York: Alfred A. Knopf, 1983.

Sullivan, Denis G., Jeffrey L. Pressman, Benjamin I. Page, and John J. Lyons. *The Politics of Representation: The Democratic Convention 1972.* New York: St. Martin's Press, 1974.

Thompson, Paul, and David McHugh. *Work Organizations: A Critical Introduction.* London: Macmillan Education, 1990.

Tocqueville, Alexis de. *Democracy in America.* Edited by Richard D. Heffner. New York: Penguin Books, 1956.

Tsiganou, Helen A. *Workers' Participative Schemes: The Experience of Capitalist and Plan-Based Societies.* Westport, Conn.: Greenwood Press, 1991.

Warner, Malcolm. *Organizations and Experiments: Designing New Ways of Managing Work.* New York: John Wiley & Sons, 1984.

Young, Karen M., ed. *The Expanding Role of ESOPs in Public Companies.* Westport, Conn.: Quorum Books, 1990.

Zager, Robert, and Michael P. Rosow, eds. *The Innovative Organization: Productivity Programs in Action.* New York: Pergamon Press, 1982.

INDEX

Alchian, Arman, 18–19
Aristotle, 145, 151
Avis, Inc., 16

Bachrach, Peter, 2, 15, 23–24; attack on Greenberg's work, 43–45, 158
Barber, Benjamin, 33
Bernstein, Paul, 38–39
Botwinick, Aryeh, 23–24
Burawoy, Michael, 13 n.9

Capital, power of, 4–7, 12
Cohen, G. A., 38
Cooperative Home Care Associates, 5
Cotton, John, 19, 37, 44
Cynicism, American, 9

Dahl, Robert, 33, 35
Demetz, Harold, 18–19

Economic success, and participatory experiments, 79–80, 93, 137–141
Edwards, Richard, 107–108, 111, 147
Efficacy, 2, 17–19, 24, 48, 134, 137; defined, 47; efficiency debate and, 18
Elden, Maxwell, 46
Ellerman, David, 44, 49

Elster, Jon, 110–111, 154–157
Employee ownership: capital control and, 5, 49–51; corporate view of, 3; employee satisfaction and, 19, 50. *See also* Capital
Employee Stock Ownership Plan (ESOP), 16, 47, 49–51, 55, 82, 92, 96, 99
Equality: as historical undercurrent, 6, 11; research defintion, 47; in Tocqueville, 29. *See also* Liberty
Exit behavior, 37, 126, 146, 155

Fred Schmid Appliances, 16
Fukuyama, Francis, 123

Garfield, Charles, 6
General Motors Corporation (GM), 4
Gould, Carol, 149–150
Grady, Robert C., 33–35
Gramsci, Antonio, 33
Greenberg, Edward S., 16–17, 34, 43–45, 120, 158
Gunn, Christopher Eaton, 16–17, 19

Habermas, Jurgen, 7–9, 11, 28, 156
Hall, Rosalie J., 50–51, 152–154
Harrison, Bennett, 18

Hirschman, Albert O., 21, 46, 108, 146, 155–157; explanation of employee difficulties in determining how to act, 128–129, 134, 141, 150; idea of moral resources in, 112. *See also* Exit behavior; Loyalty behavior; Voice behavior

Individual identities, effects of on participation, 3–4, 51
Individualism, 7, 27–29, 32, 34–36
Industrial democracy, 17. *See also* Participatory theory
Irrational expectations, of employees for participatory experiments, 50–51, 120–121, 134; rational interpretation of, 128–129

Jackall, Robert, 19, 20–21
Jones, Derek, 19, 41 n.7
Justice: market conception of, 33–36; society's different measures of, 31–32

Kanter, Donald L., 9, 12
Kaufman, Arnold, 145
Klein, Katherine J., 50–51, 152–154
Kohn, Alfie, 6

Lane, Robert E., 31–33, 35, 37, 74, 124
Lawler, Edward E., 150
Levin, Henry M., 19, 20–21
Liberty, 3, 7, 11–12; Dahl and, 33; Lane and, 33; Rousseau and, 25–27; Tocqueville and, 29–30
Lowes Companies, 5
Loyalty behavior, employees and, 21, 37, 127–128

MacLaury, Bruce K., 19
MacPherson, C. B., 15, 24, 35–36
Mansbridge, Jane, 145, 147
Market relations, 4, 31–32, 36
Marshall, Ray, 5
Mason, Ronald, 120
Methodological issues, 44–46, 52–54, 68–70, 161–164
Mill, J. S., 145–146
Mirvis, Philip H., 9, 12

National Center for Employee Ownership (NCEO), 16, 92–93
Northeast Ohio Employee Ownership Center, 5

Orange Handling, 95–114; distrust in, 96–98; employee attitudes in, 100–102, 104–107; labor–management relations in, 96–98, 100, 106, 128; ownership structure in, 98–100

Participation: byproducts of, 121; corporate view of, 3, 5, 16, 18; defined, 17, 47; definitional difficulties, 46–52; effects of trust and, 128; employee recogntion of economic rewards for, 130, 140; employee view of, 8, 50; external influences on, 4, 133; internal company influences on, 20–21; maximal definition of, 46–48; participatory personalities and, 149–150; perversion of its effects, 127–129, 148; productivity and, 18–19; public activity and, 131–132
Participatory democracy. *See* Participatory theory
Participatory theory, 1–2, 9–10, 17–18, 120–122, 124, 133, 148–149; educative component of, 22–24, 51–52; testing hypotheses in case studies, 70–72, 87–90, 109–112
Pateman, Carole, 1–2, 15, 24, 26–27, 146; educative effects of participation in, 22–23, 121
Pitegoff, Peter, 49
Plywood firms, of the Northwest, 16, 34, 43
Politics versus markets: different aims of, 80–81; different ideas of justice for, 31–36
Possessive individualist ideology, 34, 36
Profit maximization, 5
Putnam, Robert D., 38, 112, 119

Quad/Graphics, 77–93; employee attitudes for, 83–87; employee support of participatory experiment in, 82–84, 129; ownership structure in, 79, 82, 92
Quadracci, Harry, 79, 82, 93

Reich, Charles, 6
Rosen, Corey, 113
Rothschild, Joyce, 21, 122
Rousseau, Jean-Jacques, 22–23, 25; characteristics of democracy in, 95; description of general will, 26–27, 77–79, 90–92, 145

Sampson, Anthony, 119
Schumpeter, Joseph A., 23–24
Size of firms, effects on participation, 95–96
Standard Knapp, 55–74; employee attitudes in, 62–65; employee lack of trust in, 61, 63, 67, 135; employee participation in, 59–61, 128; management–labor relations in, 66–68; ownership structure in, 59–60
Stone Construction Equipment, 16

Tocqueville, Alexis de, 7, 65; associational life for, 11, 28; equality concerns for, 29; manufacturing aristocracy

Tocqueville, Alexis de *(continued)* concerns for, 11–12, 30–31, 123; Rousseau comparison and, 28–31

Union, presense of in participatory workplace, 55–56, 63–63, 128, 135–136
United Airlines, 6

Voice behavior, 46, 155; as employee option, 21, 141; general theory of, 36–38; without choice, 38, 60, 80, 129, 146

Walzer, Michael, 7
Whitehall Laboratories, 6
Whitt, J. Allen, 21, 122
Worzalla Publishing Company, 6

Zaritsky, Herb, 98, 100, 114
Zaritsky, Stan, 98, 100, 114

ABOUT THE AUTHOR

S. LANCE DENNING received his Ph.D. from the State University of New York at Albany in Political Theory.